Big Culture

Big Culture

TOWARD AN AESTHETICS OF MAGNITUDE

David Wittenberg

The University of Chicago Press CHICAGO AND LONDON

The University of Chicago Press, Chicago 60637
The University of Chicago Press, Ltd., London

Published 2025

34 33 32 31 30 29 28 27 26 25 1 2 3 4 5

ISBN-13: 978-0-226-84290-5 (cloth)
ISBN-13: 978-0-226-84292-9 (paper)
ISBN-13: 978-0-226-84291-2 (ebook)
DOI: https://doi.org/10.7208/chicago/9780226842912.001.0001

This book was made possible with generous support from the University of Iowa's Office of the Vice President for Research and College of Liberal Arts and Sciences.

Library of Congress Cataloging-in-Publication Data

Names: Wittenberg, David, author.
Title: Big culture : toward an aesthetics of magnitude / David Wittenberg.
Description: Chicago ; London : The University of Chicago Press, 2025. | Includes bibliographical references and index.
Identifiers: LCCN 2024058418 | ISBN 9780226842905 (cloth) | ISBN 9780226842929 (paperback) | ISBN 9780226842912 (ebook)
Subjects: LCSH: Magnitude (Philosophy) | Aesthetics.
Classification: LCC BH301.M27 W47 2025 | DDC 111/.8—dc23/eng/20250201
LC record available at https://lccn.loc.gov/2024058418

Contents

1
Fear of Bigness

The impetus for this book came in the form of some troublesome but stimulating thoughts I had while living in Oakland, California, as a graduate student in architecture. I would regularly visit the Oakland Museum, designed by Kevin Roche and John Dinkeloo in the 1960s, a building that I, like many others, greatly admired.[1] The Oakland Museum exhibits few markers of the monumentality and civic self-importance that tend to characterize museum architecture. Roche and Dinkeloo designed a meandering assemblage of concrete tiers and terraces with landscaped roofs. The building has no overall symmetry, no obvious front or back, no fully clear distinction between its interior and exterior spaces, no single main entrance, and no strictly defined circulation path through the exhibits. "The galleries are arranged," as the architects write, "so that the roof of one becomes the terrace of another," and each of the museum's sections "opens directly onto lawns, terraces, trellised passages, and broad flights of stairs."[2] This design reflects a program merging several progressive agendas: a blending of disparate museum types at a single site (art, history, science); a connection, both physical and ideological, to urban redevelopment projects in Oakland; a regionalist ethos, epitomized by the ecologically minded landscaping and allusions to the tiered architecture of California's coastal hills; and a general aspiration to engage with Oakland's economically and ethnically diverse communities. The result is, in the best sense, a diffuse building, in which museum functions typically denoted by architectural form and iconography—exhibition, pedagogy, historical preservation, civic high-mindedness, tourism—are distributed amid a scheme more closely resembling a public garden or town bazaar than a cultural shrine. At every step, the Oakland Museum offers an enlightened reinterpretation of the usual solemn or strident claims about the institutional status and purpose of museums.

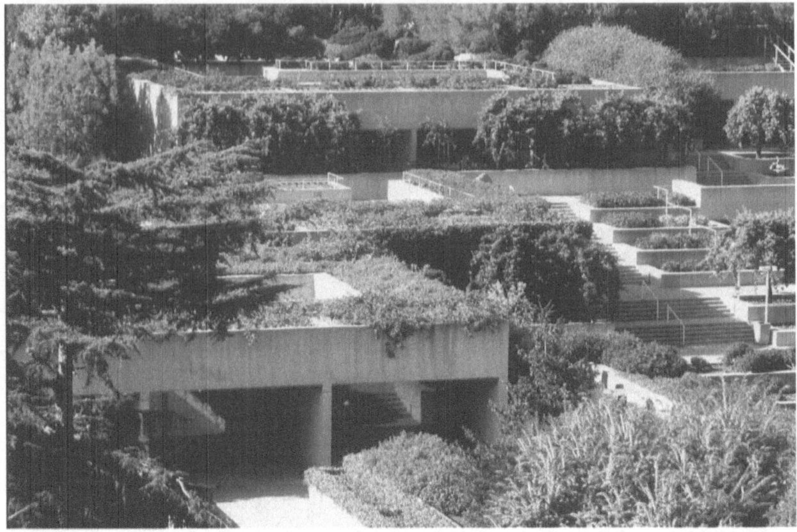

FIGURE 1.1 Oakland Museum, Oakland, CA, 1969 (photo courtesy of Kevin Roche John Dinkeloo and Associates)

Yet, despite all its subtlety, the Oakland Museum still represents a distinctly contrarian polemic.[3] What the building argues against, in fact with some degree of hostility, is the conventional *bigness* of traditional museums, their "ruthless monumentality," which even the most self-conscious modernist museum designs tend to inherit from neoclassicism and other imperial traditions, and which Kevin Roche calls "pompous and repelling."[4] At the Oakland Museum, a visitor can scarcely fail to recall this conventional monumentality by virtue of its conspicuous absence. What he or she encounters instead is what the museum's own promotional materials call a "non-building," the effect of which is to recast traditional museum design, with its assertive massing, symmetry, and forceful orchestration of circulation, as a lamentable obstacle to a citizen's free participation in culture.[5] Roche and Dinkeloo bluntly assert their "belief that traditional museums were not only poorly designed to preserve and exhibit objects, but their designers also ignored the comfort, convenience, and psychological needs of the museum visitor."[6] The Oakland Museum's "non-building" is thus a benchmark for the progressive repudiation of the antiegalitarianism of traditional civic architecture and planning. The last traces of "museal" monumentality disintegrate into a naturalistic landscape as though in a flash-forward from a postapocalyptic movie, surrendering themselves to the ecosphere.[7] "Since the building was finished," Roche and Dinkeloo observe with a few years' retrospect, "the planting has done what it was hoped it would, growing over the entire building, gradually submerging its form."[8]

I return to my own troublesome but stimulating thoughts, such as they were. While I continued to admire Roche and Dinkeloo's Oakland Museum, I was uneasy with what seemed to me a strong presumption at the core of its revisionism or self-abnegation: the notion that bigness, whether in a museum building or any other civic structure or space, *victimizes* the citizen, and therefore ought to be combated, dissimulated, or, as Roche suggests, "submerged"—in short, that architectural monumentality is the natural enemy of what he and Dinkeloo call people's "comfort, convenience, and psychological needs." Bigness, per se, is construed as reactionary and antihumanistic, even a spontaneous expression of authoritarianism, and so citizens indubitably benefit from its diminishment or destruction. In the domain of modernist architectural theory, such a stigma upon bigness appears frequently in the reflexive association of monumentality with histories of royalist, imperialist, clerical, or militaristic iconography. In standard architectural histories, links between monumentality and tyrannical politics may be sustained by reference to midcentury paragons of "architectural megalomania" such as Albert Speer's plans for Nazi government buildings in Berlin, the Stalinist Empire style employed by architects under the sway of the Soviet Central Committee, or even well-intentioned urban mega-projects such as Oscar Niemeyer's capital city of Brasilia or China's One City Nine Towns development outside of Shanghai.[9] In a word, architectural bigness is *fascist*, and hence inappropriate for any public structure meant or supposed to be authentically civic-minded. In light of such a reflexive distrust of architectural monumentality, Roche and Dinkeloo construe their Oakland Museum not merely as a self-critical or self-deprecating building; it is a direct moral attack upon the "pompous and repelling" oppressiveness, the fascism, of bigness itself.

But are such inferences about the evil of bigness correct? Is big architecture, even bigness as such, oppressive and antihumanistic, possibly fascistic? Is a big museum building really antithetical to the "comfort, convenience, and psychological needs" of its public? On the contrary, isn't the raw appeal of architectural monumentality, the pleasure that people take in the sheer massiveness of big buildings and public spaces, a vital part of what enables such architecture to serve (or in turn to be criticized) as an effective ideological symbol of the city, state, church, corporation, or culture itself? Is there not something disingenuous and paternalistic in the impulse to protect the citizenry from the menace of bigness? Don't people actually *like* cathedrals, palaces, enormous train depots or airports, immensely tall skyscrapers, grandiose capitals or courts, oversized shopping malls, and monumental museums, regardless of whether these structures metaphorically or metonymically subjugate the polis? Indeed, don't people like them *because* they are big? Is there not a basic pleasure or thrill in bigness itself, without which even Roche and Dinkeloo's contrarian attack on the oppressiveness of museum architecture would lack all force or rationale?

Such questions suggested a need to interrogate more scrupulously the category of bigness, and more generally the aesthetics of magnitude. I was further encouraged by the corroboration that architects such as Roche and Dinkeloo, who vehemently oppose bigness in one building, may cheerfully embrace it in another, for instance, in their own Ford Foundation building in New York City or their Knights of Columbus building in New Haven, Connecticut, both roughly contemporaneous with the Oakland Museum. This telling inconsistency confirmed my impression that architects and cultural critics alike still lack a basic theory of bigness alongside the repertoire of conceptual, aesthetic, or moral scruples they may express about it.[10]

When one encounters a contradiction of this sort—that bigness can simultaneously appear to be, on the one hand, a seductive pleasure or thrill and, on the other hand, an enemy of "comfort" or "psychological needs"—one suspects that remnants of unconscious motivation still animate critical language and ought to be excavated. A glance at both academic and mainstream critiques of popular culture, in which the sheer bigness of phenomena is constantly observed or lamented but rarely directly theorized, reinforces this suspicion. For instance, videos of atomic bomb blasts, rallies at Nuremberg, planes crashing into skyscrapers, or tsunamis leveling port cities furnish outstanding popular icons of horror or menace, but at the same time loci of visceral attraction, formal gratification, and (this is given initially as a mere hypothesis) outright pleasure, not only despite but because of the violence and destruction they proffer. One scarcely need scrutinize one's own discomfiting fascination with horror or violence to observe such a paradoxical combination of affects, as well as the difficulty of adequately representing them in formal, structural, or ideological terms. The practically infinite availability of depictions of overweening bigness in popular culture gives sufficient data at least to confirm the sociological cachet of such tableaux, not to mention their appeal to "psychological comfort and needs," even if such a baldly empirical observation represents the merest segue to theoretical analysis. Likewise, a certain blank maximalism of mainstream cultural production—the most popular song, the most expensive film, the best-selling book, the most widely viewed television program, the tallest building, the most crowded concert, the most visited tourist attraction, or the most profitable fad—is a commodity that sells its own exorbitant magnitude virtually regardless of content. Considering such phenomena, and many others, this book intends to begin theorizing bigness more fully and, as my subtitle suggests, to make strides toward an aesthetics of magnitude adequate to its object.

✷ 2 ✷

Postulates of an Aesthetics of Magnitude

Taxidermy

When my child was about two years old, we took them to the Farm-in-the-Zoo in Chicago. The Farm-in-the-Zoo is a scaled-down replica of a sort of American family farm that scarcely exists outside the fantasies of urban dwellers like ourselves: colorfully painted silos and sheds, tidy vegetable beds, corrals full of congenial pigs, chickens, ponies, and so on. Wandering around, we eventually entered a small barn containing a single animal behind a heavy metal gate. I leaned over and told my child, "it's a cow." Their reaction to this cow, the bulk of which dominated both the interior of the barn and my child's tiny figure in the stroller, was a stiff hush, which I immediately interpreted as a sign of real fear, followed by this anxiously voiced appeal: "Daddy, can we see a different animal, come this animal is *too big*."[1]

For my child—of course, I now reconfigure their response even as I recollect it—this was a primal experience of what Kant calls the "absolutely large" (*schlechthin groß*), an immensity surging up amid otherwise manageable spaces and objects, overwhelming their immediate environment.[2] Prior to our excursion to the Farm-in-the-Zoo, my child already knew what cows looked like, more or less. But their acquaintance with them, as with most animals large or small, was through picture books, in which all creatures are depicted roughly the same size or at least within the same order of magnitude: cows, horses, mice, elephants, birds, bumblebees, dinosaurs, dragons. In other words, my child's understanding of big animals was purely formal, an "aesthetic" comprehension in the restricted sense in which we have come to use that term, since Alexander Baumgarten's writing in the mid-eighteenth century, to refer to constructed and framed representations of objects and scenery.[3] This living beast, intruding upon the otherwise cordially diminutive setting of the Farm-in-the-Zoo, was something quite other than a carefully framed visual image. It was an all-too-material *thing*, a looming, synesthetic threat of flesh, heat, odor, and shuddering weight. Not merely big, it was, in my child's precise words, "*too big*," or in Kant's corresponding terminology, a "magnitude that is equal only to itself."[4]

As a strictly amateur cognitive psychologist, I would suppose that every child, even one less cloistered than ours by town sidewalks and overcautious guardians, must at some point have undergone such a primal experience of magnitude, shattering the cozy schemata through which humans are initially prepared to assimilate their worlds. The possibility of appraisal or comparison with a prepared aesthetic image ("it's a cow, like the one in your book") is outstripped, and what lingers is the emotional charge of bigness itself, the disquieting thrill of the proximal entity distilled to sheer mass and menace.[5] Deferring to my child's evocative literalness, I wish to adopt their terminology as technical language for a first postulate of an aesthetics of magnitude. Big things are first of all *too big*, which is to say, inescapably present and physical, irreducible to form or schema, immeasurable, incomparable, like the abruptly encountered living cow that surpasses any received image or category that might function to contextualize it. As the fretful parent reflexively infers, the child confronted with something "too big" has no recourse to adult-minded assurances about proper scale or, in other words, to the understanding that all beasts, like all other material things, persist faithfully in being just the size they ought to be, serenely in conformity with natural law and an aesthetic decorum grounded in physics and logic. They are never truly miniature or gigantic except through fantasy or fiction—in Kant's terms, never "absolute," always manageable, comparable, measurable.

The child grows up; their world evolves into its expanded but adulterated future. They learn a range of accommodations between their own body and the decreasingly intimate environs that comprise a developing human's sphere. Among other accomplishments, the child learns how to reckon objects in their appropriate scales, so that nothing is, nothing can be, a "magnitude equal only to itself." Big animals become relatively unremarkable amid the plethora of stuff in the broadened environment, estimable and classifiable by what Freud calls "secondary process" thinking or what Nietzsche calls the "fiction" of a "world that is calculable, simplified, comprehensible, etc., for us."[6] Presumably there comes a day when a cow no longer embodies—no longer *can* embody—the absolute "too big," and dwindles to the conventional stature of yet another measurable object.[7] Cows, then, are bigger than some animals, smaller than others, but generally speaking the proper size of themselves, a happy medium given even sketchy parameters of physics and biology. We might say that the adult's polite sense of scale, in its modulation of the primal threat of the big thing, is an acquired skill in *taxidermy*. By comparing and classifying objects and their relative magnitudes, humans learn to kill the imposing materiality of the thing and preserve its mere form.

The elemental terms for a scalar taxidermy are given by Hegel in the early sections of the *Phenomenology of Spirit*, along with his more general account of the development of objectivity. The initial response of consciousness to its environment is a "sensuous certainty," in which each thing appears fully and inexorably present, "a pure *this*" or just "*what is*."[8] Consciousness soon learns to treat such immediate impressions as fleeting and ultimately false. Each sensuous thing is in fact a mere instance of objective perception, what Hegel terms a "universal," sharing its attributes in whole or in part with any number of other things that might have been perceived instead.[9] This learned act of reducing immediacy to universality, or of annulling the thing's sensuousness so as to preserve its reusable form, is what Hegel calls "experience," and incidentally it also provides the logical basis for Marx's analysis of the general "estrangement" of sensuous material through human labor.[10] The primordial bigness of the thing is sculpted, eviscerated, bestilled, and ultimately subordinated to its usefulness in or as an object. And so, as the cow becomes measurable and scalable, it also becomes manipulable and repurposable, a *type* in lieu of a singular thing, in essence, a mere icon or statuette of itself. Its primal impact is recalled only hazily, like the cathexis of images in dreams that, as Freud says, "come from the past in every sense," an affective residue reserved for preconscious redeployment in some future accidental moment in which bigness and its potential violence might irrupt.[11]

Scalar taxidermy is a skill in seeing *more* than the sheer, overweening presence of bigness; yet in another sense it is a skill in seeing *less*, or in *not* seeing, a proficiency at stuffing down the primal sensuous attributes of things in order to assure their use value. The literary critic Viktor Shklovsky, analyzing the propensity of language to formalize or standardize the inconveniently rich domain of sense perception, speaks of "algebra" or "algebrization," an "economical" reduction of the objective world in which "perception becomes habitual, it becomes automatic," and the thing is known only "by its configuration" or by "its silhouette."[12] In psychoanalytic terms, which will continue to be useful for this topic, the taxidermy we perform on the big thing, as we grow out of its terror, amounts to separating cathexis from object, or emotional charge from image. This is Freud's "secondary process," an acquired skill in distinguishing things in the objective world from whatever subjective passions originally drew us to them—in a word, repression.[13] But presumably one never disposes of that primary cathexis entirely. Like everything else repressed, it remains in, or more precisely it *is*, the unconscious of our experience, still capable of reanimating the object at any moment we find ourselves fascinated by big things or by bigness itself. Like the eerie vitality of the stuffed animal posed and mounted by the taxidermist, bigness lives uncannily close to the surface of things, intimating or awaiting a fortuitous revival of its original force.

For the adult, if an occasion arrives when some creature, a big cow or anything else, manages to puncture the rational schematism of proper scale and impose itself as terrifyingly gigantic—"absolutely large," a "magnitude equal only to itself"—this will always appear to be an aesthetic rather than an ontological consequence, resulting from some defamiliarizing *perspective* that momentarily reactivates infantile phenomenology: an optical illusion, a special effect, perhaps a sudden shock during a horror film or thrill ride, perhaps some accident of proximity at a rodeo or state fair. An animal or anything else that appears gigantic is a situational event, surfacing out of a necessarily obscure technics of psychology or viewpoint; in phenomenological terms, we might call this a primal intuition of "possibly-being-crushed," a violent momentary foray of body into mind, an inkling of "the productivity and resilience of matter"[14]—perhaps a memento of the erotic.[15]

What Is Big Is Too Big

In a famous series of experiments, the Swiss psychologist Jean Piaget investigates whether humans have an a priori conception of magnitude or quantity. Piaget places in front of four- and five-year-old children an assortment of cylindrical vessels of varying heights and diameters. He then invites the children to pour liquids from some of the containers into others, changing the amounts and configurations. For example, Piaget asks one child to pour lemonade from a short, wide container into a tall, narrow one, and another child to reapportion the coffee from one large container into several smaller ones. Piaget then asks the children to tell him what has happened to the liquid: "You both have the same amount?"; "Who has more?"; "Will there be the same amount to drink?"; "Show me with your finger where I should pour."[16]

To correctly respond to such queries, presumably a child must grasp that the most immediate perceptual clues—for instance, the height of the liquid in a tall, narrow glass or the number of glasses sitting on a table—do not, in and of themselves, determine how much liquid is present. In brief, the child must be able to distinguish a quantity of liquid from the qualities of its container, comprehending that a specific amount of lemonade or coffee is not strictly proportional to the width or tallness of the glass holding it. But the answers the children give to Piaget demonstrate that, before the age of about six, they are unable to conceive of a substance fully separate from the form of its vessel. Instead, as Piaget asserts, "the quantity of liquid transferred increases or diminishes depending on the shape or the number of the containers," and the child is "not at all inclined to admit that the same given quantity of liquid can remain unvarying through [the] changes of shape associated with its being transferred."[17] Thus, at one moment the child asserts that the taller glass contains more liquid, and a moment later believes that multiple glasses contain more, even though that very child has just poured the same liquid from the single tall container into the several shorter ones. "When the child contemplates the unequal levels," Piaget writes, "he forgets the widths, and when he observes the unequal widths, he forgets what he has just thought about the relations [between] levels."[18] At other moments, the children change their minds or oscillate between incompatible deductions, seemingly "insensible to contradiction."[19] Piaget concludes that children at this age are incapable of perceiving anything but a "gross, unidimensional quantity" (*quantité brute unidimensionelle*), as though they were able to "reason about only one relation at a time."[20]

We might speculate that the "gross, unidimensional quantity" to which Piaget refers is close to our most primordial and unmediated experience of bigness. Encountering a one-dimensional indicator of magnitude, such as the height of liquid in a particular glass, the child does not think to compare this datum with other information observed before or after. As Piaget writes, when the child makes a claim about an amount of liquid, she expresses "a perceptual relationship of difference between two qualities" and has no interest in any "logical multiplication of relations."[21] Mere sensory data and ontological deduction implicitly correspond: the height of the liquid simply *is* its magnitude. In Hegel's dialectical terms, no negativity intrudes upon the child's intuition of a sensuous certainty.[22] She neither measures discrete units nor compares present experience with past or future, but only reproduces an unadulterated sense impression. "Even when the child's criteria [for quantity] include the relation of 'big' [*gros*] or 'large' [*grand*]," as Piaget writes, such a relation remains a "simple perceptual given," and could as easily be describing the thing's color, texture, or shape—bigness belongs immanently to the thing itself.[23] And as an unreconstructed attribute, bigness is akin to a *tactile* experience, more like a direct contact with the body than a visual *quale* occurring at some modulated distance. The water in the glass *feels* tall, or *feels* more, just as the cow *feels* (too) big.

The child is thus an instinctive positivist, having no aptitude for negation or diminution, no mechanism for understanding, in Piaget's terms, either "relationships of differences" or "composition by partition."[24] And so we can also say, there is initially bigness *but not smallness*; bigness is sheer presence, but smallness would be a species of lack, something missing from the thing, a negation for which the child does not yet have categories. In short, *bigness precedes size*, on the same phenomenological level that, for Hegel, sensuous certainty precedes truth, or for Freud, the unconscious precedes thought.

What is big is too big. This postulate is essentially a psychological claim, even if the theoretical terms supporting it will be drawn chiefly from philosophy and aesthetics. Bigness is the cathexis of the object or image, its force or emotional gist, therefore also its abiding vitality, and as such is necessarily a superfluity or an embarrassment, viewed from any perspective of objectively proper (adult) scale. A consideration of the too-bigness of the thing—"baldly encountered" yet "not quite apprehended"[25]—helps illuminate some experiences that cultural theorists may otherwise find difficult or awkward to explain. For one thing, we seem frequently to be drawn to big objects and images *as* big; we are attracted by bigness, per se, independent of the function, purpose, or propriety of objects. At the same time, we seem to lack fully adequate critical tools for explaining such unalloyed attraction to magnitude. As a consequence of that lack, from the perspective of cultural theory—let us momentarily and polemically call the latter the taxidermic practice of analyzing the phenomenality of things as components of a system of objects—the quality of bigness tends to appear as infantile, blank and inarticulate, as it were without a dialectic. If so, we will have done well to commence our approach to an aesthetics of magnitude from the perspective of the child, endeavoring to access what Freud calls the "past" of our perceptions. Bigness is the unconscious non-delimitation of the thing, its tacit adverbial potency—its "*too*"—quite regardless of its nominal or adjectival content.

What Is Big Is Small

In May 2015, a team of photographers led by Filippo Blengini created what may have then been "the world's largest photo," a panoramic view of the Mont Blanc assembled from seventy thousand individual shots taken over several days.[26] The size of a record-setting photo is determined not by width or area, as it might be for a physical print, but rather by the quantity of digital information contained in the image: 365 gigapixels, as compared to, say, a 320-gigapixel panorama of London stitched together from about forty-eight thousand individual shots.[27] One could try to imagine printing an extremely large-format version of such a digital image—a journalist, presumably quoting information from the Blengini team, calculates that "the resulting 365-gigapixel photograph would be as large as a soccer field if printed at 300 dpi"[28]—but for obvious reasons such enormous prints are never produced. Indeed, the scale at which we end up viewing the "world's largest photo" is more or less that of a conventionally sized image, for instance, a photograph in a magazine or newspaper, or a screen image on a personal computer or phone.[29] Therefore the picture's bigness remains entirely a conceptual abstraction, never a direct experience. To put this another way, the Blengini team's photo of the Mont Blanc is big only in the same sense that the object of a cinematic special effect is big—the Hometree in *Avatar* or the *Giganotosaurus* in *Jurassic World Dominion*—by virtue of an iconography or signification of enormity that an audience correctly interprets. To be sure, the actual Mont Blanc is a very large mountain, but the world's largest photo of that mountain has no greater physical extension than a film image of Mount Olympus in *Clash of the Titans,* Mount Doom in *The Lord of the Rings,* Snake Mountain in *Masters of the Universe,* or Mount Wundagore in *Doctor Strange in the Multiverse of Madness.*

By contrast, the world's smallest image is a strictly physical object that can be measured in precise lengths and widths, a reproduction of a *National Geographic Kids* magazine cover "nano-chiseled" from a polymer at eleven by fourteen micrometers.[30] However, unrescaled though it may be, this reproduction is no more available to be seen by human eyes than the hypothetical football-field-sized print of the Mont Blanc, except through the assistance of a prosthetic technology such as a microscope or computer program that can enlarge it for us. Like the magnitude of the world's biggest picture, the magnitude of the world's smallest is graspable only as information, gleaned through media that compensate for the limitations of human senses. In either case, the version of the picture we ultimately view belongs, to use a term Joshua DiCaglio aptly borrows from the field of statistics, to the same "scale domain" as all other images humans are likely to encounter in everyday life.[31] Aside from a handful of explanatory captions or gauges placed next to it on its web page, and even if we learn that it was originally intended to be viewed "live" through a microscope, the world's smallest image for the most part "looks much like any other cover of the children's magazine" it depicts.[32]

Assuming that any image, qua image, requires at least the potential to be viewed by a human (or other) subject, it may be reasonable to assert that extremely large or extremely small pictures are not yet "images" at all, not even objects, but rather blank data sets awaiting reimaging to adjust their dimensions to the scale of a sensorium. As Friedrich Kittler argues, following Lacan, "art and media are fundamentally about the deception of sensory organs."[33] Like sound recordings pitched to the range of frequencies perceptible to the human ear (approximately 20 to 20,000 Hz), or projections employing colors within the visible light spectrum (approximately 380 to 750 nm), pictures are almost always sized or resized for the convenience of human apparatuses, or more precisely, for their illusion. Kittler's point can be supplemented with the theoretical caveat that the type of object we generally call a "picture" is something we might be within range to *touch*: the "beholder's body," as Michael Fried notes, is inextricably "part of the situation in which objecthood is established."[34] Thus even an image as extravagantly large as, say, a stellar constellation, when it gets viewed by a person as a single picture or icon rather than as an arbitrary selection of discrete stars, is rescaled approximately to the size of the worldly object it is imagined to duplicate (bear, dog, water dipper, crab, or harp). We then readily juxtapose the outlines of that replicated object over its configuration of stars as we observe them from earth using some device like a constellation diagram or smart phone app, reifying the iconic shape of that segment of the firmament. A single atom, too, when it becomes an image, is roughly human-scaled, perhaps the size of a marble or a golf ball. Not by coincidence do pictograms of atoms resembles solar systems or galaxies, equally convenient to human eye or hand when represented as ball-size.

In brief, *all pictures are the same size* or, to again employ DiCaglio's borrowed term, in the same "scale domain."[35] Let us say, to accommodate the outermost limits of pragmatic dimensionality, that all pictures range from a few millimeters narrow (rice-grain paintings from Turkey, India, and China) to a few hundred meters wide (the Nazca geoglyphs in Peru), but never much more or less than that, and nearly always within a much narrower range than those extremes. A picture is the size of a human body like a dollhouse is the size of a doll. Here we encounter the strange dialectic of bigness that will haunt all discourses of the sublime: what is big is in effect *small*. To become an image of excessive magnitude, to be perceivable or comprehensible as enormous, the image must first be small enough to conform to the magnitude of the body perceiving it. Even in the case of the world's smallest picture, its enormous smallness, so to speak, is "reduced" (which here means "enlarged," although arguably the magnitude of images is an absolute value) to the dimensions of a consumable image on a manipulable screen. And when its original magnitude emerges via the reproduction, it can do so only as reconfigured, sublimated, remediated, strictly a connotation of excess, or a figuration of the vastness of its miniaturization. Whatever thrill of extremity the image still possesses—and presumably it must possess some such energy if it generates interest in its being the "world's most" of anything—that thrill appears only in the nebulous guise of something slight, residual, infantile, id-like, only the vaguest hint of "possibly-being-crushed" haunting the taxidermic reproduction of a once-living enormity, evoked here via the subject's tentative or faintly erotic fascination with the now diminuted magnitude. Bigness is the residual cathexis of the image as a (physical) thing, never its real size or dimension: Bigness is *small.*

Uncompromising Bulk

In the opening scene of *Star Wars,* as we gaze into a vast field of stars, the camera "tilts down to reveal a planetary surface from a low orbit."[36] I am quoting from Scott Bukatman's brief reading of this scene in his essay "Zooming Out: The End of Offscreen Space." From the upper corner of the film screen, emerging as though from over the audience's right shoulder, "a spaceship enters the frame" and zips past, heading toward the planet. As the ship moves away from us, lasers (or some exotic weapons) shoot after it, and we are alerted to the presence of an attacking ship approaching from the rear: "Its pursuer enters from above and behind the camera. A triangular prow glides into view. And glides. And glides. And glides."[37] As Bukatman's repetition suggests, the massive attacking ship does not so much appear on-screen as *continue* to appear, consuming, as reckoned by the scale established by the first ship's passage, a surprisingly long time to complete its journey through the frame. The set designers have skillfully detailed the great ship to enhance its steadfast emergence. Its bigness seems to increase exponentially as portions of its workings—for instance, what appears to be a huge loading bay in the underside of the hull—are successively dwarfed by ever larger machinery coming into view. At long last, the "uncompromising bulk" of the ship devours almost the entire screen, then heads away toward its target as we finally view the glow of its colossal afterburners.[38]

Once the huge ship traverses the frame, the camera is done concentrating on detail and immediately cuts to a wider shot showing explicitly what the audience has already surmised, that a terribly lopsided space battle is taking place. With its David-and-Goliath motif established through this visual contrast, the *Star Wars* franchise is underway, along with all the calculated genre play that will be its stock in trade. Arguably, the films will never rediscover, here or in any of the sequels, a shot of such formal splendor and visual impact as this opening scene—certainly not in later counterparts such as the explosions of the planet Alderaan or the Death Star, spectacles of vast, genocidal violence as undistinguished and sterile as one might ever encounter in popular cinema. In a sense, the conceptual and ideological potency of the subsequent epic of empire and rebellion is already achieved with the juxtaposition of the two ships, and above all by the emergent magnitude of that imperial cruiser, its sheer, outrageous bigness, exemplifying whatever thrill may continue to inflect the melodrama of overweening power confronted by underdog resistance.[39]

Yet, to state a kind of open secret, one presumably too obvious to be avowed in most film critiques, the ship we see on the screen is not a physical thing at all. It is not even *big*, except by virtue of an illusion: mattes, models, and camera tricks are employed to construct an image that strictly neither varies in size nor, as Bukatman suggests, "slides over" the viewer in anything but a figural sense. The tricky phenomenological task therefore prompted by the shot is to locate within this undeniably powerful spectacle a cathexis of physical massiveness that animates the impression of sublimity conveyed by the clever filming of the model. To put this another way, the task is to locate the precise point of distinction in the ship's dual status as literal and figural "object." A full explanation of why this image of (a model of) a big ship on a fixed-size screen can seem to loom like an actual *thing* would require much more than a treatise on the phenomenology of representation; it would also need to address our most basic unconscious imbrication of reality with image, and of consciousness with fantasy. For present purposes, the fleeting yet powerful moment of the "too big" provided by this brief scenario—"You remember the shot," Bukatman writes, "I'm sure you do"—at least exposes a few of the most visible distensions, so to speak, of the psychological problem of an aesthetics of magnitude.

We may continue to consider Bukatman's fine description by noting a slight but telling discrepancy in the figural registers he employs. Far from being a specific fault of Bukatman's language, this discrepancy exemplifies an entirely customary means of describing film imagery, one to be rediscovered perhaps in every account, including my own, of size differences on-screen. The *ship* increases in magnitude until it becomes an "uncompromising bulk," but the *image* of the ship, by necessity, remains the same size throughout. Both film theorists and film viewers presumably attribute such a juxtaposition of orders of magnitude to the intervention of the film camera, which modulates the apparent size of the moving object through the changes of lens, editing technology, and so on. It would be especially pointless to state such truisms were it not for the fact that they tend to remain submerged in the rhetoric that critics typically employ to describe the cinematic image, a rhetoric that defaults to a referential mode that speaks of the object on the screen as actual and "suspends disbelief" in its great size or other fantastic attributes, to use an old-fashioned term for this old-fashioned problem.[40] Thus, Bukatman's language implies that the big ship comes to appear close to the body of the film viewer—"sliding over us," as he says—much in the same way the too-big cow was close to the body of my child at the Farm-in-the-Zoo: "its uncompromising bulk—which is still appearing, its expanse is still sliding over us—throws our learned sense of scale onto the scrap heap."[41] Sufficiently visceral or "close" still to spur emotion, it is nevertheless sufficiently anodyne and distant to be consumed and enjoyed, even reduplicated in the form of posters and toys.

It might be fair, then—not only within some hackneyed movie-review language, but in precise philosophical terms—to describe the effect of the opening of *Star Wars* as one of "childlike wonder," albeit tenuously linked to what Mary Ann Doane names "the castrating tendenc[y]" or "a radical violence to the body" implied by the unseemly scale of the close-up.[42] The infantile or adolescent aspect of the giant ship, or of its sheer bigness, represents a nondialectical *blank* for cultural theory, a fruitfully obtuse flagrancy, which makes Bukatman's endeavor to analyze its formal features, and his portrayal of the physical experience of seeing *Star Wars*, all the more constructive. Any critical approach to bigness in the image must embrace the tactics of an archaeologist presented with a fascinating but obscure physical artifact, in the same sense in which Freud describes the practice of psychoanalysis as akin to "the technique of excavating a buried city."[43] We seek the latent "too" in the bigness of the image. What makes a big thing fascinating or provoking must be the vestigial feeling of the possibly-being-crushed, its immemorial phenomenological root, dissimulated in secondary processes of representation. We seek to explain the uncanny vividness of its taxidermy.

Finally, then, we might observe the peculiarly circumscribed potency of such sublimation when we look, as Bukatman invites us to do, at cinematic media that aim to produce a more "real" phenomenological immersion, such as 3-D or IMAX. Contrasting the IMAX experience favorably with, say, that of a portable computer screen, Bukatman writes: "While IMAX films present an 'unframed' image, the Web (like GUI'S [*sic*]—graphical user interfaces—in general) is *all* windows, frames, borders, and boundaries."[44] One sees the contrast Bukatman is aiming for, as well as the blatancy of the divergence between these two types of media, although even this dichotomy may be drawn too starkly. One might opt to treat the quotation marks that Bukatman places around the term "unframed" as scare quotes, connoting the necessarily partial degree to which this term actually describes IMAX or any other existent cinematic technology. For one thing, IMAX, too, is of course very well framed within its theatrical location, and restricted to a repertoire of visual and aural stimuli, *distanced* senses, despite efforts in some theaters or amusement parks to add tactile, bodily, and other sensations to the show.[45] For another thing—in the end, this may be the governing limit upon all immersive mass media insofar as they are "harnessed" to the context of late capitalism, which so far remains the only context in which such media are likely to be manufactured[46]—the sense of immersion in an IMAX film must be carefully delimited by the constraints of the marketability of its commodity form. Bluntly, the viewer cannot literally feel he or she is hurtling out of control down a bobsled track or swinging through canyons of city buildings on a spiderweb thread, any more than an Oculus Rift or Meta Quest headset could afford to replicate realistically the horror of meeting monsters or demons in a virtual reality game, the terror of falling off a cliff or skyscraper, or the nausea of weightlessness in outer space, while still hoping to sell itself to a broad swath of consumers. Yet even here—one is tempted to say, even *more* so in the IMAX theater or with a VR headset than in a conventional theater environment, let alone on some portable screen—the secret phenomenological heart of the image potently animates its eventual effect upon the viewer. One might even assert that its bigness is the index of its realism, the magnitude of our tendency to treat it as objective and therefore to allow it, always momentarily and always in a manner circumscribed, formal, and ultimately consumable, to evoke a primal terror in which the child's body is beset by the looming bigness of the thing. And this may finally be what Bukatman means when he says that immersive (or "hypercinematic") media "make quite a fetish of physical presence."[47]

It has become sometimes useful, following Timothy Morton, to identify very big things as *hyperobjects*, "massively distributed in time and space relative to humans."[48] With due deference to Morton's critique, and for reasons that will become gradually clearer, I argue something like the opposite: big things are always smaller than they seem, always resolutely contained within the determinate capacities of human perception and aesthetic comprehension. Bigness therefore emerges as an ambivalent critical category for reasons somewhat different than those Morton gives. Bigness is an attribute always not quite itself, even as its object may be all too exactly what it appears to be. Objects and images only become big by conforming to domains of perception or imagination that constrain their magnitudes effectively within sets of attributes "relative to humans," in Morton's own terms. The result is a counterintuitive reductionism, even a certain parochialism, of scale: insofar as things are perceivable by us—which is also to say, insofar as things are formed into images—they are all, more or less, the same size.

Hence my second postulate: *what is big is small*. Indeed, big things are *small* even as they are, per my first postulate, *too big*. With this paradoxical pairing, I gesture toward a framework for a theory of magnitude, but mindful that the stubborn resistance of bigness to categorical or systematic treatment, its persistent self-contradiction or self-subversion, is part of what makes it an interesting critical topic in the first place. Respectful of such resistance, instead of designing a theory of bigness in successive steps or polite linear order, the book opts to wend its way through a series of examples, drawing what potential claims it can from each in turn. For the most part, I do not collate my discussions into conventional chapters; they remain as short or long as a given example or subtopic warrants, in turn suggesting multiple possible routes through the aphoristic material. Consider this perhaps a critical analog to the meandering form and circulation pattern of the Oakland Museum, a building prompted by misgivings about forthright monumentality. As in the Oakland Museum, such variability seems at once well suited and fruitfully hostile to the question of bigness, which can, sometimes like the very big thing itself, and not coincidentally, emerge into visibility only in fits and starts even alongside its own blatancy. My hope is that the book's composition therefore reflects a core trait of "big culture" over and above my own limitations as a theorist, and moves determinedly if haltingly toward an aesthetics of magnitude.

What is big is *too big*; (therefore) what is big is *small*.

✷ 3 ✷

Unsublimity

THE ATOMIC BOMB

The Bomb Is Too Big

The first atomic bomb test, named for obscure reasons "Trinity" by the administrators of the Manhattan Project, was conducted secretly in Alamogordo, New Mexico, on July 16, 1945. At that time, the horrors to be visited upon Hiroshima and Nagasaki were still weeks away, and the enormity of the bomb still a mathematical abstraction to be estimated, appreciated, even joked about. Los Alamos scientists ran a betting pool on how big the Alamogordo blast would be, wagering—one may view this as typical military euphemism or as an epitome of the scientist as naive adolescent in a high-tech playground—whether the Trinity "gadget" would be a "boy" or a "girl," by which the scientists meant a success or a dud.[1]

By nearly all accounts, the magnitude of the Trinity test greatly exceeded expectations, a surfeit that lent itself to the impromptu task, among the scientists and military personnel who were its first witnesses, of describing the explosion's bigness.[2] "Words are inadequate tools for the job of acquainting those not present with the physical, mental and psychological effects," General Thomas Farrell comments in a description quoted by General Leslie Groves in his memorandum to the US secretary of war.[3] "The lighting effects beggared description," Farrell says: "It lighted every peak, crevasse, and ridge of the nearby mountain range with a clarity and beauty that cannot be described but must be seen to be imagined."[4] General Farrell does not shy from figures of classical aesthetics: "It was that beauty the great poets dream about but describe most poorly and inadequately . . . and made us feel that we puny things were blasphemous to dare tamper with the forces heretofore reserved to the Almighty."[5]

Alongside stock theology and somewhat sketchy logic (the bomb "must be seen to be imagined"), synesthesia is a typical feature of eyewitness accounts at Alamogordo, prompted both by the intensity of the flash and by the destructiveness to real objects and bodies (so far mainly potential) of the bomb's radiation and shockwave. The multisensory or extrasensory quality of the bomb's light is almost invariably the first focus. The physicist Isidor Isaac Rabi, who was located at base camp approximately ten miles from ground zero, writes: "There was an enormous flash of light, the brightest light I have ever seen or that I think anyone has ever seen. It blasted, it pounced, it bored its way right through you. It was a vision which was seen with more than the eye."[6] Rabi's colleague Philip Morrison, similarly positioned, writes that the flash "was like opening a hot oven with the sun coming out like a sunrise."[7] William Laurence, a *New York Times* reporter on the scene, describes "a sunrise such as the world had never seen, a great green super-sun."[8]

A month later, survivors of the atomic bombings of Hiroshima and Nagasaki offer similar depictions of a transcendently potent flash, attempting to capture the superfluity of its radiance with metaphor or simile. Eyewitnesses describe "a sheet of sun"[9]—"that dreadful brilliance seemed enough to melt me; the whole world turned a lightless white"; "I thought, 'the whole world is dyed orange' "; "I was enveloped by a blue flash, like lightning at the bottom of the sea."[10] Yoshito Matsushige, a newspaper photographer in Hiroshima, writes that "a bluish-white light filled the room, as if someone had ignited a huge amount of magnesium right before my eyes."[11] Witnesses less familiar than Matsushige with photographic equipment still frequently employ the simile of a camera flash: "like a powerful ribbon-flash of magnesium"; "like the magnesium flash of a camera"; "very like a photographer's flare"; "burning magnesium."[12] The uncanny pairing of this mundane image of the camera flash with the tremendous intensity of the bomb's light suggests a paradox parallel to that of the sublime, an image or object for which, in Kant's terms, "no presentation adequate to [it] is possible" but which is nonetheless "present[ed]" in a single idea.[13] The bomb's bigness is tantamount to, and expressed by, the "insufficiency of language" itself; but therefore a certain modulation of linguistic ineptitude may be deployed dialectically to relay, if not precisely to describe, the event's magnitude.[14] Incongruously but nonetheless lucidly, linguistic failure in the face of an atomic bomb explosion is equivalent to rhetorical success.

Such a paradox is readily observable in one of the most detailed narratives of the Hiroshima bombing and aftermath, Toyofumi Ogura's *Letters from the End of the World*. Ogura was a history professor at Hiroshima University; his memoir begins as he is walking to work on the morning of August 6, several kilometers from what will momentarily become the bomb's epicenter. Ogura's tone is lush, verging on histrionic, as he describes the weather almost like a movie backdrop for the impending cataclysm:

> It was a fine morning, windless and sultry, typical for the area around Hiroshima, as you know. The midsummer morning sunlight filled the sky to the point of overflowing. The brilliance of the light glinting off the mist in the blue sky was almost painful. The air-raid alert had been lifted about thirty minutes or an hour before and I was walking absentmindedly along the dusty paved road. I came to the east side of Shin'ozu Bridge.[15]

The explosion, when it comes, transfigures the scene even as the cadence of Ogura's narrative continues weirdly unaltered: "I stopped there for a minute, and just as I looked toward the sea and noticed the way the waves were sparkling, I saw, or rather felt, an enormous bluish flash of light, as when a photographer lights a dish of magnesium." The ironic inadequacy of language emerges first in Ogura's modest qualifying phrase, "or rather felt," by which he adjusts the assertion that he "saw" the explosion's light, followed by his almost contemplative use of the standard simile of the camera flash. However, in the next two sentences, Ogura accomplishes a poetic coup, dire and magnificent in its merging of the quotidian and apocalyptic:

> Off to my right the sky split open over the city of Hiroshima. I instinctively flung myself facedown onto the ground.

The brutal catachresis of Ogura's phrase, "the sky split open," supplants the several trifling moments of personal disorientation that precede it: the equivocal assertion that he "saw, or rather felt" the flash; the slightly fussy tone with which he employs the photographic simile; even the eerily mundane qualification that the explosion happened "off to my right." The morning sunlight had already been "overflowing" and "almost painful," but now the very firmament disintegrates, and both Ogura's individual gaze and the sentimental language of the weather are annulled. The volatility of Ogura's figural chains conveys this cosmic upheaval; "instinct" is the sole remaining subjective response. Indeed, the impropriety of the language that Ogura employs, both in its catachrestic excesses and in its vacillation between lavish analogy and finicky detail, comprises its poetic triumph. The too-big thing emerges not directly, nor even dialectically through metaphor or analogy, but rather only ecstatically through the eccentricities and fissures of language itself. Certainly, for Ogura, words are "inadequate tools," as they were for General Farrell, yet their cumulative malfunction comprises a fair revisualization of what otherwise must remain obscure, not because the big thing was too dark or distant to be seen, but because it was far too visible.[16]

Middle Distance

The closer eyewitnesses are to the epicenter of an atomic blast, the more confusedly but tellingly their narratives enact the impossibility of description. The following account is from an "ordinary . . . A-bomb victim," as the writer and chronicler Kenzaburo Oe names him, a butcher working about two kilometers from the Hiroshima epicenter, who suffered terrible radiation sickness and eventually went blind. More fully than Ogura, and in proportion to his more drastic proximity, the butcher forsakes any visual perspective that might furnish even the partial lucidity required of an image:

> At the time of the atomic bombing, I was working in a butchery near the Otagawa Canal in western Hiroshima. I heard a great *dokan* [bang] sound, and in an instant was blown flat on my back on the concrete floor. Owing to the summer heat, I was wearing only a work apron over a sleeveless undershirt; and in the butchery we went barefooted, so many glass splinters stuck in my feet. Even though I was unconscious, I kept hearing a strange sound.[17]

This story echoes other close accounts from Hiroshima and Nagasaki; it might even be called a typical narrative of atomic bombing from a middle distance, which is to say, originating at a site sufficiently far from ground zero for the witness to have survived the blast yet close enough for him or her to have been powerfully stricken by the *pikadon* ("flash-boom").[18]

I will pause to remark that, strictly in the capacity of retrospective critic or theorist, I now write in an entirely mercenary mode. At the middle distance where Oe's butcher stood working in his shop, close enough to the epicenter, but not too close, or in George Bataille's blunt words, "enduring the effect without dying," his retrospective narrative fulfills certain aesthetic demands convenient to the reader or critic.[19] First, the narrative simply exists, because its speaker is not among those tens of thousands instantly killed or mortally wounded. Second, in its depiction of a specific proximity, the narrative productively fails, even more evocatively than Ogura's, to observe the magnitude of the event. At this middle distance, the bomb is too close, *too big*, to be seen at all, and can only be felt. At the risk of a callous analogy, I would compare Oe's narrative, in its formal shape and delimitation if decidedly not in its effect, to my child's experience of the cow in the Farm-in-the-Zoo, an infantile-phenomenological encounter with the possibly-being-crushed. The bomb, for Oe's butcher, is a direct and destructive impact upon the body, its violence transmittable through a synesthesia no less lucid for its illogic or incoherence, in which the butcher's very inability to assimilate what has happened signifies the event's potency and the narrative's realism.

Unlike Ogura or the Trinity scientists, the butcher sees no flash, let alone any naturalistic or quasi-biblical spectacle. Instead, his whole body is blown down, seemingly by the *sound* of the "bang"; shards of glass embed themselves in his feet, or rather appear already embedded there, as though cause and effect were indistinguishable; uncannily, he recalls both being "unconscious" and "hearing a strange sound." In reconstructing his experience, the butcher therefore situates himself neither as an eyewitness nor, frankly, as the "ordinary victim" that Oe names him, but rather as a blunt and unalloyed object of his own narrative, a being abruptly separated from his own awareness by something so great as to overwhelm his individual sensory capacities, or maybe to fuse them together. Even the boundary between conscious and unconscious is disarticulated.[20] Thus, at the extreme inner edge of a potentially narratable distance from the epicenter, one encounters what Bataille calls the "very human vertigo" that at most connotes the catastrophe, and which presupposes (regardless of their incompatibility) both "the sort of proximity created by the sensory imagination" and "a minimum of distance" needed to generate a story.[21] Synesthesia and catachresis, the productive malfunction of sensation and figuration, compose the narrator's accurate yet unreadable rhetorical gauge of the event's bigness, as it were the pressure of the real referent violently forcing its way back up through the screen of the signifier.

For "the citizens of Hiroshima," as David Nye writes, remaining guardedly sardonic about what is extremely obvious, "the bomb did not reveal a new landscape, nor was it the ultimate in spectacular lighting."[22] One might assert that a revelatory *viewpoint* from middle distance in Hiroshima is strictly impossible, regardless of the fact that it remains the optimal basis for the narrative reconstruction of an eyewitness account. In its lieu is the unassimilable, even uninterpretable, juncture of proximity and detachment, a rhetorical non-site at which somebody is assailed by too-big sensations—not yet by "the bomb," per se, but only by its *dokan* or *pikadon*—yet some mind survives to tell the tale. And this determinate failure of viewpoint reminds us why we are still too close for anything like the sublime, quite unlike in the accounts from Alamogordo or even from Ogura's comparatively safe vantage at Shin'ozu Bridge, several kilometers further away than Oe's butcher. The bomb is still much *too big*, which is also to say, it is not yet *small* enough to be merely sublime.[23]

A common impression relayed by middle-distance A-bomb victims is that only their own houses had been struck, or that some conventional weapon had detonated next door or somewhere down the street. The impact of an explosion larger than anything ever made by humans is first encountered as a local, even individual phenomenon, prompting a misjudgment that Bataille consistently observes in the accounts relayed by John Hersey, and which other writers have identified as "one of [the] trademarks" of atomic explosions.[24] Thus Bataille suggests:

> What we learn from John Hersey about the arrival onto the scene of the atomic bomb is no different from, or differs little from, what has been reported of thousands of large bombs. The impression is not much stronger; it only requires multiplying by the large number—more than two hundred thousand—of those who, in varying degrees, experienced the bomb.[25]

Pursuing Bataille's provocation about the unreliability of eyewitnesses, we are invited to consider that the atomic bomb's unprecedented bigness is strangely irrelevant to narrative, and that the objective scale of the event, as it is conveyed well after the fact, is fundamentally disconnected from any phenomenology of the actual bodies of its victims. Indeed, the disconnection, in Hersey and elsewhere, between the first recollections of middle-distance survivors and the scale of annihilation they discover when they finally emerge into the destroyed city confirms what Bataille identifies as a kind of solipsism of trauma, described again with characteristic impudence:

> The individual in the streets of Hiroshima, dazzled by an immense flash . . . learned nothing from the colossal explosion. He submitted to it like an animal, not even knowing its gigantic scope.[26]

A bomb story "has only sensory value, since what there is of *intelligence* in it is mistaken."[27] Paradoxically, the bomb is both too close and too far away to be reckoned with. Like the unconscious itself, which, as Freud suggests, knows "no negation, no dubiety, no varying degrees of certainty," the primal quality of bigness can scarcely enter any conscious "human" story able to adequately measure it.[28]

Yet what most concerns Bataille, in his capacity as both literary and political critic, is what happens after the initial responses, when Hersey's eyewitnesses draw back and rediscover a "human" perspective, as it were a taxidermic reconfiguration of their prior "animal" immersion. This drawing back occurs almost like a truncated phenomenological history of the invention of consciousness itself, perhaps an analog for the coalescence of the adult's sense of measurement or proportion out of the child's sensuous immersion: "The interest of John Hersey's remarkable book has to do with the slowness of a revelation that gradually changes a catastrophe, which strikes in an isolated, animal way, into an intelligible representation."[29] Now, as the victims grasp the magnitude of the event and relinquish the "animal" mode exemplified by the fertile wrongness of synesthesia and catachresis, the bomb acquires its correct scale, along with the attributes of an objectivity perhaps sufficient to identify a "hyperobject." It has become *big*, which is to say, with deep irony, that it has become *small*, a mere "intelligible representation" of something that annihilates whole cities. And therefore we verge on the very different horror of a disaffected understanding of what has occurred in Hiroshima on August 6, 1945, akin to the understanding that Claude Lanzmann famously calls "obscene" in narrative reconstructions of the Holocaust.[30] Not by coincidence, it is at this stage of any given chronicle we may finally arrive at a sublime image, by virtue of which the mind forms what Kant calls a "representation . . . of quantity."[31] Sublimity requires, with that same deep irony, the manageable and narratable *smallness* of the depiction of what is absolutely large.

And on this ambivalent basis, the belated and distanced fruition of the sublime, begins the long cultural-historical project of "accurately" representing the bomb's magnitude, of graphing it, quantifying its effects, tallying its casualties both immediate and postponed, gauging its power in kilotons and megatons of TNT, comparing it to other powers both natural and human-made, and so on.[32] In this domain of measurement and instrumentality, formal elegance and propaganda are practically indistinguishable, and scale becomes the tool of regulation, commodification, and proliferation. In essence, we have returned to the spirit of the wager that amused the Los Alamos scientists as they prepared for the first atomic test at Alamogordo. We *represent* the bomb's excessive bigness, composing of it an estimable and calculable tableau, as convenient and well framed and consumable as you like, until finally we are able to send postcards of mushroom clouds or draw children's cartoons of A-bombs or H-bombs with only the vaguest residual intimation, if any at all, of their real violence. In phenomenological terms, the bomb becomes *big* only when it is sufficiently no longer *too big* that it is permitted to become *small*.

The Sublime

The canonical seventeenth- through nineteenth-century European theories of the sublime (more precisely, of the "natural sublime") exhibit a chronic equivocation in terminology that I would suggest is akin to our most elemental relations to bigness.[33] Thomas Burnet asserts that "there is something august and stately in the Air" of the "greatest Objects of Nature," but he can identify only "the Shadow and Appearance of INFINITE" as its cause: "as all Things that are too big for our Comprehension, they fill and over-bear the Mind with the Excess, and cast it into a pleasing kind of Stupor and Admiration."[34] For John Dennis, "ordinary Passions" become "Enthusiasms" in the contemplation of an uncommonly "vast and glorious Body" such as the sun, yet neither a psychological rationale for this shift from ordinary experience to sublime "Meditation," nor the source of "Enthusiasms," ever becomes fully accessible, as Dennis admits: "I call the very same Passions Enthusiasms, when their Cause is not clearly comprehended by him who feels them."[35] The third Earl of Shaftesbury, cataloging the "vast," "ponderous," "huge," and "deep" spectacles of the natural landscape, suggests that "thoughtless Men, seiz'd with the Newness of such Objects, become thoughtful," and Joseph Addison suggests that we are "struck . . . with that rude kind of Magnificence" or "flung into a pleasing Astonishment" in the presence of "stupendous Works of Nature."[36] Yet both Shaftesbury and Addison ultimately rest with merely rhetorical connections between the sublime object and the extraordinary "thought" it provokes, opting for what Philip Shaw calls "a piling up of subordinate clauses with no apparent center."[37]

Throughout these speculations, perhaps owing to a Western-philosophical habit of rationalizing ambivalence in the guise of enquiry, a pair of theoretical tenets consistently emerges. The first is the identification of a "fear" or "terror" located somewhere at the core of the sublime experience, and the second is a "distance" permitting one to modulate or mitigate such terror with the assurance of ultimate security. The big thing is received, in Addison's words, "at the same time, as Dreadful and Harmless," and therefore the subject's response, as Kant eventually writes, "is, in view of the safety in which [the spectator] knows himself to be, not actual fear."[38] However, distance is no less theoretically indefinite than the sublime's more primal terror, and both attributes tend to be slippery or even self-contradictory, producing fruitful oxymorons. John Dennis calls the sublime a "delightful Horrour" or "terrible Joy," while Frances Reynolds suggests that the mind "seems to stand, or rather to waver, between certainty and uncertainty, between security and destruction."[39] Neil Hertz, observing such prevailing mystifications in the classic terminology of the sublime—he notes the consistent use of "verbs like 'baffle' and 'check' or nouns like 'astonishment' or 'difficulty'"—substitutes the psychoanalytic term "blockage" for the variety of expressions used by the seventeenth- and eighteenth-century writers.[40] In something akin to a psychological defense, the impression of real threat underlying an experience of the sublime is recast as hypothetical, figural, unreal; or it is merely reduced or distilled; or it is alloyed with compensatory opposites.

In the more systematic theorizations of Edmund Burke and Kant, the ambivalence of the sublime is elevated to the status of a philosophical category, regardless of what may seem the risk of conceptual self-contradiction. What Burke, following Dennis, names "delightful horror" or "tranquility tinged with terror" is now identified as the consequence of a delicate negotiation between sensation, perception, and object: "When danger or pain press too nearly, they are incapable of giving any delight, and are simply terrible; but at certain distances, and with certain modifications, they may be, and they are delightful."[41] A careful distinction between tactile and visual senses is key to the modulated "distance" of Burke's theory, as it is to Kant's. Objects of nature too close are painful because they are so gigantic at such an intimate range as to "make our capacity to resist into an insignificant trifle in comparison with their power."[42]

Kant suggests that, although we can have a direct and immediate "feeling" (*Gefühl*) for what is beautiful, the sublime instead offers only an indirect "pleasure" (*Lust*), arising through an inhibition and subsequent release of emotion that he says "is all the stronger" for having first been impeded: "the mind is not merely attracted by the object, but is also always reciprocally repelled by it."[43] Therefore the sublime is what Kant calls a "negative pleasure."[44] Its ambivalence arises because the object is "beyond all comparison" and can never be directly seen: "nothing therefore that can be [an] object of the senses is . . . to be called sublime."[45] Nevertheless, the very impossibility of perceiving the sublime object, its "infinity" for the human sensorium, is still grasped as an attribute integral to a single "presentation" (*Darstellung*), because, whether or not the whole *thing* can "be contained in any sensible form," reason tends to insist on cognizing objects in single strokes.[46]

Kant's list of objects that we might call sublime—more precisely, of objects that "excite the idea of the sublime" in the perceiver's mind[47]—somewhat confutes, or perhaps confirms by way of contrast, his reputation as a Königsbergian homebody:

> Bold, overhanging, as it were threatening cliffs, thunder clouds towering up into the heavens, bringing with them flashes of lightning and

> crashes of thunder, volcanoes with their all-destroying violence, hurricanes with the devastation they leave behind, the boundless ocean set into a rage, a lofty waterfall on a mighty river, etc.[48]

To this catalog of natural marvels, Kant adds some human-made objects, presumably also encountered by him secondhand: St. Peter's Basilica in Rome, the Egyptian pyramids, and a few others.[49] However, even this brief compendium raises problems, perhaps reflecting a general difficulty in pinning down the sources and precise effects of sublimity. For example, despite including a stormy ocean in his list, just earlier Kant had averred that "the wide ocean, enraged by storms, cannot be called sublime," ostensibly because, again, "the proper[ly] sublime cannot be contained in any sensible form, but concerns only ideas of reason."[50] And having mentioned human-made objects such as cathedrals and pyramids, a few pages later Kant sees fit to assert that "the sublime must not be shown in artistic productions (e.g., buildings, columns, etc.), where a human purpose [*Zweck*] determines the form as well as the magnitude."[51] In each such instance—this is to some degree characteristic of all of Kant's critiques—reconciliations may be possible between such conflicting statements, but the means or method to accomplish them is not wholly obvious. The convolutions of Kant's descriptions of psychological phenomena tend to reflect both their inherent complexity and the newness or inelegance of the philosophical terminology available for their formulation.

However, what more profoundly characterizes Kant's examples, whether natural or human-made, is the structural ambiguity of their relationship to the perceiver. When we draw sufficiently back from these threatening vistas—note that we have by no means worked out the precise literal or metaphorical gauge of the "distance" that a subject places between itself and the thing—the threat is controllable in the same formalistic sense as a sadomasochistic game with pain: "the sight of them becomes all the more attractive the more fearful it is, provided we find ourselves in safety."[52] Hence "negative pleasure" is produced by the disagreeable inadequacy of the imagination faced with "great magnitudes" and a corresponding gratification on the part of the reason in judging that same inadequacy from an ostensibly superior vantage. The dialectic of sadomasochistic abjection before bigness reconnects the child's ontological certainty of what is *too big* with the adult's epistemological conciliation in a single concrete moment somewhat analogous to a worked-through trauma. In the end, all theories of the sublime remind us that the remnant of unmediated, sensuous, infantile terror, the possibly-being-crushed, is reserved as emotional cathexis, awaiting reanimation in the adult's sporadic or accidental encounter with extraordinarily large objects.

So, in theories of the sublime, we reconfirm what Piaget observes in the responses of children to questions about magnitudes, that *bigness precedes size*. Somewhere in the heart of the static and desiccated "object" lies this primal cathexis, the feel of that dynamic mass of the too-big, too-close *thing*, a magnitude fundamentally different from anything measured and prior to all scale. If big objects, qua big, still succeed in fascinating the adult, then presumably the unconscious persists in asserting, in some inscrutable proportion to that adult responsiveness, the childlike feeling of possibly-being-crushed, a primordial yet amorphous threat of violence reactivated in the sublimated sadomasochistic game of "negative pleasure." Thus at the root of all theories of the sublime lies the embryonic impression that the "terror" of the *too big* abides in the potted imagery of pragmatic adulthood, ever capable of irrupting as a thrill or intimation of real emotion, rendering the object suddenly and (always) unexpectedly sublime.

Finally, in light of all this obscurity and complication, here is Kant's aptly convoluted summary of the ambivalence into which the mind is thrust by the unassimilable magnitude of the sublime object:

> The feeling of the sublime is thus a feeling of displeasure (*Unlust*) arising from the inadequacy of the imagination, in aesthetic estimation of magnitude, [for] the estimat[ion] through reason (*ästhetischen Größenschätzung zu der Schätzung durch die Vernunft*), and a pleasure (*Lust*) that is thereby aroused simultaneously from the agreement of this very judgment of the inadequacy of the greatest sensible faculty with ideas of reason, insofar as striving for them is still a law for us.[53]

The mind "feels itself moved"—note the vagueness of the terms—by the "idea of infinity," or by the excessive *quantity* of the thing's size, even if its bigness itself can never be perceived as a *quality*. This equivocation, the modulation of "displeasure" and the making-safe of "terror," is what I have figured as taxidermy, the adult's habit of stuffing (down) the vivid phenomenon of childhood and preserving only the outline or signifier of its prior force. The thing's primal bigness is bestilled, dematerialized, deanimated, made into a consumable image, or even just the silhouette or précis of such an image. Yet the object retains some of the material threat of possibly-being-crushed that provoked our primal response, and presumably continues to cathect our "negative pleasure."

The Bomb Is (Too) Small

Leaving behind the dreadful middle distance of Oe's butcher or Hersey's victims in Hiroshima and returning to something like the fully framed long shot of a film, we evolve a perspective that is, so to speak, much more possible but much less actual. From this vantage, and in the greater breadth of comprehension it enables, the atomic bomb can be a sublime object, even an icon, but its actual or potential trauma is sublimated away, distilled from phenomenological registers into the formal, statistical, and narratological. A little farther away from the epicenter, one might be able to observe something like the entire transition from *too big* to *small*, or the construction, out of the initial or primal "animal" trauma of the event, of a balanced, dialectical, even humanistic vocabulary of sublimity, akin to the "elision of difference" that Zachary Horton calls "scalar collapse."[54]

Toyofumi Ogura stood at such an apposite distance when the bomb exploded over Hiroshima, and he therefore finds himself capable within mere moments of reconstructing Bataille's "human perspective"; his firsthand account evolves rapidly into a secondhand drama of relatively aloof observation. Like all narratives of atomic aftermath, Ogura's story continues to exhibit vast suffering and horror, even as he wrestles with the disconnect between the fluency and even beauty of his own chronicle and the unutterable, almost notional agonies of the victims he encounters. The chief one of these victims is Ogura's own wife, Fumiyo, whom he eventually finds dying of radiation poisoning, and to whom the letters of the book's title are addressed. But even prior to Ogura's Dante-like trek into the center of the city, and long before he locates Fumiyo—indeed, commencing mere seconds after his first view of the blast from the Shin'ozu Bridge, four kilometers away—his letters strive to build a fairly conventional picture of a destroyed Hiroshima, opting for a sequence of images leading to the most iconic of all atomic figurations, the mushroom cloud:

> Then I raised my head and looked up over the city. To the west, in the sky that had been blue a minute before, I saw a mass of white clouds—or was it smoke? Whichever it was, it had taken shape in an instant. Then a halo of sparkling lights, a little bit like the ring that forms around the moon as a sign of rain, appeared near the cloud mass and expanded like a rainbow. . . .
>
> A massive cloud column defying all description appeared, boiling violently and seething upward. It was so big it blotted out much of the blue sky. Then the top of it began to spill down, like the breakup of some

> vast thundercloud, and the whole thing started to seep out and spread to the sides. The first cloud mass set down a foot like a huge waterspout, suddenly growing into the form of a monstrous mushroom.[55]

Ogura's leisure to begin, as he says, "mulling over" the scene, is underscored by the incongruous casualness of his own literary ambition, allusions to which accompany his voice throughout the story that follows.[56] Moving on from naturalistic similes, and contradicting his own conventional synoeciosis that the mushroom cloud "def[ies] description," Ogura opts for classical and theological terms: "I thought that it must be a manifestation of the *shumisen* cosmos that . . . the Buddhists of India talk about"; and immediately after: "I tried to visualize the cloud pillar seen by Moses that is mentioned in the Old Testament."[57] Eventually, Ogura joins these sentiments to a brief homily similar to Thomas Farrell's plea of linguistic inadequacy, acquiescing both to the impossible scale of destruction at hand and to the vexing (but in literary terms, entirely fruitful) misrelation it exposes between image and word: "the unsophisticated concepts and fantasies dreamed up by the ancients were useless to describe this horrible pageant of clouds and lights staged in the firmament."[58] A decisively modern cataclysm ("maybe it was some kind of flame projection, or a death ray?") makes classical or biblical literature "pale into insignificance," yet such imagery and style ("pageant," "firmament") continue to furnish a literary foil for Ogura's project of conveying, through a precisely determinate failure of modern terminology, the bomb's immensity.[59]

For Ogura, in keeping with his literary project of relaying a readable portrait of the enormity of the event, the bomb has now become sublime, precisely in the equivocal sense offered by Kant in his tellingly awkward description: "[What is] sublime is that which, even to be able to think of [it] demonstrates a faculty of the mind that surpasses every measure of the senses."[60] The luxuriousness of Kant's mild version of sadomasochism, a pleasure at one's own displeasure in a cerebral incapacity, resonates with the self-confessed wrongness of Ogura's narrative. Discovering himself constantly disengaged from the agonies he observes, Ogura remains, as he himself sometimes fully, sometimes hazily realizes, altogether too calm, too contemplative, too literate.

Ogura's writerly misalignment, allied with and yet so different in perspective from the misjudgments of victims at middle distance who thought "that a bomb had exploded in their immediate vicinity," might be termed the secondary wrongness of the sublime: the drastic inaptness of even an intimation of pleasure in reason (the faculty of retrospective literary composition) in light of the tremendous violence and suffering occurring virtually alongside it.[61] The novelistic chronicle of a destroyed world ("in those hours Hiroshima had ceased to exist") continues to be irreconcilable with the "world-destroying"[62] suffering of victims who were too close either to see or to care about any such expansive tableau. Ogura's deductions are somewhat like those which Heidegger, albeit in a very different context, calls "logically correct but metaphysically untrue."[63] And now Kant's own term "displeasure" may itself appear veritably obscene, to again invoke Claude Lanzmann's apt censure of conventional language and narrative at such moments, in plain sight of the extremity of suffering all too close at hand.

Yet "displeasure" is still an appropriate term for the narrow range of emotion Ogura exhibits as he tries, throughout the meandering course of his search for his wife and colleagues, to reconstruct the "stark spectacle" of Hiroshima.[64] Ogura's pseudo-suffering—this is not my own judgment but a paraphrase of Ogura's own persistent self-criticism—is expressed as a necessarily meager privation accompanying the survivor's task, whether pragmatic or literary: "I was struck dumb"; "I had lost all confidence"; "a crippling sense of insecurity"; "anxious"; "worried"; "cynical."[65] The primary agony of other people is translated into the secondary distress of Ogura's failure to do justice to that suffering, and yet the result is an apt rhetoric of aftermath, perhaps a type of exploitative inspiration. As Ogura approaches the city center, he confronts portraits of such transcendent misery that, as it was for Dante approaching the bottom of hell, the world-destroying violence at the obscure root of the sublime simultaneously arrests and revivifies his dialectical capacity for poetic description:

> I saw something that brought me to an abrupt halt. A swarm of people, all of them burned or injured, was teeming up the long, wide roadway. They looked like fragments or scraps of living organisms, motivated not by any personal desire to seek refuge but by some vast, tenacious "life force" that transcended individual will. I can't describe the scene adequately.[66]

The wrongness of Ogura's stance determinately fails even in its own failure to be the primary wrongness of the victim, an obscene dialectical gap of which Ogura is shrewdly aware: "I stood riveted to the spot, fascinated by what one could perhaps call the 'monstrous magnificence' of it all"; "It was relatively easy to walk on the roads of the incinerated city center"; "I noticed what looked like a long row of corpses laid out side by side along the streetcar line. . . . It was just like being at the fish market"; "I was amazed by the geometric consistency of the destructive force."[67] His fluent callousness belongs to the constitutive paradox at the heart of bigness; its sublimated and attenuated symptom, finally, is the paltry negative pleasure of sublimity.

Marketable Euphemism

It took some time for political and pop-cultural handlers of atomic bomb imagery to learn how to exhibit the bomb's sublimity in pictures. Early attempts are tellingly muddled. A well-known declassified film of the original Trinity test, made by a photographer for the US Department of Energy, reveals an almost comical failure to accommodate itself to the event it tries to document.[68] The explosion severely overexposes the film and is therefore first recorded only as a pure whiteness, the bomb's "magnesium flash" ironically rendering the literal photographic equipment completely ineffective. About fifteen seconds in, the blank monochrome of the overexposed image wanes and the outlines of the mushroom cloud begin to emerge, really because the explosion is now finished. But the camera operator is

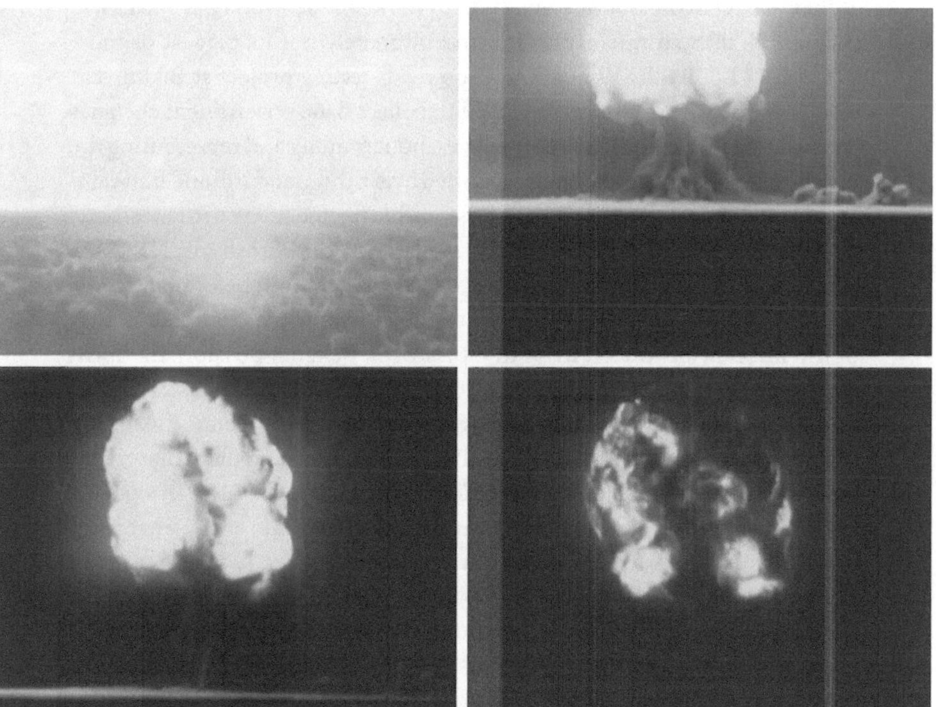

FIGURE 3.1 Trinity atomic test, New Mexico, July 16, 1945 (film by US Department of Energy)

compelled abruptly to tilt the lens upward, having realized, once he is able again to see at all, that the phenomenon has already exceeded the frame of his initial setup. Only alongside the failure of the equipment to capture a primary image of the explosion is some modicum of its incongruous size and violence recorded, in a way analogous to the potent failure of rhetoric in the firsthand accounts of Hiroshima discussed above.[69]

But both telemetric and aesthetic lessons were learned in due course. Photographing and measuring the bomb had been integral to its development and use from the beginning, and even at Hiroshima, telemetry was nearly as well planned as the bombing run itself. Indeed, what eyewitnesses in the city saw first, well before the explosion, were the parachuted measurement instruments dropped in anticipation of the *Enola Gay*'s arrival with the bomb. We ought therefore to consider any photographic or film footage a pointed ideological argument about how to view the bomb's spectacular bigness, or, by extension, about the political and cultural meaning of the sublime.

A year after Hiroshima, the American Joint Army/Navy Task Force One conducted Crossroads Baker, the second of twenty-three nuclear bomb tests at Bikini Atoll in the South Pacific Ocean between 1946 and 1958. Baker was the world's fifth atomic explosion, and ultimately not its biggest or most powerful.[70] But by the time of the Crossroads testing project at Bikini, and alongside the vast resources deployed to collect data, government agencies had become meticulous, even obsessive, about framing and representing the bomb. Scientists and documentarians used over a thousand still and film cameras to record the Crossroads Baker test, and corrected many of the aesthetic mistakes made trying to take pictures at Alamogordo, Hiroshima, Nagasaki, and even at the first Bikini test, Crossroads Able, a month before Baker.

For a number of reasons related to the convenience or marketability of the imagery produced from it, Crossroads Baker is possibly the most recognizable and iconic atomic explosion. The setup of the test, through both accidental and intentional design, was highly photogenic. The bomb was detonated under water, which damped the blinding flash that might have obscured the explosion's initial silhouette, as it did at Alamogordo. Yet the underwater blast, unlike underground atomic tests, enabled a dramatic above-surface viewing of its secondary effects, specifically, an immense plume that metonymically adduced, and even improved with a broader proportion and more satisfying symmetry, the expected shape of the mushroom cloud.[71] Both film and still photographers were then able to capture, or at least very directly to evoke, the event's immediate aftermath, albeit from a safe and aesthetically profitable distance and with a detail and clarity unique in such footage before or since.

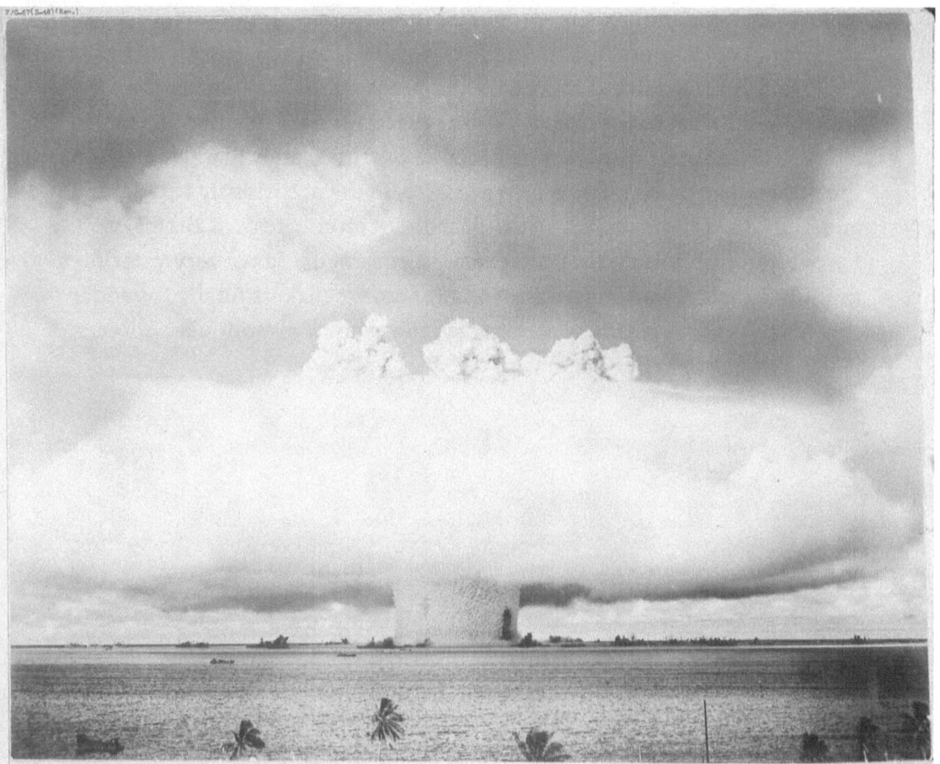

FIGURE 3.2 Crossroads Baker bomb test, Bikini Atoll, Marshall Islands, July 25, 1946 (film by US Department of Defense)

Other aspects of Bikini Atoll lent themselves to a clarifying revision of A-bomb photography. Details such as palm trees, grass huts, and a white beach sit placidly in the foreground, and the small, puffy clouds of a pleasant tropical day in the background, augmenting the massiveness of the explosion and some, but decidedly not all, of the ironies of its Edenic scenery.[72] The most familiar images of Crossroads Baker are taken from readily comprehensible positions either on the beach or from airplanes, and the explosion is in all cases symmetrically framed. If one compares the less composed photographs of Trinity, Hiroshima, and Nagasaki, the latter two taken from the returning planes that had dropped the bombs on Japan, the excessive degree to which the Baker test is constrained by the lens and frame becomes very apparent. In addition, because the Bikini projects were partly intended to gauge potential damage to ships and other equipment from an atomic attack, a number of large naval vessels, including decommissioned battleships and an aircraft carrier, were positioned close to the Baker blast site, providing indicators of scale otherwise absent from typical mushroom cloud photos. Hence the Crossroads Baker explosion is nicely suited to leaflets and promotional posters or, if we are watching the film, to the twenty or thirty seconds of a narrative "scene," in all cases delimited, finished, transportable, and ultimately marketable.[73] To the obscenity of such incongruity, as well as to the notoriously vast natural and human damage caused by the decades of atomic tests at Bikini Atoll, I would add only this: that pictures of Crossroads Baker very carefully modulate distance and light, allowing the image makers finally to render this blast as *big*—which is also to say, to make it, in political and even

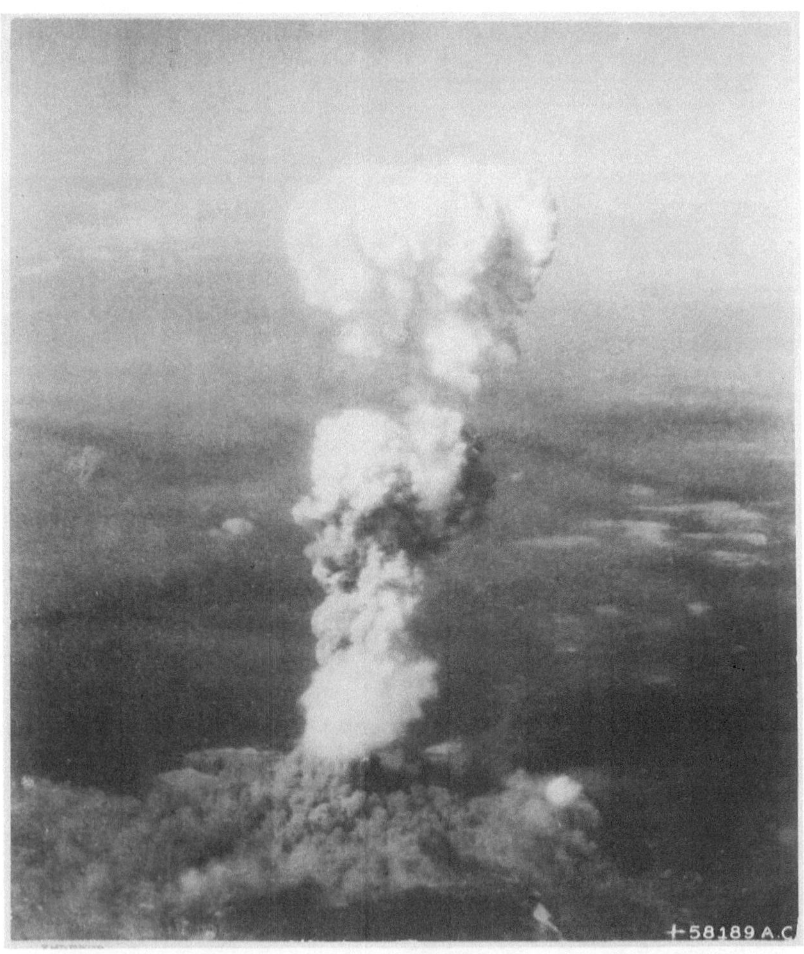

FIGURE 3.3 Hiroshima mushroom cloud, August 6, 1945 (photo by George R. Caron, from the B-29 bomber, *Enola Gay*; US National Archives at College Park)

ethical terms, altogether *too small*—"safe," in Kant's or Burke's language, but therefore, in political terms, catastrophically trivial. The sublime is *marketable euphemism*. It occurs only when the unsublime bigness of the bomb is already over and done, when the immediate power of the blast (but certainly not of its radiation or its medical or environmental effects) has subsided, and whatever hints remain of its crushing violence become susceptible to the taxidermic sublimation of the well-framed image.[74]

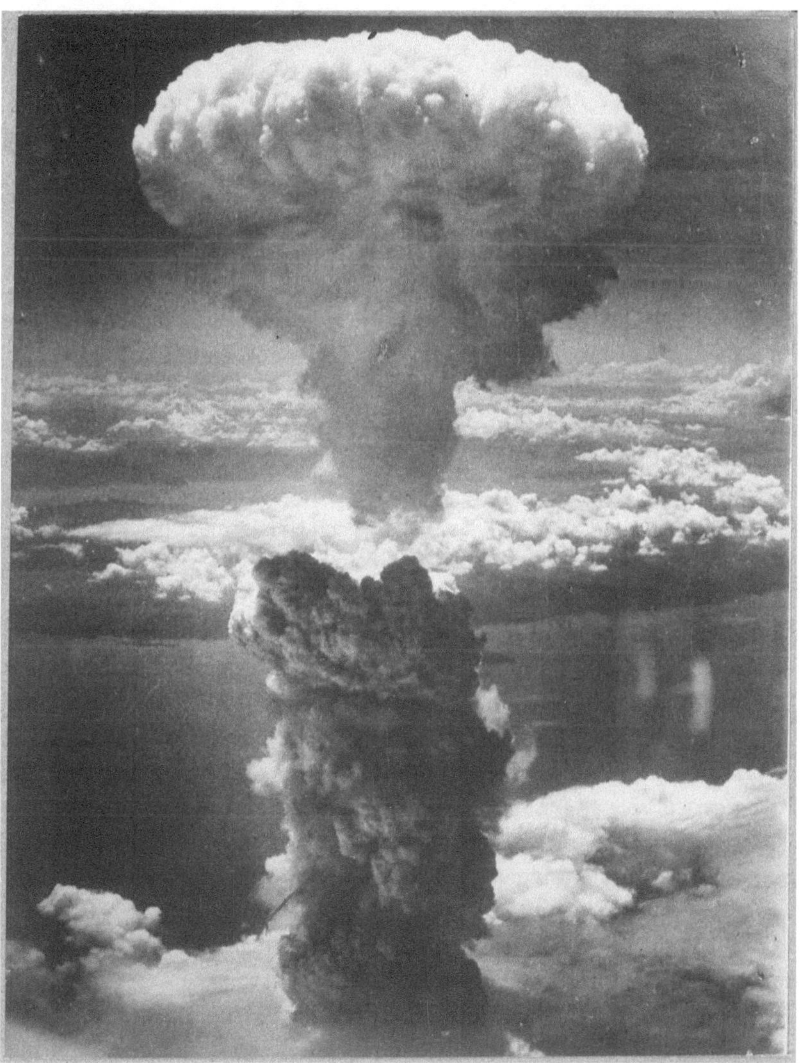

FIGURE 3.4 Nagasaki mushroom cloud, August 9, 1945 (photo by Charles Levy, from the B-29 bomber, *Great Artiste*; US National Archives at College Park)

✷ 4 ✷

Antinomy of an Aesthetics of Magnitude

Could Be Bigger

In Plato's dialogue *Parmenides*, a young Socrates converses with two of the best-known Eleatic philosophers of the prior generation, Parmenides and his student Zeno, discussing possible objections to a theory of forms. During the exchange, issues of size come to exemplify broader questions about the relation between objects and attributes, and between general and particular. Parmenides shows Socrates that if a big thing "partakes" of the form of bigness (*mégethos*), then it becomes difficult to think cogently about what the quality of "bigness itself" might be; in essence, bigness must be both a "certain single character" in itself and a mutable quality of many different things "by virtue of which they appear big."[1] Therefore Parmenides suggests that the form of bigness is both "one" and of "an indefinite number," a logically untenable situation, as Socrates agrees. For instance, if the form of bigness proves to be "divisible," such that we can attach it to any number of things of different magnitudes, then some instances of bigness turn out, perversely, to be smaller than others.[2] The conclusion of the dialogue finds none of the three thinkers, least of all Socrates, inclined to resolve this conundrum; as a result, bigness retains its equivocal role as simultaneously present and absent in the thing.[3]

In part because of the rigor of its indecisiveness, the *Parmenides* succeeds in presenting the general terms of a conceptual problem that will echo in speculations about forms and attributes throughout Western philosophy in the guise of a vexing dualism. The difficulty philosophers confront is in determining how an object can be said to have a certain quality and how we simultaneously know, independent of the specific configuration of the object, what the perceived quality itself is supposed to be. Thus the problem of magnitude is connected to the broader issue of the immanence of material attributes or qualities, and therefore also to debates that will reemerge in Cartesian, Kantian, and Hegelian metaphysics of subject and object, right up to contemporary modalities such as object-oriented ontology and new materialism. This is among the reasons Alain Badiou identifies the *Parmenides* as the touchstone for the fundamental Western-metaphysical problem of "the one and the multiple."[4]

For the purposes of my narrower discussion of the aesthetics of magnitude, and also sidestepping the most severe convolutions of both the *Parmenides* and the history of metaphysics that ensues from it, we can follow a hint of Plato: When the inquiry into forms encounters such a crisis of objectivity, or when its theorist strives to persuade an especially worthy dialectician such as Parmenides, bigness is among the first attributes put at stake, a simultaneously passing and exemplary quality, especially useful because it seems so closely connected to basic metaphysical categories such as extension and substance. Following Plato, the question of magnitude never fully escapes this impression of exemplary crisis, amid which it seems to represent less a problem in and of itself than the sign of continual theoretical frustrations of a broader nature, the symptom of a troublesome materiality not yet assimilable by philosophical terms. And finally, we continue to see echoes of this exemplary difficulty especially where size takes on a political significance, which may be the same as to say, where the erotics of bigness most directly impinge upon the social sphere, or where the scale of the multitude demands theorization.

A second occurrence in Plato of the question of magnitude, no less troublesome in its way although seemingly less immediately debatable, comes in the relatively more straightforward discussion of forms in the *Meno*, where the matter of bigness appears so fleetingly that we must pause our reading of the dialogue to catch its implication. Socrates and Meno are discussing the topic of virtue, asking, in much the same mode as in the *Parmenides*, whether virtue is a single or a multiple sort of thing, and in any case how it might be taught.[5] The conversation leads to the dialogue's most famous digression, in which Socrates sets out to demonstrate that knowledge (such as "knowledge of virtue") inheres in the immortal soul, and that therefore "seeking and learning are in fact nothing but recollection."[6] At this point, by way of an instructive analogy, Socrates steers the conversation to geometry.

Sketching some figures in the sand, Socrates asks one of Meno's slaves, who happens to be standing nearby, some questions about geometry that the boy appears able to answer correctly in the absence of any mathematical training. In other words, the boy, seemingly drawing upon some internal reserve of knowledge, and certainly without the benefit of a formal education, "recollects" his "true opinions" about the composition of squares, sides, diagonals, and areas:

SOCRATES, *drawing figure in the sand*. Now boy, you know that a square is a figure like this?

BOY. Yes.

SOCRATES. It has all these four sides equal?

BOY. Yes.

SOCRATES. And these lines which go through the middle of it are also equal?

BOY. Yes.

SOCRATES. Such a figure could be either bigger or smaller, could it not?

BOY. Yes.

SOCRATES. Now if this side is two feet long, and this side the same, how many feet will the whole be? Put it this way. If it were two feet in this direction and only one in that, must not the area be two feet taken once?

BOY. Yes.

SOCRATES. But since it is two feet this way also, does it not become twice two feet?

BOY. Yes.

SOCRATES. And how many feet is twice two? Work it out and tell me.

BOY. Four.[7]

For the moment, I leave aside questions (there are several) about what might motivate a slave repeatedly to answer "yes" to leading questions posed by an Athenian citizen, as well as about the role of the numerous visual and oral hints Socrates provides the boy during this catechism. For whatever reasons, perhaps including, but hardly limited to, native mathematical intuition, the boy is able to arrive at correct answers about the area of the square divided in various ways. Certainly he is a cooperative interlocutor.

I will dwell instead on a seemingly incidental question arising near the start of Socrates's conversation with the boy, a question that is easily disregarded once the dialogue moves on to the specific mathematical inquiries proposed. Just after sketching the square on the ground, and having assured himself that the boy understands the equivalence of its sides and widths, Socrates interjects the following query: "Such a figure could be either bigger or smaller, could it not?" The boy, whether because he "recollects" the definition of a square or because Socrates has proportioned the sides sufficiently neatly in the sand, or for both reasons, again answers "yes" to this apparently superfluous question about the size of the drawing. But why does Socrates even ask the boy this question, which is the only one he poses about the figure as a whole rather than about its parts or proportions?

Here, something profound sneaks its way into the otherwise perfunctory setup of geometrical pedagogy. On the face of it, Socrates is merely confirming that the boy will cooperate with his method of demonstration, which requires drawing and comparing larger and smaller figures of various sorts. But a more essential principle lies at the root of this exercise, the affirmation of which is absolutely required if Socrates's experiment is to succeed in exhibiting true geometrical knowledge on the boy's part as opposed to mere empirical observations of drawn lines and shapes. Geometers identify this principle by the term "similarity": two figures of unequal size are "similar" when their angles are the same and their sides proportional. For instance, any two triangles of different sizes will be similar if composed of the same three angles.[8] Squares are a special case: since their four angles are always ninety degrees and their four sides always of equal length, all squares, regardless of magnitude, are similar.[9] What the slave boy is therefore confirming for Socrates at this moment, and in turn for the reader of the *Meno,* is the purely exemplary status of this particular figure in the sand, a figure that in principle will be similar to any other square of any other size that Socrates (or anyone else) might draw at another time or place. In effect, replying to the question "could the square be bigger or smaller?" the slave boy infers—more properly, he recollects—that no geometrical figure is ever big or small, per se.[10] In essence, a geometrical figure does not *have* size (*mégethos*), rather, only relations or proportions. In this sense, the square is never a specific *thing* at all, but only the representation of one.[11] Thus, when Socrates asks the slave boy further questions about the square—"So doubling the side has given us not a double but a fourfold figure?"—we can be certain that the boy's answers rely not upon a measurement of this specific empirical shape, but only upon the proportions of an ideal figure that the drawing exemplifies.

Yet the size of particular figures used in a given pedagogical exercise may matter a great deal, not to geometry as such, but rather to the success of the demonstration, and therefore ultimately (albeit indirectly and seemingly accidentally) to the feasibility of a doctrine of recollection or even of a theory of "eternally existent" forms.[12] If Socrates is correct that the slave boy's intuitions are already "somewhere in him," the process of "arousing" them requires the boy to practice his reasoning on actual shapes somewhere in time and space and then to answer questions about them "in order."[13] And while it may be true that "if the same questions are put to him on many occasions and in different ways, one can see that in the end he will have a knowledge on the subject as accurate as anybody's," it seems equally true that without *some* readily visible figure in front of him at some definite location, the slave boy would remain in the dark, whatever latent knowledge his immortal soul might harbor.[14]

Thus there are at least two distinct senses of "mattering" put in play by Socrates's perfunctory question about size. In one sense, the strictly geometrical, it does not matter at all how big a particular square is: our conclusions, or the slave boy's, about its parts and proportions will be true or false regardless of magnitude. In quite another sense, call it the material or phenomenological, it matters a great deal that this particular square in the sand is big enough (but not too big) for the demonstration to proceed.[15] If the slave boy must bide for a while alongside this signifying illustration, cognizing its angles, areas, and so on, if only to recollect "eternally existent" truths about the ideal proportions it represents, then the sand square must be rendered within an order of magnitude compatible with the boy's sensorium, and in some relatively happy medium for engaging the "proper way to recollect"—the proper "order," as Socrates says, of pedagogy.

These two senses of mattering in the *Meno*'s brief digression on geometry represent two divergent metaphysical notions of magnitude, perhaps corresponding to the divergent senses of the form of bigness so inconclusively proposed in the *Parmenides*. In the sense that magnitudes never matter for geometry, the sand square sacrifices itself, so to speak, to the general knowledge it is employed to elicit. It has no thinghood of its own, but only a connotative status or a temporary use value. But in the sense that *some* empirical example is required for a slave boy (or anyone else) to "recollect" geometrical forms, the size of the square matters very much, as it were in the social world of pedagogy or in the material world of real human bodies through which forms are recollected in the "proper way" and teaching conducted in good "order." In this latter sense, diagrams such as the sand square have precisely the function of "apparatuses," which Karen Barad describes as "specific material configurations, or rather, dynamic (re)configurings . . . through which intelligibility and materiality are constituted (along with an excluded realm of what doesn't matter)."[16]

Phenomenologically or even pragmatically speaking, if a square must belong to the "scale domain" of a human body in order to be seen adequately[17]—in short, if geometry must be *depictable* to convey truths to a subject—then the barely suppressed "apparatus" of visual culture now intrudes upon the metaphysical pretension of the geometer, even exposing his or her antimaterialistic bias. Were one too careless about the bigness of squares drawn in the sand—for instance, if they were too small to be seen distinctly or too large or distant to be grasped as wholes—geometry as a science, or even as a mere repertoire of hypotheses, would not get off the ground, and certainly would not arrive at the metaphysically privileged position from which it might dismiss the merely contingent magnitudes of "similar" figures. In a word, size must always be *viewed.*

Thus, despite Socrates's sanguine dismissal of the *topos* of "bigger or smaller" from the purely formal realm of geometry, we reencounter the same dilemma with which Parmenides had confronted him in less assured times: size belongs neither to the form nor to the object itself, yet it *must* belong somewhere. Put another way, we are obliged to sacrifice the materiality of the example in order to see the proper (non-)scale of geometrical objects, yet the pesky materiality of a specific apparatus comprises the trace of its own erasure within a metaphysics founded on the axiomatic generality, and therefore the rescalability, of geometry. In brief: I employ some useful drawing of a square—I sacrifice it to its own merely exemplary status as a medium of pedagogy—and only then do I (re)establish an ontology of geometrical squares founded on its determinate exclusion.

Here, then, is a metaphysical hypothesis gesturing toward an aesthetics of magnitude, and partly accounting for the paradoxical status of my initial pair of postulates: Bigness is the sacrificed materiality of the thing, the ambivalently secreted *body* of the image, appearing, within the metaphysically determinate proportionality of objects, as the symptomatic residue of a superseded physical past. To adopt and possibly to pervert the pedagogical ordering laid out by Socrates: the bigness of the specific figure is the preconfiguration of the thing, a quasi being prior to its availability for measurement or rescaling, prior to any sense in which the object is either similar or different from any other. Bigness is the object's singularity, its nonsimilarity, its *unconscious.* Far from a reckonable magnitude or quantity, it is closer to a primary *quality* in its mere infancy, as Piaget was able to confirm. Or, again to borrow Barad's terms, bigness is the "dynamism" of the matter of the (figural) apparatus, "inexhaustible, exuberant, and prolific."[18] No wonder that in any context in which a sociological, psychological, or economic need to institute proper (or at least socially manageable) scales—in effect, to "collapse" the extreme divergences of magnitude that are characteristic of "manifold material existence" into a "productive and profitable" interplay of "functionally unique entities at different scales"—bigness may persist in signifying the unproductive, the unformed, the nascent, the weird, the infantile, even the terrifying.[19] And in turn, for any ostensibly well-adjusted metaphysics, bigness will emerge in the scandalous guise of *antinomy.*

Size Is Relative

The bigness of our solar system might be imagined using something like the following model.[20] To represent the sun, place a bowling ball in the middle of Manhattan, say, on the sidewalk in front of the New York Public Library at Fifth Avenue and Forty-First Street. Then walk eighty feet north, about the length of two city buses, and place a peppercorn on the sidewalk to represent the earth. Continue walking up Fifth Avenue, placing objects to represent the other planets—a pinhead for Mars, a chestnut for Jupiter, a hazelnut for Saturn, and so on—until you have gone about 2,250 feet, slightly less than half a mile. A coffee bean at Fifth Avenue and Fiftieth Street can represent Neptune, the outermost planet in the solar system, or, if you wish to include the dwarf planet Pluto, a sesame seed near Fifty-Third Street. Now picture all these objects orbiting around the bowling ball back at Fifth Avenue and Forty-First Street, encompassing a circle about twenty-four city blocks in diameter, and you have a reasonably good scale model of our sun and its planets.[21] This twenty-four-block circle represents the only region of space human beings are ever likely to traverse, given that the nearest significant objects beyond our solar system are distant by many thousands of times its diameter. However, if you feel like adding the closest major object outside the solar system—Proxima Centauri, a small star located slightly over four light-years from the sun—you can place a walnut approximately four thousand miles from the bowling ball in Manhattan, say, somewhere in Berlin, Germany.[22]

Even such a model conveys only the vaguest hint of the true size of the cosmos once we leave our local region of space, in part because the model neglects to account for the vast stretches of time required to cross the distances it depicts. Space travel is limited by whatever maximum velocity humans can achieve using actual vehicles and fuel. If we decline to consider such material constraints, our model remains far too abstract, its clear-cut juxtapositions falsely implying that we might hop across tracts of celestial space as easily as we stroll up Fifth Avenue or board a plane to Berlin, or as easily as we sweep our eyes over an atlas, globe, or orrery, or use a mouse wheel in Google Maps to zoom out from a screenshot of a city street to the entire earth. Arguably, expanses of space are always depicted far too easily, and expanses of time with far too much difficulty, to illustrate cosmic size with real lucidness. In other words, only by way of a conditional suppression of time—a strategic sacrifice of some, but only some, material dimensions—can a functional scaling of celestial space emerge.[23]

To more adequately incorporate the dimension of time, we might supplement the model as follows. To travel through and beyond the solar system, let us imagine flying in a real spaceship. Among the fastest ever built by humans is the Juno probe, launched in 2011, which can achieve speeds upward of 155,000 miles per hour.[24] Departing from our peppercorn earth, eighty feet north of Forty-First Street in Manhattan, and traveling full throttle up Fifth Avenue in our scaled-down Juno probe, we would arrive at Neptune, the coffee bean at Fiftieth Street, in about two years. It would take us another eighteen thousand years to get to our walnut in Berlin, the neighboring star Proxima Centauri.[25] In other words, properly accounting for time at the scale of this model, the fastest technology humans have ever created would convey us from downtown New York to our nearest celestial neighbor in Berlin at the speed of a moderately fast glacier.[26] And we are still considering only a voyage to the *nearest* star. The Milky Way galaxy contains perhaps four hundred billion stars, and the Milky Way itself is one of as many as two trillion galaxies in the observable universe.[27] If we were to continue traveling only to the very nearest of those galaxies, Andromeda, the tiniest baby step into the greater cosmos, our voyage in the speedy Juno probe would take ten billion years.

All this is to say, when we begin to consider the bigness of things in our "remote corner of the universe"[28]—mountains, oceans, monuments, buildings, crowds, battles, disasters, film images, landscapes, even the earth itself or entire planetary ecologies or solar systems—we deal with magnitudes that, in any absolute sense, are so vanishingly minute that even the factors or exponents required to construct analogies of their status in the cosmos strain the capacities of human intellect. If a skyscraper, a city, an animal, or an SUV can be called "big," but also a star or a galactic cluster, or if we are able to use a term like "numerous" to describe both the number of droplets in a cup of water (about 5,000) and the number of atoms in a single droplet (about 5,000,000,000,000,000,000,000)—then it may seem fruitless to theorize magnitude as anything but a purely relative convention, arbitrarily dependent upon some fleeting context, speech act, or picture-thought, and having nothing essential to do with the real objects or spaces to which it refers.[29]

Such a relativist doctrine is the logical extension of what I earlier called an "adult" (or "taxidermic") contemplation of size: no judgments of size are generalizable, but arise only from the coincidental perspectives of individual subjects. The bigness or smallness of things is a matter of the comparative dimensions and positions of *other* things, and therefore contingent upon the situation in which an object emerges for the perceiver. Of course, the solar system may seem fantastically large viewed from a sidewalk in New York City but fantastically small looking back from Andromeda, just as an elephant appears enormous up close and tiny from across town. Objects can always be resized or rescaled through comparison or from differing viewpoints, a mutability that accounts for what can seem like our nearly infinite capacity to condense the scale of time or space to suit a local perspective, as we did initially with the bowling ball model of the solar system, above. In effect, a relativist metaphysics of size removes any basis for the potential scalar error that so exercised Parmenides in Plato's dialogue. It now becomes perfectly reasonable to speak of especially large mice or especially small whales, or even about tiny galaxies or enormous molecules, just as we can readily agree that a big crowd on a train platform represents a small portion of the throng that just left a football stadium, or that an undeniably huge cruise ship is dwarfed by the sea. We would decline to say that any of these objects—elephant, mouse, whale, stadium, crowd, ship, galaxy, or molecule—is big or small in an absolute or strictly immanent sense.

Regardless of the nonchalance it may breed concerning dimensions of actual space and time, such a noncommittal attitude toward the size of things, which I have also suggested is a routine "adult" way of thinking, a useful scalar taxidermy, agrees with some classic philosophical approaches to the theory of magnitude. Aristotle adopts such an approach: "a mountain is called small yet a grain of millet large, because one is larger than other things of its kind while the other is smaller than other things of its kind."[30] For this description, any inference about bigness or smallness is strictly a local judgment, entailing a perspective coincidentally or accidentally connected to the object at hand. The same mountain we just called small becomes big, or the big grain of millet small, when the viewpoint shifts, so that a single object in effect exhibits contrary attributes: "the same thing turns out to be at the same time both big and small," as Aristotle asserts, echoing the objections of Parmenides without quite the equivalent reproach.[31] Aristotle reminds us that we also speak this way about quantities, avowing that "there are many people in the village" even though the same number of people would be "few in Athens."[32] And because, in strictly logical terms, nothing can "admit contraries at the same time," attributes of size, like quantities, belong to the class of what Aristotle calls "relatives," meaningful only in relation to some "correlative" to which they are connected in specific speech acts. In short, magnitudes are invoked only "*of* or *than* other things, or in some other way *in relation to* something else."[33] Mountains or millet grains are big or small only with regard to their correlatives, in the same way that "by 'double,' [we mean] the double of a half," or "by 'less,' less than that which is greater."[34]

Once we accept the premise that bigness or smallness is relative—never immanent; always a *seeming* rather than a *being*—we are free to produce images or concoct stories that manipulate size with virtually no constraints upon time, space, or materials, a predilection Zachary Horton calls "an aesthetics of freescaling."[35] If one's perspective grows large enough, the entire earth seems small or, if one shrinks small enough, a cell or molecule is gigantic.[36] No wonder it is so easy to imagine flying to Proxima Centauri, or even to other galaxies, disregarding physical constraints on travel for any spaceship with actual fuel and mass. And no wonder writers or filmmakers so readily expand and shrink bodies at the whim of a potion or ray, transforming material things with the same effortlessness with which we operate a knob or slider to alter the magnification of an image in a microscope, telescope, zoom lens, or computer browser, "to make the great tiny and the tiny great in an effortless zoom."[37] Size is not a thing but a viewpoint, not *in* the world but only "of" relative positions or proportions.

Size Is Absolute

Galileo Galilei, in *The Two New Sciences*, his final major work, sets out to counter exactly such an Aristotelian relativism, both in order to correct habitual prejudices in matters of resizing and to give a more accurate account of the attributes of materials.[38] The book is a dialogue between three interlocutors, Sagredo, Salviati, and Simplicio, who meet in the Venetian Arsenal amid a bustle of working shipbuilders.[39] This setting is significant, for although historians customarily praise Galileo for "lay[ing] the groundwork . . . for all of the science that followed" him, his text rather credits the expertise of these practicing artisans performing their physics on the ground, so to speak, who therefore grasp intuitively the limitations of the materials they are obliged to use.[40]

As the dialogue opens, Sagredo, a well-intentioned but fairly uncritical scholar, scolds these very artisans for adhering to what he calls "an idle notion of the common people," namely, "that one cannot reason from the small to the large, because many mechanical devices succeed on a small scale that cannot exist in great size."[41] In opposition to this "common" prejudice, Sagredo offers something like an Aristotelian metaphysics of size centered on the principle of geometrical similarity:

> All reasonings about mechanics have their foundations in geometry, in which I do not see that largeness and smallness make circles, triangles, cylinders, cones, or any other solid figures subject to different properties. If the large machine is built with all its members conforming to the proportions of the smaller [one], and if the smaller is sound and

> stable for the use for which it is designed, I cannot see why the larger should not also be exempt from adverse and destructive encounters that may come to it.[42]

This theory may sound sensible enough, but any worker dealing with actual machinery will immediately perceive why it is utterly false. Salviati, the interlocutor representing a viewpoint closest to Galileo himself, expends mere minutes convincing Sagredo, along with the even more ingenuous Simplicio, that any too-direct analogy between geometry and mechanics must fail to account for the "misbehavior of machines in the concrete as compared with their abstract ideal counterparts."[43]

For example, if one doubles the size of one of the "solid figures" mentioned by Sagredo, that object's volume, and consequently its mass, increase not linearly but cubically. A wood beam doubled in size in all its proportions is not twice but eight times (2^3x) as heavy as its original, and to that same degree more vulnerable to the "adverse and destructive encounters" that must worry builders or artisans. This principle is commonly known as the square-cube law. From it "there clearly follows," as Salviati eventually affirms,

> the impossibility, not only for art, but for nature herself, of increasing machines to immense size. Thus it is impossible to build enormous ships, palaces, or temples, for which oars, masts, beamwork, iron chains, and in sum all parts would hold together; just as nature could not create trees of immeasurable size, because their branches would fatally weaken, burdened by their own weight; and likewise it would be impossible to create skeletons for men, horses, or other animals which could subsist and carry out their functions proportionably when such animals were increased to immense height.[44]

In short, "the larger the structure is, the weaker in proportion it will be."[45] Salviati shows all this fairly easily; the geometry and mathematics required are elementary.

One might therefore surmise that the revolutionary character of Galileo's insights about magnitude reside less in their implications for engineering than in the degree to which such calculations are capable of shocking an otherwise reasonable intellect such as Sagredo's. Salviati's rudimentary analysis of materials, already grasped intuitively by the philosophically uneducated Venetian artisans, challenges metaphysical preconceptions so deeply entrenched that their repudiation verges on a spiritual crisis: "Already I feel my brain reeling," Sagredo declares, "and like a cloud suddenly cleft by lightning, it is troubled."[46] Throughout the discussion that follows, Sagredo dwells on the "marvelous," "remarkable," and "wonderful" qualities of Salviati's demonstrations and claims, which, as Salviati himself declares, "are so far from the opinions and teachings commonly accepted, that to broadcast them publicly will excite against them a great number of contradictors."[47] By the end of the dialogue, one might conclude that, alongside Galileo's many scientific discoveries, the book's most striking proof is of the prevailing incapacity of humans to conceive size and scale adequately, and of our reliance on fixed ideas that hinder even the simplest comprehension of real magnitudes.[48]

Such habits are especially conspicuous in biology and zoology, as Galileo's reference to "horses [and] other animals" anticipates. Several centuries later, as the field of what will come to be named "allometry" is getting off the ground, writers still lament the failure of "common" people, but also of many of their fellow scientists, to properly account for the sizes of material things, despite the simplicity of the math involved. In 1917, D'Arcy Thompson declares that "the zoologist or morphologist has been slow, where the physiologist has long been eager, to invoke the aid of the physical or mathematical sciences; and the reasons for this difference lie deep, and in part are rooted in old traditions."[49] As Thompson suggests, even erudite biologists, from Linnaeus in the eighteenth century to William Kirby and William Spence in the nineteenth, seem to have "remained ignorant" of Galileo's elementary deductions:

> K[irby] and S[pence], like many less learned authors, are fond of popular illustrations of the "wonders of Nature," to the neglect of dynamical principles. They suggest, for instance, that if the white ant were as big as a man, its tunnels would be "magnificent cylinders of more than three hundred feet in diameter"; and that if a certain noisy Brazilian insect were as big as a man, its voice would be heard all the world over: "so that Stentor becomes a mute when compared with these insects!" It is an easy consequence of anthropomorphism, and hence a common characteristic of fairy-tales, to neglect the principle of dynamical, while dwelling on the aspect of geometrical, similarity.[50]

Thompson's tone is courteous, but surely it is a damning criticism of his colleagues to accuse their work of either "anthropomorphism" or "a common characteristic of fairy-tales," and Thompson continues to express amazement that scientists can make claims "so easily seen, on physical grounds, to be unnecessary."[51] Fifteen years later, Julian Huxley, in a similar vein, observes that despite the important work of Thompson, to whom

Huxley's own book is dedicated, "the subject [of differential growth] has received little consideration," and "there appears still to linger a distrust of the application of even such elementary mathematics to biological problems."[52]

In 1926, in a widely read article in *Harper's Monthly Magazine* titled "On Being the Right Size," J. B. S. Haldane offers a reproach lifted directly from Thompson, and in a similarly nonplussed tone: "Although Galileo demonstrated the contrary more than three hundred years ago, people still believe that if a flea were as large as a man it could jump a thousand feet into the air."[53] Haldane's article is especially helpful because of the detail with which he expands Galileo's ruminations on gigantic "men, horses, and other animals," exposing the discrepancy between the sizes of actual creatures and our seemingly limitless capacity to imagine them enlarged:

> Let us take the most obvious of possible cases, and consider a giant man sixty feet high—about the height of Giant Pope and Giant Pilgrim in the illustrated *Pilgrim's Progress* of my childhood. These monsters were not only ten times as high as Christian, but ten times as wide and ten times as thick, so that their total weight was a thousand times his, or about eighty to ninety tons. . . . As the human thighbone breaks under about ten times the human weight, Pope and Pagan would have broken their thighs every time they took a step.[54]

Haldane's point, in line with his advocacy of a correct allometry, is that a thing's physical magnitude is inextricably tied to its configuration, so that "a large change in size inevitably carries with it a change of form."[55] Far from being an artifact of mere perspective or context, as in Aristotle, for whom "nothing is called large or small just in itself, but [only] by reference to something else," size so strictly adheres to the properties of objects that it ought to be considered the *cause* of their form. "The higher animals are not larger than the lower because they are more complicated," as Haldane asserts; "they are more complicated because they are larger."[56] John Tyler Bonner reiterates the ontological investment of this claim: "size is the supreme regulator of all matters biological"; "Size is the prime mover"; it "dictates the characteristics of all living things. It is the supreme and universal determinant of what any organism can be and can do."[57]

With allometrists such as Huxley, Thompson, Haldane, and Bonner, we could not be farther from an Aristotelian scalar relativism, and therefore also from our customary "adult" metaphysics, which treats size as something subjectively produced from a contingent or coincidental perspective. Yet it is worth remembering that the biologist's essentialist mode is, every bit as much as Aristotle's, an everyday and intuitive way of thinking, regardless of the level of an individual's acquaintance with either biology or geometry. We speak like Galilean essentialists whenever we distinguish fact from (scalar) fiction, for instance, every time we judge the fictionality of some inflated animal, realizing that "a hare could not be as large as a hippopotamus, or a whale as small as a herring."[58] Our allometric capacity to determine that imaginary beings are miniature or gigantic, in fantastical stories, special-effects films, or cartoons, is necessarily founded upon a comprehension of their proper sizes in the physical world. We know that a heron does not dart about like a hummingbird, nor a mouse shake the earth like a *T. rex*, unless we are deliberately positing superpowers, monstrosities, allegories, or parodies.[59] And even in these latter cases, pictorial exaggerations directly exploit our implicit grasp of the proper sizes of things, by which we gauge the rightness or wrongness of both images and our judgments about them and generally collate the differences between subjective impression and objective reality. In fact, even Aristotle, the exemplary relativist of magnitude, readily switches to an essentialist mode, sounding like Galileo or Bonner, when this latter way of thinking is expedient, for instance, in the *Poetics*, where he declares that there are proper and improper sizes for artworks depending on their forms, a rule famously applied to the length of tragedies: the "limit for the magnitude (*mégethos*) of a story," as Aristotle asserts, is "set by the actual nature of the thing."[60] Aristotle even proceeds to compare the length of a tragedy to the size of a well-constructed animal, gainsaying the relativism of his *Categories* and *Metaphysics*: "To be beautiful, an animal or anything else structured with parts, should not only have its parts arranged in order, but also be of a definite magnitude. Beauty is a matter of magnitude and order."[61]

Here then are two metaphysical proposals about size, each of which appears sound in its turn, but which contradict each other: first, an Aristotelian relativism (notwithstanding the vacillations of the *Poetics*), in which a thing's bigness is never an immanent attribute but determined solely through relations to other things; second, a Galilean essentialism, in which not only is a thing's bigness intrinsically part of it, but magnitude determines structure and form. If compelled to choose between these competing metaphysical proposals as a matter of theory, it would be sensible (as it usually is) to opt for the Galilean, not only for its demonstrable accuracy, but also because it can still be reconciled with the scalar relativism of our perceptions provided we treat the latter strictly as a domain of appearances or imagination, a species of illusion prompted by the vicissitudes of the senses or by merely temporary positions. Our metaphysical contradiction would then be resolvable among levels or registers, or what Hegel most concisely describes as the difference between the object "in itself" and the object "for consciousness." On one level (the object in itself), size is strictly immanent and all scalar variation is delimited by material constraints; on a second level (the object for consciousness), material constraints fall away by one or more dimensions, depending on representational expediency.[62] The images of things—but not things themselves—become susceptible to expansion and contraction by virtue merely of the scenarios in which we discover them; infinite scalar variability becomes startlingly easy to contemplate, and physicality or materiality startlingly easy to suppress. Such a dialectical or phenomenological resolution accords with most histories of science, in which something like a "Galilean era" supplants the Aristotelian, and modern science is convened on the basis of theoretical and, most crucially, experimental corrections of perceptual phenomena, a kind of generalized Copernicanism.

For the Galilean, whose metaphysics the theorist might prefer for its empirical defensibility, the error or imprecision of Aristotelian relativism is thus correctible by directed scientific study, for instance, employing good physics and physiology, good allometry. However, since in the present setting we aim not for rigorous materials science but for a functional aesthetics of magnitude, a resolution between competing metaphysical schemas, however well it may serve the physicist, zoologist, or engineer, will be no more adequate than merely postulating that what is true of an object in itself would account for the full set of that object's phenomenological relations for consciousness. For one thing, both of the metaphysical positions I have depicted, and for which I offered the shorthand "Aristotelian" and "Galilean," emerge artlessly in everyday cognition, quite regardless of their demonstrable truth or error. Indeed, in routine perception and imagination, we require *both* schemas, frequently at the same time, to form useful judgments about magnitudes.[63] Consider the confusion into which perception would fall were it obliged to deduce the size of an approaching or receding object strictly from the magnitude of its present silhouette, without recourse to immanent properties. Yet consider also the difficulty we would encounter describing relations between objects if all factors determining their *relative* sizes—spatial positions, quantities, degrees of interaction, and so on—were dismissed as mere illusions or artifacts of viewpoint. Often, perhaps most often, we are correct to judge a thing as bigger or smaller based on its position rather than on some immanent quality, and a great deal of our basic comprehension of the world would have to shift were this not the case.[64]

When everyday language exhibits a discrepancy accompanied by such obscure or ambiguous rationales, we can suppose its derivation to be unconscious, ideological, metaphysical, or some combination of these.[65] Indeed, the continuous juxtaposition of this pair of propositions about magnitude appears to be of the kind that Kant calls "a wholly natural antithetic, for which one does not need to ponder or to lay artificial snares, but rather into which reason falls of itself and even unavoidably."[66] Neither merely a contradiction nor some historical or phenomenological correction, then, this is an *antinomy*—two governing tendencies of thought, each of which is "natural" in its own right, but the combination of which reveals an incompatibility between underlying metaphysical postulations. We are both Aristotelians and Galileans of magnitude, not entirely unlike the (anxious) sense, in a more general psychology, in which we are both selves and others to ourselves.

✷ 5 ✷

Hyperfacticity

THE BIG-BUDGET FILM

Waste

To the degree an aesthetics of magnitude has existed, its prevailing mode has been the theory of the sublime, at least since the European seventeenth century. I have suggested several ways in which models of the sublime fall short of an adequate account of bigness. In a nutshell, to be big enough to be sublime, the thing must no longer be *too big*, which is to say, no longer big at all in a primary sense. More exactly, the thing's bigness, conceived as an attribute of a real physical object, becomes ambiguous, if not radically ambivalent, at the moment the subject becomes capable of evolving a perspective sufficiently distant to receive it *safely*, to invoke the odd term that Kant shares with nearly all other theorists of the sublime. The profound irony of such safety, or of the "negative pleasure" it enables, emerges in proportion to the sheer violence or terror, the *too*-bigness, of the thing at hand. For this reason, in the second chapter, I described pictures of atomic bomb explosions, such as those taken at Bikini Atoll, as "*merely* sublime," because the very aspect they distill away in order to represent a big object is the force, the proximal violence or terror, of bigness as such.

This consistent psychological equivocation, the ambivalent modulation or making-safe of terror, corresponds nicely to what I called "taxidermy," the adult's habit of stuffing down a more lively terror of childhood, preserving only the silhouette or signifier of its prior animism. The thing's bigness is bestilled, dematerialized, deanimated, made objective. Yet presumably the object still retains some infantile germ of "terror," or at least of some emotion sufficient to provoke our continued fascination with its bigness as adults. What theorists of the sublime generally do with this complex and ambivalent emotional situation is what people often do with complicated emotions or with their own imaginative limitations—they displace them from the subject onto the object and rediscover them, as it were, phenomenalized. The inclination of theorists of the sublime to locate incompleteness or lack *in* the object, or in other words, to discover the object's in-principle imperceptibility, is a powerful inheritance for literary and cultural theory. Even in models that do not employ the exact terms of a Kantian or Burkean sublime, this basic projection tends to bias the understanding of bigness. For one example, consider Timothy Morton's "hyperobject," still among the most familiar contemporary iterations of sublimity. For Morton, a principal characteristic of the very big object, what he identifies as its "hyper" attribute, is that it is "nonlocal," and therefore can never be fully sensed, like a geological timescale or the global environment.[1] Such sensuous lack in the object—its partiality, its absence, its ambivalence—is especially convenient for the theorist; such an attribute lends the thing a dialectic, a gap to fill. However, to rediscover phenomenalized absence or lack in the object is especially peculiar here because we are speaking of things that are, on the face of it, anything but lacking. And what if such a gap is not there, if the big thing is not (merely) sublime or hyperobjective, not ambivalent or nonlocal, but just straightforwardly, bluntly, even obscenely *huge*? Then what it might expose is the unconscious of theory itself, its own inherent incapacity, its "navel," to use Freud's term, into which theory cannot see, possibly because bigness is too utterly visible for the theorist, too ingenuous, too crude.[2]

We therefore do best to scrutinize bigness on the ground, so to speak, where the peculiarity of its simultaneous perceptual blatancy and psychological density might be most directly observed. As a pointed alternative to the sublime, I opt for a theoretical mode derived from habits of mainstream cultural consumption, necessarily less discomfited than philosophical aesthetics or cultural critique at the sheer blatancy of very big things. Such a mode may be observed in the reception of architecture and mainstream film, two contexts in which bigness tends toward something like the opposite of the absence, secrecy, or lack constitutive of the sublime. For instance, a big-budget film may initially flirt with distance or incomplete perceivability, perhaps to create suspense for a potentially sublime image to come. We glimpse a shadow of King Kong, or of the giant aliens in *Cloverfield* or *Super 8*; we see the ground tremble or a puddle ripple at the approach of the *Tyrannosaurus rex* in *Jurassic Park*; we see the looming shadows or roiling clouds heralding the arrival of a mothership in *Close Encounters of the Third Kind* or *Independence Day*; we glimpse the advent of Godzilla beneath ocean swells or behind office buildings in a plethora of remakes. But ultimately, these very big things decisively and fully appear; the rationale of bigness in popular film, and probably in nearly all mainstream cultural production, is to be fully *seen*. The big object must exhaust itself for the senses, so to speak, fulfilling its tacit promise to render itself available for complete consumption. Bigness is not hyperobjective but *hyperfactical*.

The motives for the total presence of bigness in popular cultural production, its lack of any lack, or its emphatic *is*, are plainly both aesthetic and economic. The big thing in a mainstream film must be seen, not least to warrant the expense of having produced, displayed, and advertised it. Referring to *Waterworld* and the 1998 *Godzilla*—the latter film, incidentally, furnishing the obligingly unequivocal tagline, "Size Does Matter"—the film critic Tom Shone writes that "more than a few of us were curious to see what wasting 200 million dollars looked like."[3] But most of the audience is interested precisely in that, and, in the production and marketing of a big-budget film, some such schadenfreude is certainly planned in advance. The audience, after all, pays to see the big money spent, and the extreme size of the film image is a literal mark of its own cost-effectiveness, just as (in the paradigmatic tautology of mainstream marketing) the best-selling book is the one to read, the top-selling song the one to download, or the most popular fashion the one to wear.

We might call this species of hyperfactical bigness in popular film, along with its analogs in visual and other popular media, an "expenditure spectacle," given its unembarrassed flaunting of its own extreme cost. Indeed, it scarcely matters what particular species of bigness the money has been spent on—explosions, huge sets, vast crowds, some CGI city or planet or monster—provided we *see* the $200 million used up. Any list of big things in cinema includes an arbitrarily broad variety of images, delimited only by extant technologies of magnification, duplication, or scenographical exploitation: for instance, the gargantuan Babylonian palace in D. W. Griffith's *Intolerance*, the napalming of a jungle in the opening of Francis Ford Coppola's *Apocalypse Now*, the immense funeral crowd in Richard Attenborough's *Gandhi*, the fantastical four-dimensional cityscapes of Christopher Nolan's *Inception*, the swarming fighters of *Avengers: Infinity War*, or the dizzying verticality of synthesized vistas in *Titanic*, *The Matrix*, or *Avatar*.[4] "There is nothing," as Susan Sontag writes, "like the thrill of watching all those expensive sets come tumbling down."[5]

The spectacle of bigness tends to pause the progress of a film in much the same way that the erotic image of the woman on screen momentarily freezes narrative, as Laura Mulvey famously suggests in her analysis of the film spectator's gaze.[6] Consider a type of cinematic shot one could call a "waste reveal," in which the camera roams over extravagantly multiplied commodities or bodies, showing off, alongside climactic plot events, the sheer profligacy of sets, effects, or extras.[7] A fine example is the ending of *Citizen Kane*, in which the camera roves through the seemingly infinite stock of

Kane's crated-up possessions; an even more famous one is the crane shot across acres of wounded Confederate soldiers in *Gone with the Wind*. Post-CGI, consider the vast digitized armies of *Star Wars Episode II: Attack of the Clones*, *The Lord of the Rings: The Return of the King*, *Troy*, or *Dunkirk*, or the seemingly endless masses of undead warriors in *Game of Thrones*.[8]

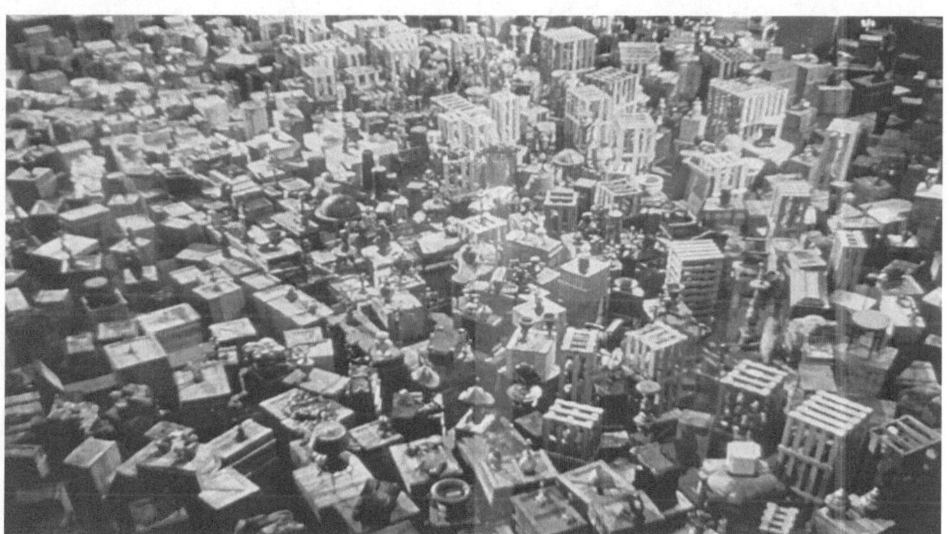

FIGURE 5.1 *Citizen Kane* (1941): Kane's crated-up possessions

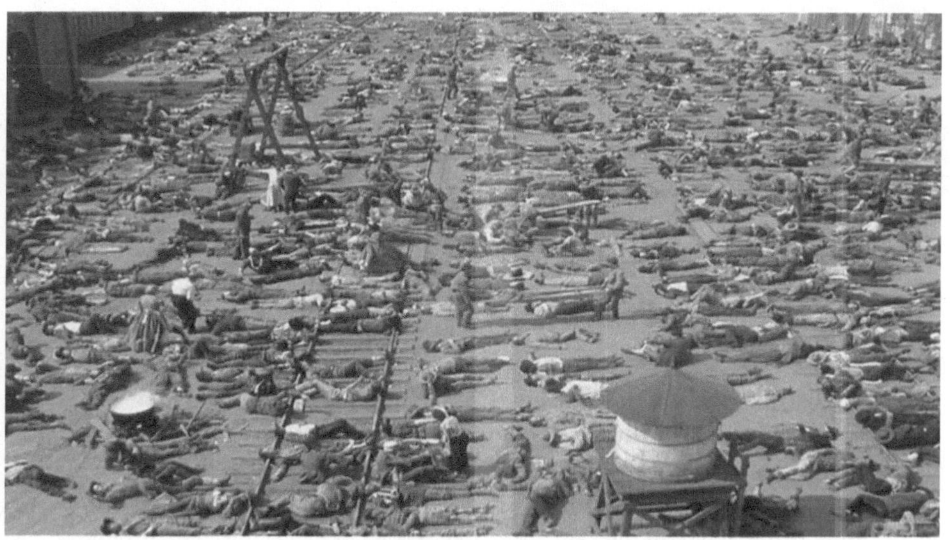

FIGURE 5.2 *Gone with the Wind* (1939): wounded soldiers in Atlanta

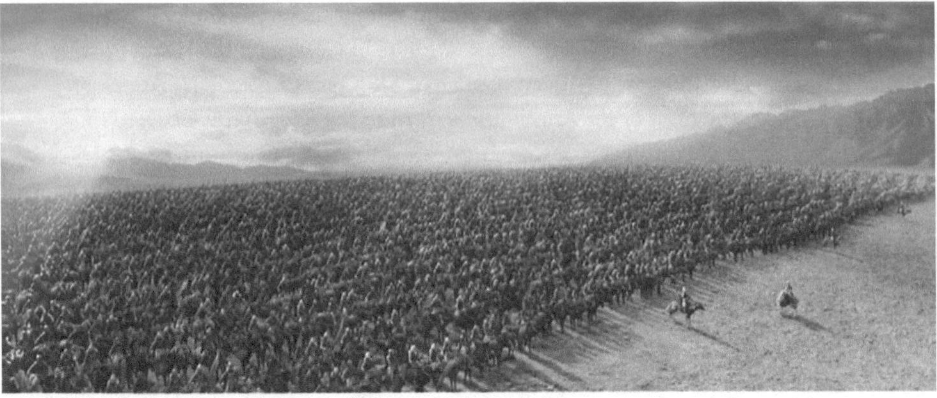

FIGURE 5.3 *The Lord of the Rings: The Return of the King* (2003): digitized army

The blockbuster epic (*Star Wars, Lord of the Rings, Independence Day, Jurassic Park*) tends to contain multiple instances of waste reveals, so that it is almost possible to reconstruct the narrative of the film strictly as a story about the production and destruction of big things. But this is difficult to talk about in critical language, since it is essentially an account of two registers, infantile cathexis and investment capital, both of which emerge all too bluntly or non-dialectically in acts of spectatorship. The first register concerns the emotional charge, and the second the *shadenfroh* wastefulness, that must animate the presentation of cinematic bigness, almost (as with Mulvey) regardless of its contribution to the narrative. These registers concern the production of spectacle and its consumption by real or quasi-real audiences and through real or quasi-real media. Neither register is *in* the film; each is essentially paratextual. That is perhaps why images of the atomic bomb finally can become paradigmatic instances of the popular-cultural sublime, despite the aesthetic and even moral incongruity of such a figuration. In the atomic bomb image we see produced before us, in a consumable incarnation denuded of pollution, lingering effects, and above all of real human suffering (death, injury, disease, displacement, and generational trauma), the decontaminated picture of our desire/terror of the *too big,* reduced to the mere sterile icon of excess and waste. Above all, the chief attribute of an expenditure spectacle, of which a waste reveal is just an especially blatant example, is the very opposite of what is suggested in the analytic of the sublime: its full and excessive presence before the viewer, the utter absence of any absence. Bigness is a bald, undialectical facticity; it belongs to something decisively more *there* than any other object. The big thing is a *hyperfact,* overweeningly undeniable or irrefutable. We see all of it, even if we feel (next to) nothing.

Monster

Sitting in a dark movie theater in the summer of 1954, the moment you have anticipated finally arrives.[9] The camera has been following the female protagonist of *Them!*, lingering on her three-quarter profile while an ominous whine rises in the background. Her distracted expression hints at several of the film's melodramatic and quasi-pornographic subtexts, her figure furnishing both the archetypal innocent victim and a convenient gauge of everyday scale for whatever monster is about to emerge. Suddenly, it rears its head over the hillock a few yards away—a giant ant! She doesn't see it immediately, but the crescendo of its whine alerts her and she turns to look. And then, of course, she screams, so that we may add to this generic scenography both the thrill of the victim's terror and, as a virtually automatic consequence, the arrival of the pistol-toting male hero rushing to her defense.

Critical rigor demands that we avoid confusing the two perspectives the film invites us to consume in a scene like this. The first perspective, diegetic and plot bound, corresponds to our victim's view of an actual giant insect emerging over the hill; the second is our view, as the film's audience, of a spectacular visual tableau and the special effects deployed to

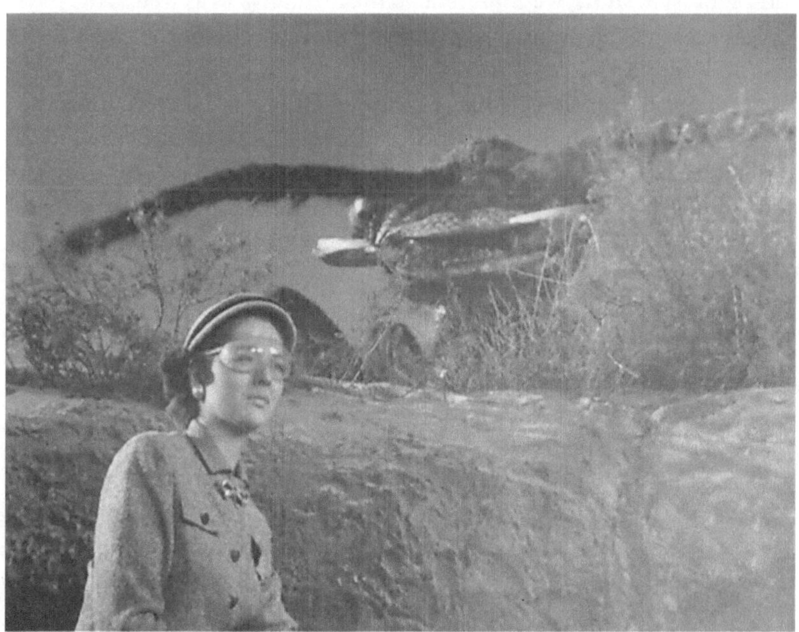

FIGURE 5.4 *Them!* (1954): giant ant

produce it. This juxtaposition of perspectives offers a nice demonstration of the antinomy of bigness. Our heroine, seeing the monster in the diegesis, receives it with something like the unadulterated shock of an amateur biologist or incipient Galilean confronted by a scalar abomination. In the material categories that cinematic or fictional protagonists are obliged to employ, a giant ant is freakishly wrong, a preternatural menace. By contrast, the film audience, viewing a summer feature at the local theater or perhaps watching television in the early morning hours, has far less at stake than she, and can afford to be more skeptical toward monstrosities. We are shocked only to the limited extent of conventional absorption in a fictional world, perhaps supplemented by the brief jolt of our first peek at the giant insect emerging on screen, a partial and short-lived cathexis that may be the maximum to which horror filmmakers can aspire in climactic moments or jump scares, given constraints of medium, genre, and skill, as well as of marketability and the Hays Code. Beyond that small instant of fright, we cheerfully observe both the unrealism of any "actual" giant ant and the (relatively) realistic cinematic effect capable of making an insect appear so huge, whether by magnifying a live animal through some camera technique or by using models or editing tricks. Therefore, unlike our heroine in the scene, we observe *size* along with the oversized thing, the rationalistic recalibration of a filmic artifact along with the ant's too-bigness. In short, we comprehend the metaphysics as well as the physics of excessive magnitude, adjudicating the dialectic of their respective plausibilities.

The pleasure in the spectacle of the giant ant is thus provoked not primarily by a film audience's terror at its appearance, at least not beyond some initial but fleeting thrill, but rather by what would seem to be the very opposite of terror, a measured admiration of the production's ingenuity. The giant ant's hyperfacticity is not quite sublime—this is not what Kant describes as "a pleasure in displeasure"—rather, the special effect appeals to what Michele Pierson calls a "culture of connoisseurship" that indulges an "appreciation of the illusion as aesthetic artifact."[10] Such connoisseurship convenes filmmakers, artisans, and fans in perpetual, cliquish debate over the merits of specific methods of illusion, presenting (or indeed selling) what Fredric Jameson calls a "supplementary bonus of pleasure in the surplus of the technological image itself."[11] From this vantage, the special effects in *Them!* belong to the "'near enough is good enough' approach to cinematic realism," a mode employing rudimentary devices such as scale models or traveling mattes in lieu of more expensive and time-consuming methods associated with stop-motion artists like Ray Harryhausen or, subsequently, with digital and postproduction tools like green-screening and CGI.[12] Members of the audience of *Them!*, whether watching in a 1954 theater or later on television or video, are surely predisposed to judge the blatancy and even outright cheapness of the techniques employed in proportion to whatever degree of fannish zeal they might summon: the ant both "really is" and "merely appears" big, a seeming contradiction in ontological terms, but not at all in the idiom of either science-fiction conventions or special-effects connoisseurship.

For the viewer, this paradox is thus resolved, at least ostensibly, as an issue of divergent but complementary levels of narrative structure or, in brief, by *how* a story is told or viewed, or by how (or how well) its image is produced.[13] On the one hand, it makes perfect sense to our Aristotelian habits of scalar relativism that giant ants should look exactly like normal-size ones, however outrageously "blown up" (or, alternatively, photographed very close in order to achieve a similar enlargement). Indeed, the entire pathos of *Them!* requires the monster to resemble a normal ant by virtue of a quasi-geometrical similarity. The filmmakers cannot afford to reconfigure the body of the giant insect by any biologically defensible change in anatomical proportions, which would render it quite un-antlike and "unrealistic," defeating the purpose of the special effect. On the other hand, our intuitive Galilean absolutism assures us that there *is not*, and never can be, such a thing as a merely "blown up" ant—that what we are seeing on screen is strictly an artifact wrought by the technology of cinema, a trick of perspective or image editing, never anything material or physical. In short, this ant is only a "thing" qua illusion, even if we may be briefly tricked or shocked at its hyperfactical irruption in the diegesis. Arguably, in all fictional scenes of drastic resizing, the simultaneous (formal) possibility and (physical) impossibility of the image are combined to produce the special significance of the object's magnitude as fascinating or "terrifying." The spectacle of gigantism rests on the apparently self-contradictory dialectic of our understanding and its symptomatic suppression: in Aristotelian terms, that this monstrous creature is exactly similar to a regular animal, only much bigger; in Galilean terms, that such amplification is inherently wrong, resulting in a grotesque perversion of real anatomy, like the famous thickened bone that Galileo uses to illustrate the potential monstrosity of enlargement. Therefore the ant, like the inflated bone, is a mere reverie, to be wondered at but then rectified as soon as the fictionalizing is done.[14]

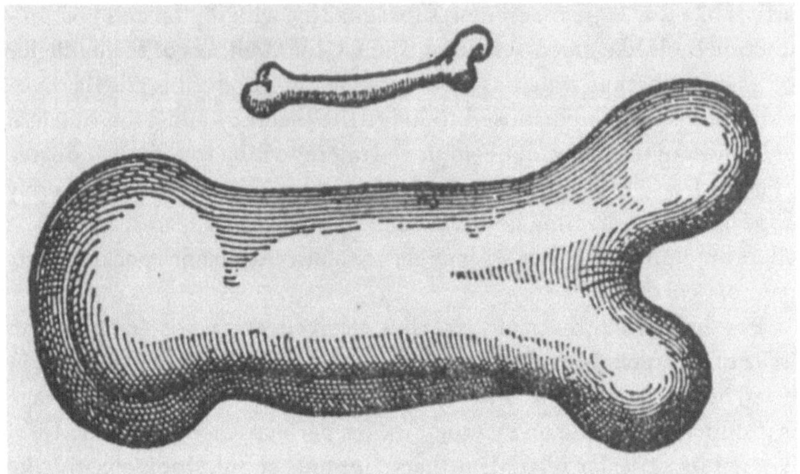

FIGURE 5.5 Galileo, *Two New Sciences* (1638): proportions of enlarged bone

Toy

Consider an updated version of the example of a giant Pilgrim and Pope that Haldane borrows from *Pilgrim's Progress*: the "jaegers" in Guillermo del Toro's 2013 film *Pacific Rim*. Jaegers are enormous fighting robots piloted by teams of human soldiers mentally linked to the robots' brains.[15] They are enlisted to battle a marauding force of equally huge alien monsters called (in tribute to Japanese monster movies) kaijus, which have apparently emerged from an interdimensional portal beneath the Pacific Ocean. In one typical scene, which also provides imagery for the film's advertisements and previews, a jaeger strides down a Tokyo street on its way to battle, snatching up a derelict cargo ship that happens to lie in its path. The jaeger handles the ship with the same practiced flair with which a human-sized action hero might scoop up a baseball bat or tire iron in order to beat down a thug, terrorist, or zombie. As the fight begins, the jaeger flips the cargo ship over its shoulder, swings it around like a club, and smashes it repeatedly into the head of the kaiju, all the while moving with a deftness that underscores both the ironic hyperbole and the generic conventionality of this tremendously inflated battle. The jaeger's great smacks seem to be effective, but the kaiju manages to grab the ship with its prehensile tail and wrest it away. Loosed from the jaeger's grip, the ship is flung down a city avenue, skipping hundreds of feet along the pavement and finally coming to rest wedged in midair between two office buildings.

The film audience presumably has sufficient intuitive comprehension of basic dynamics to sense that in reality cargo ships cannot be wielded

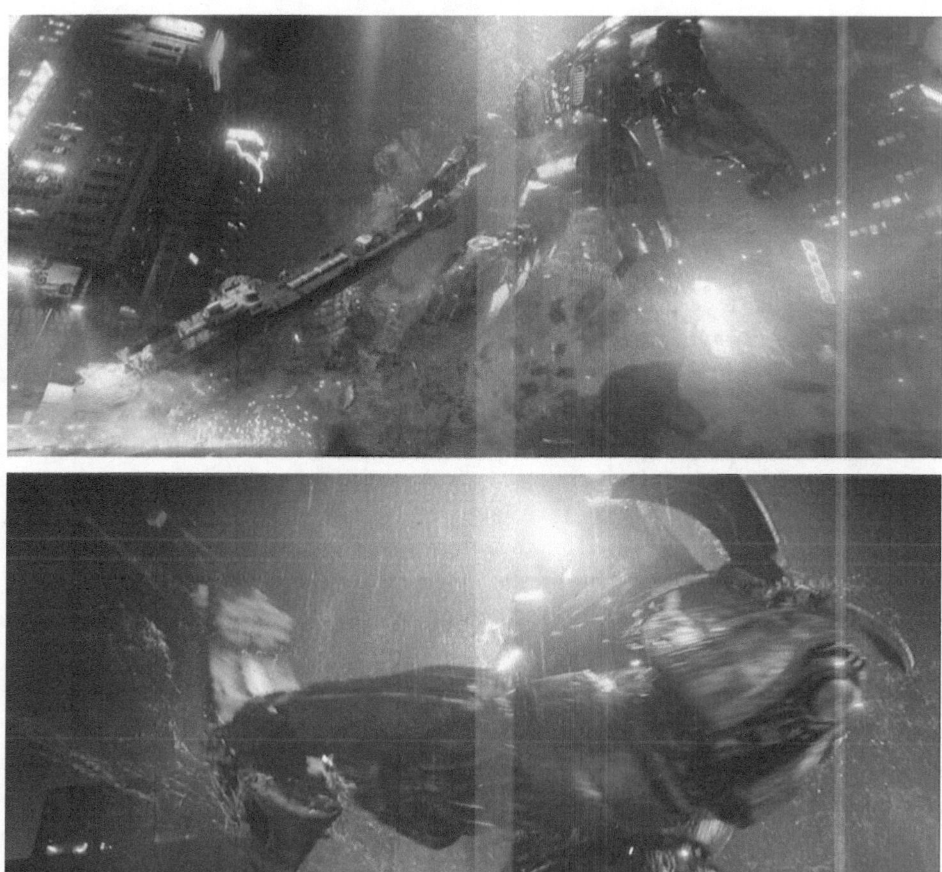

FIGURE 5.6 *Pacific Rim* (2013): jaeger and cargo ship

like baseball bats. Yet the jaeger's offhandness in brandishing the ship—the casual bravado of its swagger and its one-hand grip as it drags the hull toward the kaiju, candidly imitating the human movements and gestures on which the CGI figures are modeled—reinforces the impression of an all-but-infinite rescalability that makes such scenes good fodder for big-budget films and their trailers. The scene is simultaneously a rousing technological spectacle and a hip, even cynical joke about genre clichés. Hundreds of feet tall, and despite the colossal augmentation of its metal armature, the jaeger moves with the dexterity of the familiar overmuscled yet scrappy street fighter in post-Rambo action films, the stereotype whom Yvonne Tasker calls "the male bodybuilder as movie star."[16] Indeed, part of the audience's "distracted" knowingness surely entails our observation of the blunt unrealism of such nimble movements, the fact that all of it is done, and can only be done, with special effects.[17] As Jean Mitry observes, in the cinema "all actions are actions *as they happen* . . . [,] everything is *actual*," and so, along with protagonists, scenarios, and objects, we are always watching the film produce itself—the techniques (re)produced *as* techniques—a supplementary display that one need not be a film theorist to understand as one of the chief attractions of spectatorship.[18]

We can be more precise: the *bigness* of physical objects on the screen is not what is actual. What we are seeing are extreme scalar special effects through which small models are wrought, whether by mechanical or digital means, to look gigantic. Just how gigantic? Something in the neighborhood of three hundred feet tall, or big enough to allow robots to swing whole ships like bats—in short, *very* big.[19] Yet, in more ways than their just being the result of special effects, the jaeger and kaiju are much smaller, perhaps no larger than human size, judging from the physical mannerisms they borrow from the actors whose movements are digitized to depict them. Or perhaps they are even smaller than that, a mere eight or ten inches tall, if one considers another key rationale for their creation, as prototypes for marketable kids' action figures.

The extreme ease with which we rescale the image of the jaeger, or accept its outlandish bigness both directly in the film and indirectly as a hypothetical attribute of, say, its commodified doll form, tells us something interesting both about the deftness of human senses and about the malleability of images. The film readily admits that jaeger, kaiju, and cargo ship are already toys, and even cracks wise about such ironic rescaling by showing what appear to be injection-molded plastic figurines of jaegers and kaijus beneath the closing credits, presumably the same type of figurines the audience or their kids will be heading out to the shopping mall to buy. If we can play with jaegers as toys, then obviously their outlandish bigness—the very quality that makes them interesting enough to be sold and consumed both in theaters and at Target or Walmart—is a wholly conceptual attribute, rescalable with a near infinite ease that permits three-hundred-foot-tall figures and ten-inch figurines to *be* the same thing. The irony employed here is old, and wholly formal. It resonates with Jonathan Swift's general implication, in *Gulliver's Travels*, that even for the incredulous reader it hardly matters whether Gulliver is a giant among Lilliputians or a miniature among Brobdingnagians; the revision of "normal" size proceeds with equal adroitness in both cases, and the text establishes the critical dialectic of normality in accordance with our Aristotelian capacity for perceiving images strictly relative to contingent points of view. We fully comprehend the jaeger's "real" stature, in this sense, its inherent

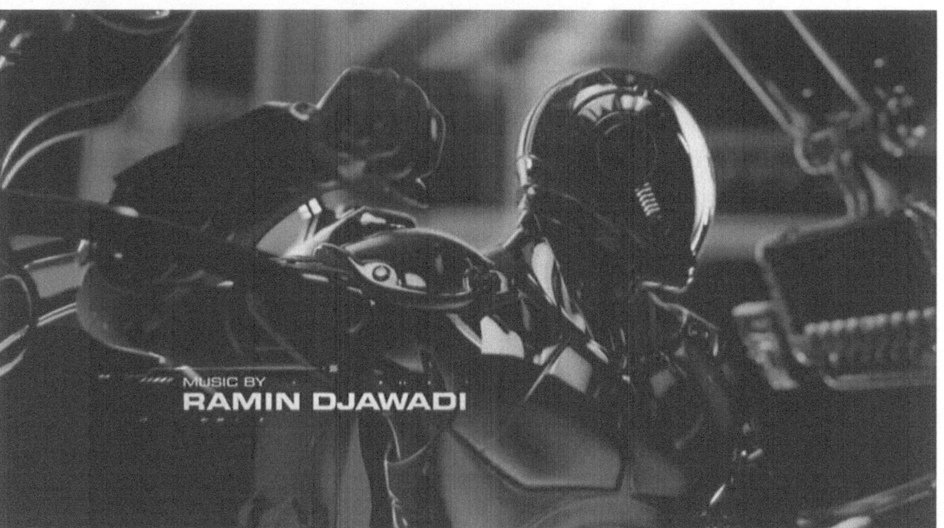

FIGURE 5.7 *Pacific Rim* (2013): "toy" jaeger

smallness, and therefore must decide what to do, theoretically, with the pseudo-fact of extreme bigness without which everything else about the figure of the jaeger that an audience comprehends or consumes would be for naught. Indeed, the miniaturization of colossal beasts and machines is not only compatible with their gigantism; these tendencies were one and the same from the start, grounded in a human deftness with the resizing of images quite aside from whatever aesthetic provincialism we might display in envisioning new forms or functions. "Cognitively the dollhouse is gigantic," as Susan Stewart remarks,[20] and the corollary is that cognitively (and, in turn, commercially), the giant is already a doll.

To continue analyzing, perhaps somewhat perversely against the inclinations of the contented film audience, we may borrow the same anti-Aristotelian tactic that allometrists like Haldane and Bonner employ against careless biologists and naive lay readers. The notion that giant robots might swing cargo ships like bats commits us to a drastic scalar mistake, one much more specific than the pro forma error of suspending disbelief in fictional plots or special effects. Consider the big ship in the scene: any large physical object so complex and delicate would crumple like foil if one tried to smash it against the head of something as dense and massive as a kaiju. In fact, the jaeger could probably not even lift up the ship without it disintegrating. And oddly enough, the audience intuitively knows that very big objects cannot behave like this cargo ship, not least from having observed what happens to similarly large things in other genre films. Consider the moment in James Cameron's *Titanic* when the huge ocean liner rears up and cracks in half merely under the pressure of its own weight.[21] Or better, try to imagine a mash-up in which a gigantic robot enters the scene in *Titanic,* lifts up the ship, and swings it around like a baseball bat. Our Galilean selves, well adapted by everyday life to recognize real constraints on the behavior of material objects, even if these selves are still incompetent (or *too* competent) at rescaling those objects in immaterial images, would, and indeed should, scoff at such liberties. And then consider the jaeger itself: blown up to these gargantuan dimensions but still retaining the proportions of a six-foot-tall human, it too would almost certainly crumple when striking or being struck by a kaiju. At the very least, facts of physics and materials science would utterly prevent it from cavorting about in the agile manner that the special effects achieve, just like a regular human-sized action hero. And the audience *gets* that. We even understand it as a certain winking irony on the part of the filmmakers about the special effect itself, which makes hyperfactical giants behave like ordinary persons or even like petulant kids, or which makes cargo ships behave like plastic toys tossed down the hallway or behind the sofa—they are brought down to size, so to speak. The *Transformers* films are an archetype for such coy commercial-ironic rescaling; in fact, one may think of the preceding analysis as Michael Bay phenomenology.[22]

Scale Is a Euphemism About Size

To reiterate some basic math, the scalar error that *Pacific Rim* invites the viewer to commit is exactly the same one pointed out by Galileo, and also the same that Haldane reinvokes to analyze the giants of *Pilgrim's Progress*: a robot fifty times taller than a person weighs not fifty times more but rather 125,000 times (50^3x) more.[23] If a well-armored, human-sized robot is, say, six feet tall and 250 pounds, a jaeger fifty times taller would weigh upward of thirty million pounds, and one can scarcely speculate on the exotic materials and energies it would need in order to run, dodge, and punch with the same dexterity as the tiny human operating its controls. The theoretical upshot of this mistake ought to be to underscore, on the one hand, the extreme ease of rescaling, and on the other hand, the hyperfacticity of bigness, its sheer, blunt, undialectical presence.

So again, here is the antinomy of bigness: two primal attributes of the object that must go together for it to work as the content of an image, but which strictly contradict each other. Nor would it matter much if one reimagined the jaeger six hundred feet tall, or three thousand feet, or thirty thousand. Its hyperfacticity and its resizability—in short, its immanent bigness and its relative smallness—are both equally essential to the image. Of course, filmmakers, whose stock in trade may be the illusory transformation of models and computer-generated avatars into representations of giants, have few allometric qualms. Their opportunistic relativism in enlarging or shrinking models generally suits our casually Aristotelian habits of thinking about size as a mere function of perspective or context. Moreover, an audience's facility in consuming special effects presumably evolves along with innovations in technique, so that our wonder at the realism of a newish effect—say, a sophisticated CGI image of giant alien bugs in Paul Verhoeven's *Starship Troopers,* the fantastically nimble giant ape in Peter Jackson's remake of *King Kong,* the macrophotographic close-ups in Darren Aronofsky's *The Fountain,* or the fluency of world-destroying superhero fights in the Marvel Cinematic Universe films—is matched by our increased disdain at the crudeness of older imagery—say, a clumsy giant insect model in *Them!* or the stuttery stop-motion of enormous beasts in the original *King Kong.* What remains consistent, regardless of the sophistication of new mimetic technologies, is the immediate interchangeability of the miniature and the gigantic, their essential *similarity,* or, in other words, the deceptively easy capacity of the viewer to accept the resizing of images along single dimensions, such that enlarged things continue to behave just like their much smaller counterparts.

The crux of the scalar mistake we continually make in resizing the image, and the engine of the antinomy of bigness, is the repression of the thing's materiality, a fantastical making-flat or making-silhouette of three-dimensional volume and mass. Actual magnitude is relegated to the residual cathexis of the image, its underlying but obscure motivation, the unconscious of its great scale. In effect, our scalar mistake politely veils the thing's massive body, discreetly overlooking its discomfiting material attributes. No wonder, as we well know, the bigger the violence gets in a film such as *Pacific Rim,* the less visceral and immediate it becomes. The colossal acts of destruction the jaegers and kaijus commit are basically comic, for instance, the tossed cargo ship that ends up lodged between two city buildings like a child's toy stuck behind the sofa. Whole cities or populations of millions annihilated at one go are far less significant for the film, and for our own emotional investment in plot or characters, than the ludicrously inconsequential question of whether the pilots Mako and Raleigh will have survived their combat mission; or whether, in *Independence Day,* Will Smith's girlfriend and son will have made it through the near-total destruction of Los Angeles; or whether, in *Armageddon,* having prevented an asteroid from destroying the entire earth, Bruce Willis will be returning home to his daughter, Liv Tyler; or whether, in *Avengers:*

Infinity War, Chadwick Boseman and Tom Holland die when Thanos kills half the living beings in the entire universe.

In a more serious vein, Elaine Scarry observes this type of scalar mistake in war rhetoric, which she identifies as "a rarefied choreography of disembodied events."[24] The indeterminate mass of actual humans involved in a war, the real agents and targets of violence, are distilled into metaphor and become a "single gigantic weapon": a "spearhead," a "hammer," an "arm," a "corps," and so on.[25] This "mythology of giants," as Scarry names it, is not just convenient propaganda, but required by the bigness of war itself.[26] Not only does "the convention express the fact that the fate of the overall army or population, and not the fate of single individuals, will determine the outcome," but "it has the virtue of bestowing visibility on events which, because of their scale, are wholly outside visual experience."[27] The bigness of war is extremely *there*, hyperfactical, yet readily and continuously revised and repressed, therefore made narratable and picturable, which is also to say, sellable and consumable. Thus, Scarry sees the bigness of war as an extreme ambivalence about bodies: the "mythology of giants" effectively "assists the disappearance of the human body from accounts of the very event that is the most radically embodying event in which human beings ever collectively participate."[28] Any properly scaled *depiction* of war is precisely the suppression of its real bigness, not to mention of its obscene violence.

In essence, the big thing is not merely absent from the scaled image, but rather, as Scarry infers, "disappear[ed]." In reaction to such disappearing, scale studies regularly insists on distinguishing size from scale, so as to account for their strange incommensurability. As Zachary Horton describes such a tendency:

> size is absolute and subject to direct measurement by the physicist. Scale, on the other hand, is relative: it requires that a relationship be stabilized between at least two entities. Scale already, then, smuggles in this process of stabilization itself. Scale is reflexive, size is not.[29]

Horton himself, pursuing aspects of Karen Barad's "agential realism," considerably complicates such a dichotomy, which perhaps references the antinomy of bigness in too abstract a fashion, declining to account for the conflict necessarily emergent when rescaled images are made. In his advocacy of a more robust scale studies, Horton observes "persistent campaigns in nearly every discipline toward scalar collapse, or the elision of difference between two or more scales when they are placed in the same medial frame."[30]

I would propose a similarly robust formulation: *Scale is a euphemism about size.* What it politely veils is the literal, hyperfactical thing and its immanent qualities—the live cow, the true violence of bodies struck by other bodies, the real mass, the real density and inertia of objects. The hyperfactical materiality of the thing uneasily persists along with the scaled image in something like the guise of a drive: bigness is both the prehistory of the image and, later, its residual infantile element, an immeasurable, unscalable quintessence. In a word, bigness is the *erotic*—the originary and now residuary presence of the body in the represented object or, if you like, of the real in the symbolic. In turn, scale is the diffident recalibration of the primal cathexis of the image, the polite, euphemistic consensus that its force can be measured, quantified, sublimated—that bigness can become something scalable, something *small.*

Because of our facility with size change, films such as *Them!* and *Pacific Rim* straddle the antinomy of bigness with the same ease with which we more generally discover ourselves capable of imagining the growing and shrinking of objects, an ease which lends the subgenre of the Gulliveresque its intuitive power, and which, not by coincidence, then permits the aesthetic contemplation of violence and war. The readiness to rescale objects, or to accept their rescaling in single dimensions, reduces the actual complexity of size change to blank spectacle, a dialectical revision or a mere echo of its primal cathexis. The realism of its too-bigness corresponds, ironically, to the measure of its fictionality. In this sense, Susan Sontag is correct to call a science-fiction film like *Them!* "one of the purest forms of spectacle."[31] Even given the complexity of phenomenological manipulation and technological praxis required to configure the antinomy of size enacted by the special-effect image, we arrive at the scene with a wholly undialectical effortlessness, and "merely watch."[32]

6

Macrophilia

THE BIGNESS OF THE BODY

Microscopical Vision

In the second voyage of Jonathan Swift's *Travels into Several Remote Nations of the World,* better known as *Gulliver's Travels,* Gulliver is visiting Brobdingnag, where he is extremely small and his hosts extremely large. In the middle of the night, he wakes in his enormous bed to find himself under attack by a pair of gigantic rats:

> I rose in a Fright, and drew out my Hanger to defend my self. These horrible Animals had the Boldness to attack me on both sides, and one of them held his Forefeet at my Collar; but I had the good Fortune to rip up his Belly before he could do me any Mischief. . . . These Creatures were of the size of a large Mastiff, but infinitely more nimble and fierce, so that if I had taken off my Belt before I went to sleep, I must have infallibly been torn to pieces and devoured. I measured the Tail of the dead Rat, and found it to be two Yards long wanting an Inch; but it went against my Stomach to drag the Carcass off the Bed, where it lay still bleeding.[1]

The vividness of the action is typical of Swift's prose, as well as a benchmark for fantasies of resizing in later literature and eventually cinema.[2] Such frightening interactions between humans and outsized animals are a staple of science-fiction and fantasy film, from *King Kong* and *Mighty Joe Young,* to *Them!* and *The Incredible Shrinking Man,* to *Honey, I Shrunk the Kids* and *Ant-Man.*[3] But Swift pursues the significance of resizing in somewhat odder directions than this long-standing convention might suggest. Gulliver's battle with the rats commences not with the attack itself, but rather with Gulliver getting up in the night with a powerful urge to urinate. Having no way to climb down from the bed, which for him is "eight Yards from the Floor," he is unable to find a private spot to relieve himself.[4] Gulliver recounts both his physical discomfort and the crisis of etiquette into which it thrusts him with a delicacy all the more ironic for its juxtaposition with the bloody violence about to follow: "Some natural Necessities required me to get down," he says, but "I durst not presume to call" for anyone in the household to assist.[5] And it is "under these Circumstances," needing to piss but too shy to ask for help, that the rats ambush him.

Yet even after the battle is finished, when the mistress of the house finally arrives to discover her tiny guest caked with blood and a disemboweled rat fouling her sheets, Gulliver's attention remains focused less on the spectacular results of the battle than on his own concern to urinate somewhere other than on the bed, regardless of how soiled it has already become. In his "Bashfulness," Gulliver continues to communicate with his gigantic hostess in diffident gestures, regardless of the further delay this adds to the already challenging conversation:

> I was pressed to do more than one Thing, which another could not do for me, and therefore endeavoured to make my Mistress understand that I desired to be set down on the Floor; which after she had done, my Bashfulness would not suffer me to express myself farther than by pointing to the Door, and bowing several times.[6]

Finally the woman grasps Gulliver's meaning and carries him outside to the garden. Once he has concealed himself and "discharged the Necessities of Nature," he proceeds to apologize at length to the reader for "dwelling on these and like Particulars."[7]

One sees that Swift's goal in the scene is something like the opposite of the hyperfactical spectacle of, say, the fight scenes in *Pacific Rim* or the waste reveal at the end of *Citizen Kane*. Gulliver continuously distracts us from bigness even as he depicts it, or draws our attention away from what is visible even as it is vividly imagined. Why so? The vaguely erotic subtext of the rat battle, arriving incongruously or metonymically through Gulliver's excremental urges and his reluctance to reveal his needs to a lady, seems coincidentally to cast questions of magnitude in terms of visual exposure and scopophilia. In a nutshell, Gulliver is more worried about being *seen* than about being dismembered or eaten. This strange priority accords with the effects of size change throughout the book. Gulliver's extreme smallness or bigness, or the relative smallness or bigness of others, almost always has the principal effect of rendering visible what otherwise would or should have remained tacit or immaterial; as ever larger things become unavoidably apparent, they tend also to become socially discomfiting or even indecent.[8] It is not farfetched to think of Gulliver's rescaled viewpoint as performing the same analytical function as the prying film camera, which, as Walter Benjamin famously argues, "furthers insight into the necessities governing our lives by its use of close-ups, by its accentuation of hidden details in familiar objects, and by its exploration of commonplace milieux."[9] Benjamin calls the camera's action an "intensive interpenetration of reality," and it is especially well achieved by the enlargement of a zoom, which "not merely clarifies what we see indistinctly 'in any case,' but brings to light entirely new structures of matter."[10] In precisely such a light, critics chiefly following Marjorie Hope Nicolson have described Swift's narrative method as "microscopy," an inherently analytical tool or lens.[11] Like Benjamin's film camera, Swift's prose discloses the "optical unconscious."[12]

Microscopical vision constantly risks seeing *too* close, and because with Swift we are always dealing with social matters, "too close" means, virtually by default, pornographic. It is possible that any literary context in which perspective is magnified by either artistic or prosthetic enhancements will eventually verge on pornography. Viktor Shklovsky, too, in discussing the defamiliarizing function of poetic language, ultimately turns his attention to sex scenes, in which "an erotic object . . . is presented as if it were seen for the first time."[13] Likewise, Gulliver's altered size tends to reconfigure human bodies around him as objects of augmented but ambivalent desire, thereby compelling a defamiliarizing redescription of the erotic itself, as well as specifying the scales at which scopophilia and sadism will tend to transact.

This decreasingly metonymic connection between bigness and the erotic crops up in scenes throughout *Gulliver's Travels*. It does so most famously in Gulliver's encounters with the "maids of honor" in Brobdingnag, who engage in sexual play with the tiny man, apparently even using him as a human dildo:

> The handsomest among these Maids of Honor, a pleasant, frolicksome Girl of sixteen, would sometimes set me astride upon one of her Nipples, with many other Tricks, wherein the Reader will excuse me for not being over particular.[14]

Gulliver's chastity or self-censorship underscores the irony of a social critique conducted through the intense focus of his resized sensorium; the reader's attention is directed not to the sex, per se—Gulliver continually narrates with characteristic diffidence, "not being over particular"—but rather to the material attributes of objects or bodies newly exposed by their enlargement, as it were a material substratum of social idealizations rendered too factical to overlook. For instance, Gulliver finds himself in extreme proximity to the "naked Bodies [of the Maids of honor], which, I am sure, to me was very far from being a tempting Sight, or from giving me any other emotions than those of Horror and Disgust."[15] The slightly odd extra phrase, "I am sure," obliquely reminds the reader that this vision of maids undressing would conventionally be an opportunity for titillation. Gulliver himself is taken aback to find the tableau thoroughly unarousing: "their Skins appeared so coarse and uneven, so variously coloured when I saw them near, with a Mole here and there as broad as a Trencher, and Hairs hanging from it thicker than Pack-threads; to say nothing further concerning the rest of their Persons."[16] Like the experience of the sublime—the following truism is simultaneously obvious and startling in Swift's incisive prose—sexual arousal requires a precise and well-regulated distance. Any too-close attention to a material body, which reactivates the potential hypercathexis of the *too big*, ironically destroys it.

In most macrophilia, which incidentally is the genre of fetish pornography that Swift's scene anticipates, both the bigness and the smallness of bodies are equally present as counterparts. But it is chiefly enlargement that is marked as erotic, both for Swift and for the macrophile, in the guise of the woman's grotesquely augmented body, and corresponding to conventional sexist configurations of desire that are simultaneously social dogma and critical target in Swift's writing. As though confirming the unconscious condensation of infantile emotions that cathect the fetish of bigness, Gulliver's experience oscillates rapidly between attraction, disgust, and outright fear, for example, in his close-up view of a nursing servant's "monstrous Breast."[17] Indeed, at any number of points during the voyage to Brobdingnag, as Susan Stewart remarks, women's breasts "represent a superfluity of nature; they will swallow Gulliver in their immediateness."[18] In addition, we can observe, in keeping with what Mary Ann Doane calls "the castrating tendencies of the close-up," that the sex scenes with the maids of honor are preceded and followed by acts of violence, namely, a pair of gory beheadings: first, that of a bird that had been harassing Gulliver, and whose neck is "wrung off" by an obliging servant, and second, the execution of a criminal whose "Veins and Arteries spouted up such a prodigious quantity of Blood, and so high in the Air, that the great *Jett d'eau* at *Versailles* was not equal for the time it lasted."[19] On the flipside, and consistent with the stereotypically heteronormative arrangement of macrophilia, when Gulliver himself is enlarged in Lilliput, his corresponding erotic cathexis adopts the barely displaced form of aggression, and one of his first waking impulses, upon seeing the tiny men surrounding his gigantic self, is to "dash them against the Ground," an urge we might compare to the augmented hostility of the motorist in a big car, observed by Theodor Adorno, who "merely by the power of his engine" is tempted "to wipe out the vermin of the street, pedestrians, children and cyclists."[20] Part of the virtuosity of Swift's method, even despite its predictable sexism, is to detail the convergence of a range of erotic and aggressive cathexes around issues of resizing, and at the same time to exhibit, in its conspicuous absence, the distance or *délicatesse* required for both "decency" and properly sublime (or sublimated) imagery. The body's bigness is unrepressed, haunting the well-scaled environs of polite society in the guise of fantasmatically tinged fetishes.

Our Ravish'd Eyes

Swift's interest in the defamiliarization of erotic ideals, but also in the critical description of excessive scopophilia, appears in other texts, especially some of his 1730s poems. In "The Lady's Dressing-Room," the augmentation of the senses, particularly the olfactory, is employed to destroy the process of idealization by which the titular lady is transformed from a strictly physical body into a "Goddess."[21] The poem's venomous misogyny is uncomfortably inextricable from its mordant critique of social ideals.[22] A lover named Strephon has stolen into the private room of his desire, the "haughty *Cælia*," just after she emerges from "Five Hours, (and who can do it less in?) / . . . spent in Dressing." Swift's verse luxuriates in the filth and distressing odors that Strephon now encounters as he conducts a "Survey / Of all the Litter as it lay" in the vacated dressing room, from the "Towels; / Begumm'd, bematter'd, and beslim'd; / With Dirt, and Sweat, and Ear-Wax grim'd" to the wafting "excremental Smell" of Celia's unemptied chamber pot. As in *Gulliver's Travels*, the intent is clearly a deflation of the too-familiar and too-hazy visual portraiture we derive from moderate or modulated distances—in this case, both an overidealized and clichéd depiction of femininity ("The Goddess from her Chamber issues . . .") and more generally the overly polite social habits that repress, rather than merely conceal, the functions of bodies. Strephon now views the detritus of Celia's makeup and toilet much too closely, and his sight is "ravish'd," as Swift declares, by sensual overscrutiny. In essence, Celia's body, even though it is absent except for its remnants, has become *too big*, altogether improperly scaled for the cult of femininity, excessively visceral and abject.

Thus even here, where the protagonist is not literally shrunk or enlarged, the detail and intensity with which Swift depicts the consequences of altering habitual perception has the effect of exposing the incompatibility of competing scales of observation: the moderate or euphemistic scale, a strictly visual rendering of Celia "Array'd in Lace, Brocades and Tissues," versus the close-in visual analysis, inevitably also more tactile and olfactory, of "The Scrapings from her Teeth and Gums" and her handkerchiefs "varnish'd o'er with Snuff and Snot." Wholes are ruthlessly separated into parts, and parts then microscopically surveilled and analyzed with each discrete sense in turn, much too big, too hyperfactical, to be effectively reassembled.[23]

"The Lady's Dressing-Room," despite its focus on one woman's body, is obviously something other than an erotic idyll, and by the end, it seems almost redundant for Swift to describe how Strephon is sorely "punish'd" for his overcurious peeping—"His foul Imagination links / Each Dame he sees with all her Stinks"—since the reader, too, has received the descriptive brunt of erotic defamiliarization.[24] Yet even amid such misogynistic bluntness, Swift's tactics shift to a disingenuous moralism by the poem's coda:

> If *Strephon* would but stop his Nose, . . .
> He soon would learn to think like me,
> And bless his ravish'd Eyes to see
> Such Order from Confusion sprung,
> Such gaudy *Tulips* rais'd from *Dung*.[25]

The sheer artlessness, even the stupidity, of this conclusion, in which Strephon is advised to unsee the "radical violence to the body" that the poem itself has rendered far too large to ignore, suggests a narrative persona very close to the oscillating naivete and coyness of Gulliver, who, having just described his own disgust at the "offensive Smell" of the Brobdingnagian maids of honor, immediately adds, "I do not mention, or intend, [this] to the Disadvantage of those excellent Ladies, for whom I have all manner of Respect."[26] A moment later, still dwelling on bodies and their smells, Gulliver declares, "I cannot forbear doing Justice to the Queen my Mistress, and *Glumdalclitch* my Nurse, whose Persons were as sweet as those of any Lady in *England*."[27] Of course, it is unlikely that "any lady in England" during this period would have looked or smelled differently than the ladies in Brobdingnag whom Gulliver has so closely analyzed in their enlarged condition. But the irony of the comparison with English ladies is clear precisely to the degree that the reader comprehends the overall antithetical thrust of Gulliver's scalar critique, and the bungled *délicatesse* of his caveats.[28] In his direct speech, Gulliver remains courteous to a fault, mimicking the uncritical acceptance of euphemisms that permit idealizations of English (and presumably any other) society, and which the fortuitous enlargements that occur during his voyages are precisely calculated to destroy.

In short, for Swift, magnitude is to correct scale what bodily impulses are to polite society: always *there*, of course, but necessarily dissimulated, diminished, abstracted, sometimes made (merely) sublime. This is a necessary process for social discourse, much in the way Elaine Scarry's "mythology of giants" is necessary for the depiction and even the propagation of war: to make bodies *visible* as opposed to *present*, and thereby to rescue what Swift calls our "ravish'd Eyes," restoring the euphemistic scalar regime of the visual at the expense of the material and tactile.[29]

If we consider precisely where Swift focuses our attention when big things are nearby, then we receive one possible answer, necessarily oblique and difficult, to the question of what magnitude *is* in the image. Consider that Gulliver continuously finds himself unable to do things: unable to escape, unable to get out of bed, unable to communicate, unable to piss, unable to speak of pissing, unable to be sexually aroused, unable to eat or drink, and in general unable to contend with the mismatch between his body and other bodies around him. In this light, Gulliver's bigness or smallness is not only a vehicle for microscopically enhanced critique, for instance, of social idealizations that do not easily survive close-up scrutiny of their material compositions. Size change is a confrontation with the hyperfactical density and opacity of *the body itself*: the body is constantly in the way, inhibiting conventional views and viewpoints, and sometimes (therefore) directly frightening. To be big, or rather to be too big—or to be compelled to confront what is too big—is to reanimate a primal erotic relationship with objects that the acquisition of correct scale sublimates or distills away. And in this sense, bigness is not something we accomplish by rescaling. Bigness comes before scale—strictly speaking, even before size. It is the infantile unconscious of the euphemistically rescaled image.

7

Racism

THE BIGNESS OF MICHAEL BROWN

Hulk Hogan

On September 16, 2014, police officer Darren Wilson appeared before a grand jury to testify about his fatal shooting of an unarmed black teenager, Michael Brown, in Ferguson, Missouri, a month before. Wilson recounts the moment he first saw Brown walking with a friend:

> I see them walking down the middle of the street. And first thing that struck me was they're walking in the middle of the street. . . . And the next thing I noticed was the size of the individuals because either the first one was really small or the second one was really big.[1]

A verbal altercation follows, during which Brown, according to Wilson's testimony, becomes hostile and tries to punch him through the open window of the police car:

> WILSON. I tried to hold his right arm and use my left hand to get out to have some type of control and not be trapped in my car anymore. And when I grabbed him, the only way I can describe it is I felt like a five-year-old holding onto Hulk Hogan.
>
> ASSISTANT PROSECUTING ATTORNEY. Holding onto a what?
>
> WILSON. A Hulk Hogan, that's just how big he felt and how small I felt just from grasping his arm.[2]

Michael Brown was undeniably a large person, six feet four and nearly three hundred pounds. But Wilson himself was not much smaller than Brown, certainly not by the order of magnitude implied by his juxtaposition of a "five-year-old holding onto Hulk Hogan." According to his own reckoning, Wilson was "just a shy [*sic*] under 6′4″" and "210-ish" in weight, in other words, the same height as Brown but slimmer.[3]

Nonetheless, Michael Brown's bigness continues to play a central role in the often confusing explanations Wilson offers of the killing. First, Wilson characterizes his initial two gunshots, fired while he was still sitting inside his car, as a defense against Brown's immense strength: "I mean it was, he's obviously bigger than I was and stronger and . . . [another punch] could be fatal if he hit me right."[4] Wilson's language becomes increasingly hyperbolic once he describes exiting his car and pursuing Michael Brown down the street; Brown is said to exhibit "the most intense aggressive face. The only way I can describe it, it looks like a demon."[5] Moments later, following a foot pursuit and several more shots, Brown has again turned toward Wilson "and made like a grunting, like aggravated sound."[6] Finally, having fired numerous bullets at Brown ("I don't know how many"), Wilson asserts: "It looked like he was bulking up to run through the shots, like it was making him mad that I'm shooting at him"; he was "going to run right through me."[7] In effect, Wilson's initial depiction of Brown as an immensely large athlete or fighter is now weirdly corroborated by images borrowed from comics or superhero films. From being "Hulk Hogan," Brown turns into the very avatar after whom that professional wrestler is named, the Incredible Hulk himself, a comic-book antihero who, by virtue of an inflatable body and inexhaustible wrath, would be capable of "bulking up" in order to "run through" a hail of police gunfire, and against whom bullets would accomplish no more than "making him mad."

The figure of Michael-Brown-as-Hulk, or the miscellany of pop-cultural fragments composing this bizarre specter, continues to populate Wilson's story about the shooting long after his grand jury testimony. Three months later, in November of 2016, presumably with ample time to reflect on the language he uses, Wilson says the following to George Stephanopoulos during an ABC News interview:

> WILSON. When I felt [his right forearm], I just felt the immense power that he had. And the way I've described it is, it was like a five-year-old holding onto Hulk Hogan. That's just how big this man was.
>
> STEPHANOPOULOS. Hulk Hogan?
>
> WILSON. He was very large. Very powerful man.[8]

Throughout Wilson's narratives and interviews, neither race nor skin color is directly mentioned, but it is easy to see why racism is widely understood to be an essential component of Wilson's fantastical depiction of this unarmed teenager. Indeed, the comic-book or cartoon avatars Wilson borrows for his characterization of the threat that Michael Brown posed are grounded in well-worn literary and dramatic stereotypes of black men that date back at least to the American Reconstruction era.[9] Even the climactic moment of Brown's death on the Ferguson street seems pilfered from genre fiction, perhaps from scenes of exorcism or vampire killing in Gothic melodrama:

> I remember looking at my sites and firing, all I see is his head and that's what I shot. I don't know how many, I know at least once because I saw the last one go into him. And then when it went into him, the demeanor on his face went blank, the aggression was gone, it was gone, I mean, I knew he stopped, the threat was stopped.[10]

Brown's body moves inexorably, as though possessed by a supernatural force or spirit, transcending individual intentions or consciousness. When this body at last expires, the force is "stopped." Wilson resorts to dehumanizing abstractions: "the aggression"; "the threat"; "it." What is finally destroyed by the officer's bullets is not a person but rather a spirit or shade, impelling isolated body parts and gestures that are paradoxically both mechanical and hyperanimated. Of course, the perverse sublimity of this narrative climax ironically depends on the continuous belief in the supernatural or superhuman quality of Michael Brown's size and strength. As in the Reconstruction stereotype of the "brute" or "buck," belligerence or savagery acts *through* the massive black body, an automatized racial inheritance.[11] The "aggression" Wilson describes is therefore not Michael Brown's per se, but belongs to his type, a nebulous or boundless force that in turn (or retroactively) justifies Wilson's terror. Michael Brown is, for Darren Wilson, perhaps literally, "a demon."

To Cry Like Children

A comparable instance of such racist demonization, remote in time but not at all in its potency as fuel for white-supremacist paranoia, is the innate savagery of the black rapist, Gus, in Thomas Dixon's 1905 novel *The Clansman: A Historical Romance of the Ku Klux Klan*. The character of Gus incidentally furnishes one of the chief "buck" stereotypes for D. W. Griffith's 1915 film, *Birth of a Nation*, among the most influential of all American racist narratives.[12] In a climactic scene in Dixon's novel, Gus, who has been hypnotized before a group of Ku Klux Klan witnesses, reenacts his rape of a fifteen-year-old white girl, Marion Lenoir. Even the mere restaging of Gus's crime prompts the Klansmen to cower in fear:

> Gus rose to his feet and started across the cave as if to spring on the shivering figure of the girl, the clansmen with muttered groans, sobs and

> curses falling back as he advanced. . . . His thick lips were drawn upward in an ugly leer and his sinister bead-eyes gleamed like a gorilla's. A single fierce leap and the black claws clutched the air slowly as if sinking into the soft white throat.
>
> Strong men began to cry like children.[13]

Like Michael Brown in Wilson's tale, Gus can "start" and "advance" through blind compulsion, a simultaneously subhuman and superhuman urge underscored by Dixon's use of animalistic metaphors ("black claws clutched the air," etc.). Given the instinctual momentum of Gus's body, the fact that he is hypnotized seems almost beside the point; neither consciousness nor intention is ever part of his "gorilla"-like behavior. It therefore becomes strangely reasonable, in Dixon's logic, for the audience of stout Klansman, whom elsewhere Dixon is keen to portray in gallant terms, to forget they are viewing a mere reenactment and "cry like children." What panics the Klansmen to the point of infantilization, apparently not at all to Dixon's embarrassment or that of his white readers, is the primal monstrosity of Gus's blackness itself, now resurfacing like a repressed memory of what Dixon calls "the eyes of the jungle."[14] The perpetual strength and brutality of the black body, lodged instinctively in the white mind like the "accursed inheritance" of "the primeval forest," rematerializes in the form of pure symptom, prompting a reflexive and (for Dixon) inevitable terror, a hyperbolic counterpart to the infamous "black and incomprehensible frenzy" of bodies that Charles Marlow sees along an African river bank in Conrad's *Heart of Darkness* a few years before.[15]

Officer Darren Wilson is not exactly a Dixon-style Klansman, but he nonetheless fits into this self-infantilizing class of "strong men who began to cry like children" at the advent of the black body, devolving from a six feet four, 210-pound (and well-armed) man into a "five-year-old holding onto Hulk Hogan." I have previously suggested that we might locate the primal cathexis of bigness—its simultaneous attraction and repulsion, resurfacing in the adult in the more placid form of a "delightful horrour [or] terrible joy" of the sublime[16]—in the child's unmediated dread of the "absolutely large" body of the other.[17] In this light, it is unsurprising to discover that the racist adult, whose perception of such bodies is already steeped in the imagery of fantasy and romance, might experience the threat of blackness as though in a scene from adolescent genre fiction, in which the "absolute" reckoning of the infantile psyche is exploited to concoct the extravagant magnitude of the other. Michael Brown in the eyes of Darren Wilson, like Gus in the eyes of the frightened Klansman, is a preconscious collage, re-imaged through half-remembered figurations from film and comic books in the way that dream thoughts are reconstructed around the miscellaneous remnants of material that Freud calls "day residue."[18]

Given its abjectly generic form, we should not be surprised to discover similar hallucinatory narratives about the magnitude of the black body, about its primordial menace and the cartoonish fantasy it provokes (or recalls) in the mind of the racist, in numerous accounts of police shootings and other violence against African Americans.[19] In 2012, Bartholomew Williams, an unarmed thirty-eight-year-old graduate student, exhibited what a police spokesperson called "super-human-type strength" before being shot to death by officers on the campus of California State University, San Bernadino.[20] In 2015, Jonathan Ferrell, a twenty-four-year-old who had been seeking help after an early morning car accident near Charlotte, North Carolina, "charged" at Officer Randall Kerrick with "crazy-looking eyes . . . like a hologram of some sort." Kerrick says: "When he got within, say, ten feet of me, I fired my duty weapon. It did not faze him. He kept coming toward me. I fired again."[21] In 2014, Dontre Hamilton, who was discovered sleeping in a public park by Milwaukee officer Christopher Manney, was shot fourteen times; according to Officer Manney, Hamilton had "super human strength" and a "thousand-yard stare," and "kept coming forward" as if the officer was "shooting a BB gun."[22] In February 2022, Officer Tou Thao, rationalizing the excessive force he and fellow officer Derek Chauvin used against George Floyd shortly before Chauvin murdered him, testified that Floyd had "super-human strength."[23] As recently as April 2023, a Kansas City homeowner, Andrew Lester, told police that he shot sixteen-year-old Ralph Yarl twice through the closed front door of his house because "he was 'scared to death' due to the boy's size."[24] Attacks on African American men, and sometimes children—from Bernhard Goetz's vigilante shooting of four black teenagers in a New York subway in 1984 to the killings of Trayvon Martin, Eric Garner, John Crawford III, Philando Castile, Tamir Rice, and many others, often seem explicable only in light of infantile fantasies about the frenzy of the outsized black body and its demonic impulse, a zombielike antagonist that must be destroyed before it spontaneously heaves and strikes.

Testifying about what may be the most famous of such racist attacks on African American men since the lynching era, Los Angeles police officer Stacey Koon, during his 1992 trial, describes his fear of Rodney King even after King had been twice tasered, beaten with batons by as many as eight police officers, and was lying face down in the street. Koon asserts that he thought King's body must be "anesthetized to the pain":

> I'm getting concerned, scared. I'm getting a little frightened here now because this gentleman has just been subjected to a multitude of blows with a metal PR24 [a law enforcement "control baton"] and there is no evidence that he is going to go into compliance mode. . . . I perceived that he was searching, he was seeking, he was a [*sic*] means to attack or a means to escape.[25]

Under cross-examination, Koon is asked whether King was a "deadly threat," and Koon replies that he supposed (incorrectly) that King was high on PCP and that "if he had grabbed my officer it would have been a death grip." The prospect of a "death grip," whatever Koon imagines this cartoonish term to signify, matches both the tone of his overall depictions of King's physical presence and the strikingly similar vocabulary of Darren Wilson's descriptions of Michael Brown. Apparently cribbing from Looney Tunes, Koon further describes Rodney King as a "Tasmanian Devil"; his arms were as "stiff as steel posts embedded in the ground"; Koon believed that King "had thrown approximately 800 pounds of officers off him." And finally, consolidating all this comic-book and professional-wrestling imagery, and directly anticipating Darren Wilson's similar allusions to cartoon antiheroes, Koon declares that Rodney King possessed "hulk-like super strength."[26]

Super-Predator

Such extreme overreaction by police (but not just police) suggests that the cathexis of racism, its merging of an infantile phenomenology of the *too big* with stock figures of the racialized other, perpetuates what Kobena Mercer calls a "a death-bearing fusion of erotic and aggressive desires in the violence that breaks against the black male body."[27] If one pursues this simultaneously generic and psychological explanation for panicked violence, which, as Mercer argues, can entail a "near-psychotic repudiation of reality," one observes that the garish stereotypes of Dixon's *The Clansman* or Griffith's *Birth of a Nation* are far from obsolete in the present day. The modern counterpart to *Birth of a Nation*, both in its overheated imaginary and in its sociopolitical influence—in other words, the counterpart of a single text that assembles a consumable motif out of the nebulous anxieties of white-supremacist culture—is John J. DiIulio Jr.'s infamous 1995 article, "The Coming of the Super-Predators," published in the neoconservative magazine *The Weekly Standard*.[28]

Dilulio's essay accomplishes the impressive but contemptible feat of transforming a vague hysteria over "the incredibly frightening picture" of a generation of "super crime-prone young males" into an ostensibly balanced, data-based disquisition *against* critiques of racism in the American judicial system, critiques that Dilulio elsewhere characterizes, ironically, as "fevered fantasies."[29] Yet whatever aura of objectivity or authority it achieves, Dilulio's portrait of black men remains saturated with uncanny dread, a reaction provoked notoriously even by "boys whose voices have yet to change":[30]

> A few years ago, I forswore research inside juvenile lock-ups. The buzz of impulsive violence, the vacant stares and smiles, and the remorseless eyes were at once too frightening and too depressing (my God, these are children!) for me to pretend to "study" them.[31]

Dilulio's language of zombielike black boys is defensively couched in the voice of rigorously self-critical academic scholarship. In a tone suggesting the resignation of a skeptical researcher confronted by stubborn facts, Dilulio speaks of "hardened, remorseless juveniles" who "reflexively dehumanize" their victims and "live entirely for the present moment; they quite literally have no concept of the future."[32] The super-predator, like the black brute of an era of (slightly) blunter racism, is so mentally deficient that his criminal actions can scarcely be called intentional. His "behavior is driven by . . . profound developmental defects," like the animalistic Hulks perceived by Darren Wilson and Stacey Koon, or like the hypnotized Gus, whose instinctive lurching terrifies Dixon's Klansmen. Dilulio asserts that super-predators "fear neither the stigma of arrest nor the pain of imprisonment. . . . So long as their youthful energies hold out, they will do what comes 'naturally': murder, rape, rob, assault, burglarize, deal deadly drugs, and get high."[33] As Dilulio finally asserts, in as self-revealing and self-disempowering a confession of "my black crime problem" as one might discover in any white-supremacist diatribe, "the fear is enormous and largely justifiable, and the black kids who inspire the fear seem not merely unrecognizable but alien."[34]

Such abject stereotyping ought to have seemed anything but "alien" in the journalistic milieu in which this language circulated once it left *The Weekly Standard*, and Dilulio should no more be forgiven his infantile overreactions (or the overreactions he abetted in others) than Dixon his bogus theories of racial inheritance. Indeed, for a culture better versed in its own social history, much of Dilulio's baleful influence might have been moderated solely through an acknowledgment of its overindulgence in clichés. The figure of the "giant negro," a subhuman creature immune to ordinary pain, forethought, or conscience, like the violent and sexually voracious buck of post-Reconstruction fiction, had been virtually a stock character in true-crime journalism for at least a century, and just as widespread in mainstream media such as *The New York Times* as in the conspiracy plots of tabloids and far-right weeklies.[35] Dilulio's awareness of his own participation in this embarrassing journalistic tradition must have contributed to his decision eventually to recant much of his argument and terminology.[36] But his work had a potent afterlife. Hillary Clinton, who, like Dilulio himself, was in an excellent position to observe prevalent overreactions to the "super-predator" myth in the burgeoning of mass incarceration during her own husband's presidency, was still invoking this term at a reelection campaign rally in New Hampshire in 1996 while discussing the administration's crime policies:

> They are not just gangs of kids anymore. They are often the kinds of kids that are called "super-predators." No conscience, no empathy. We can talk about why they ended up that way but first we have to bring them to heel.[37]

Clinton did not see fit to revisit this statement, let alone to recant it, for two decades, until directly challenged by a Black Lives Matter activist, Ashley Williams, at a 2016 campaign fundraiser: "Looking back, I shouldn't have used those words, and I wouldn't use them today."[38] Yet a couple of months after this lukewarm retraction, Bill Clinton, also confronted by BLM activists while campaigning for Hillary's presidential run, was even less inclined to reevaluate his former position, overtly espousing the talking points of 1990s anti-crime mania:

> I don't know how you would describe the gang leaders who got 13-year-olds hopped up on crack and sent them out in the streets to murder other African-American children! Maybe you thought they were good citizens, she [Hillary Clinton] didn't. You are defending the people who kill the lives you say matter.[39]

In 1993, Bill Clinton's close ally Senator Joe Biden had used similar terms, even directly anticipating some of Dilulio's language—"predators," "without any conscience," "literally have not been socialized," "beyond the pale"—during a floor speech backing the 1994 Senate Crime Bill that

Clinton eventually signed.[40] Indeed, Biden was so strong a supporter of the bill that he has frequently referred to it simply as "the Biden bill." It is worth quoting his speech at some length to gauge its somewhat fevered protofascism:

> Unless we do something about the cadre of young people—tens of thousands of them, born out of wedlock, without parents, without supervision, without any structure, without any conscience developing because they literally (I yield myself three more minutes), because they literally have not been socialized, they literally have not had an opportunity. We should focus on them now, not out of a liberal instinct for love, brother [*sic*], and humanity—although I think that's a good instinct—but for simple, pragmatic reasons. If we don't, they will, or a portion of them will, become the predators fifteen years from now. And Madam President, we have predators on our streets that society has, in fact, in part because of its neglect, created. Again, it does not mean, because we created them, that we somehow forgive them or do not take them out of society to protect my family and yours from them. They are beyond the pale, many of those people, beyond the pale, and it's a sad commentary on society. We have no choice but to take them out of society. And the truth is, we don't very well know how to rehabilitate them at this point. That's the sad truth.[41]

The sheer intractability of hallucinatory rhetoric aside, the enduring effect of the "super-predator" myth that Biden helped solidify into both shibboleth and law—as well as the more general legacy of the "giant," "hulk-like," or "super" black body that continues to animate racist fantasies both in and beyond judicial institutions—is the all-too-real death, injury, and imprisonment of actual African Americans stylized as its generic target.

8

Architecture Without Space

THE SKYSCRAPER

Automatic Architecture

In 1929, the architectural illustrator Hugh Ferriss published *The Metropolis of Tomorrow*, a compendium of his charcoal drawings of real and imagined skyscrapers, and a touchstone for theories of big architecture during the heyday of the skyscraper in the 1930s as well as during its postmodern re-emergence in the 1980s.[1] Ferriss's best-known sketches are interpretations of the 1916 New York Zoning Resolution, a set of laws that allowed developers to propose a building any height they wished, provided the volume was progressively scaled back to allow light and fresh air to reach the street. Ferriss begins his sketches as solid, quasi-sculptural silhouettes, "a representation of the maximum mass which, under the Zoning Law, it would be permissible to build over an entire city block."[2] From there, he carves away small sections, "removing those parts which were . . . found to be undesirable" and "subtleizing" the "crude masses" until he arrives at something like the Maximal arrangement of stacked stories that would adhere to the new rules.[3] The result is the "setback," one of the most recognizable visual elements of modern design and an unusually grand compromise between capitalism, urban environmentalism, and architectural form.[4]

While the setback alone does not imply very tall buildings, the specific formula of the 1916 Zoning Resolution encouraged architectural bigness; once a designer had apportioned setbacks over 75 percent of the available lot, the remaining 25 percent could be extended upward to any height desired. From this provision of the regulation eventually came the best-known "needle" designs of 1930s New York City, such as the Chrysler Building and the Empire State Building: thin, pointy towers rising out of block-wide, progressively articulated bases. In light of their reflexive adherence to the imputed silhouette of the 1916 Zoning Resolution, Rem Koolhaas calls the massing of such buildings "a pure and thoughtless

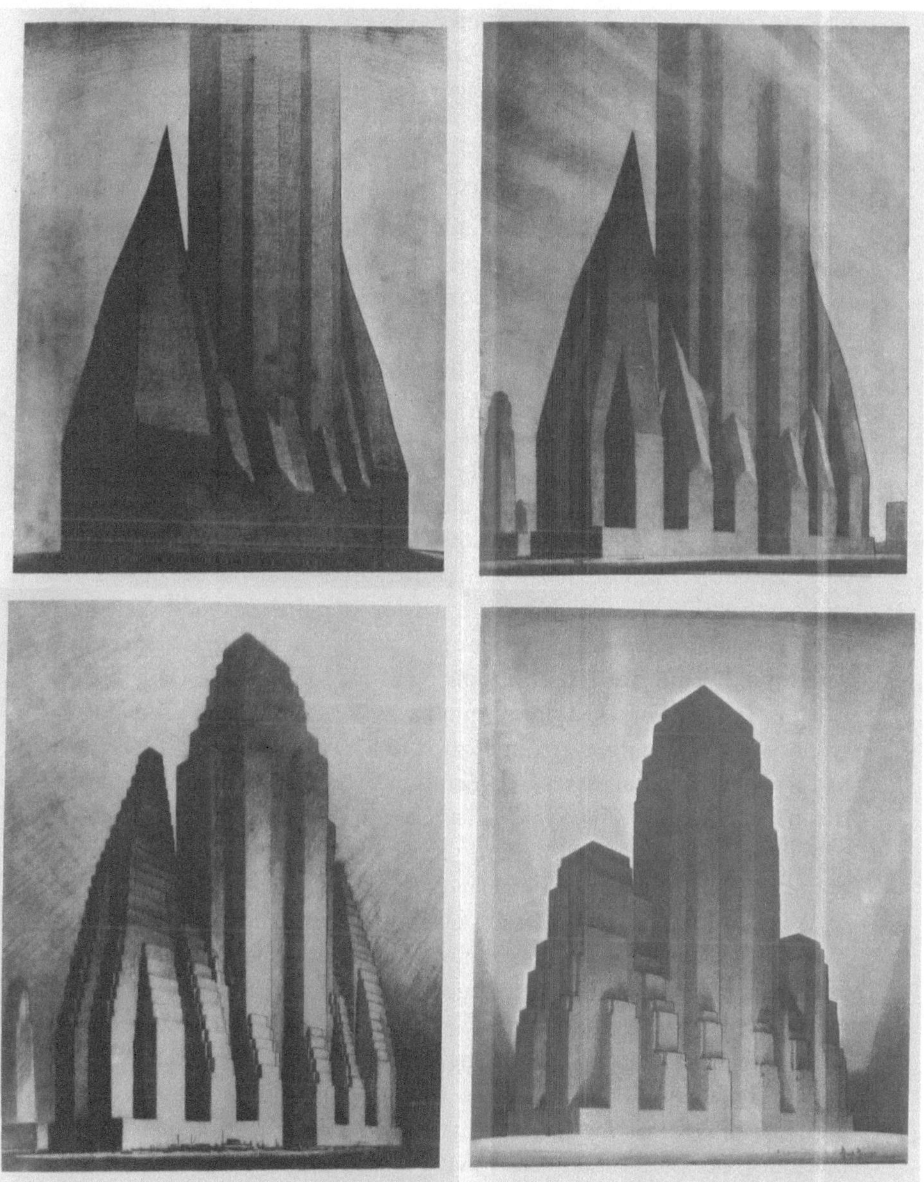

FIGURE 8.1 Hugh Ferriss, *The Metropolis of Tomorrow* (1929): skyscraper setbacks adhering to the 1916 New York Zoning Resolution

process," intended primarily to monetize the maximum commercial volume permitted by the rules—an "automatic architecture," as Koolhaas suggests.[5] Ferriss, in his formalist rigor, concurs: "Is the setback well designed?" he asks; "indeed, it is not designed at all!"[6]

The most immediate consequence of such reflexive capitalization, and in general a prerequisite for extreme bigness in commercial architecture, is the reduction of space to modular units and their repetition. For Ferriss, whose drawings express this aesthetic imperative in its bluntest conceptual guise, the tall building is more strictly a sculpture than a work of architecture. Its formal tendency suggests the following counterintuitive and wholly theoretical axiom: a skyscraper, like a statue, contains *no interior space*—in effect, it is a monolith. To lend this provocation slightly more nuance: any interior space in a skyscraper is chiefly a quantitative accumulation rather than a deliberate composition of qualitatively distinctive parts. Therefore, in a modern city, given the tendency Ferriss's drawings anticipate and the resources of capital willingly fulfill, tall buildings are to be experienced from the outside, regardless of the inhabitable or salable real estate within. Presumably this is why, among the sixty-odd drawings in Ferriss's *Metropolis of Tomorrow*, only one is of an interior perspective. And even this interior is odd: a drawing of the lobby of the Daily News Building in New York, centered around a huge pit containing a seemingly suspended globe of the earth, in relation to which the building's entrance hall serves as a kind of ethereal observation deck.[7] Ferriss himself suggests that his rendering "would scarcely be taken to refer to the entrance lobby of a newspaper and office building"; it is more like an ironic repudiation of the interior space of earthly business.[8]

We need to think antithetically, against the aesthetical and rhetorical habits of designers and developers, not to mention of the propagandists of real estate marketing. The skyscraper never did become the eclectic city-within-a-city that, from its advent, had been its explicit aspiration, one still proffered as a rationale in recent development projects. Rather, contemporary tall buildings, despite the whole history of International-Style modernism and postmodernist reactions, still hew close to the opaque monolith, the sculptural needle, that Ferriss imagined via his setbacks. To confirm this continuity, it helps to recall how many skyscraper projects worldwide have forged ahead despite the often clear unviability of selling or renting much of the multiuse interior volume they furnish. The monetizing of interior space, however necessary or desultory a goal for justifying zoning legislation or raising construction funds, may be oddly beside the point. And the bigger and more expensive the building project, the truer this ironic irrelevance may tend to become. Ultimately, the prime

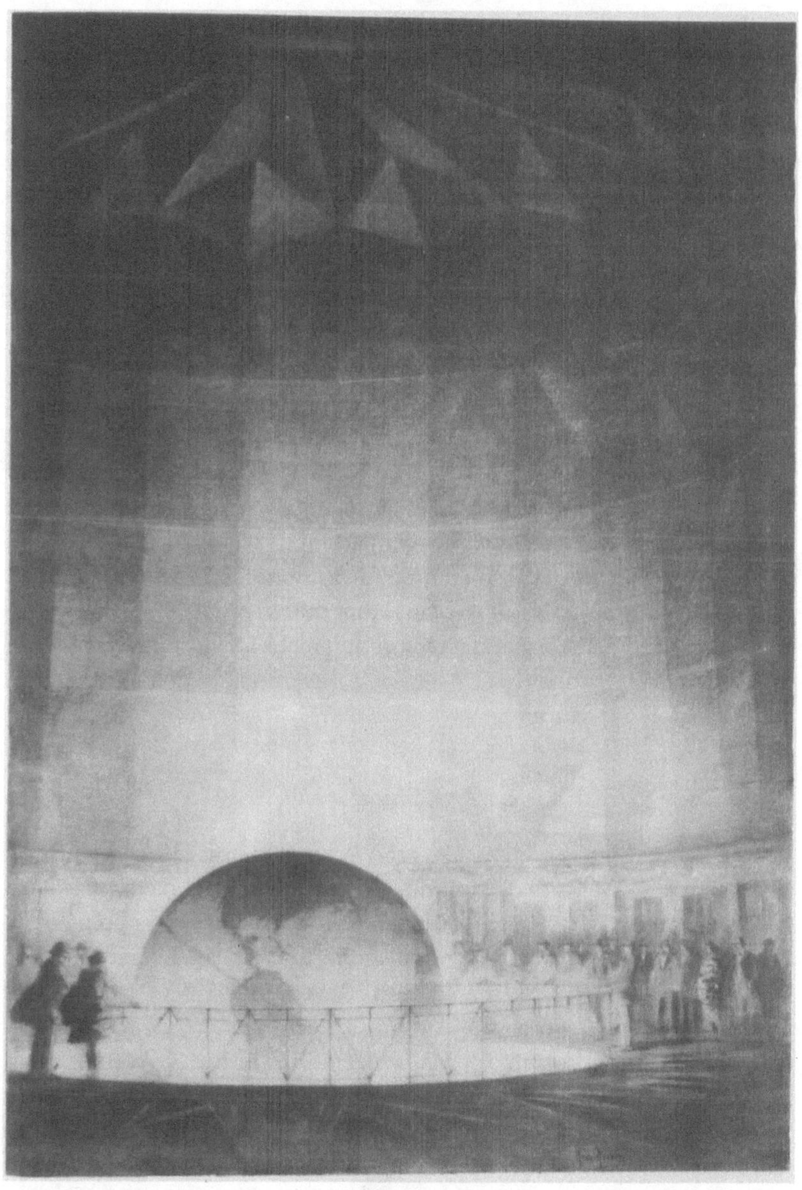

FIGURE 8.2 Hugh Ferriss, *The Metropolis of Tomorrow* (1929): lobby of the Daily News Building, New York

function of a Ferriss-inspired needle, the form I have suggested we could call a sculpture or a monolith instead of an inhabitable building, is to stand at its site and be *seen* in its unabashed magnitude. More exactly, its function is to posit, in material form and at a great but indefinite height, a visible perpendicular axis projecting from the two-dimensional grid of the urban plan. The successive floors of a skyscraper are thus generated "automatically," as Koolhaas suggests, and in indeterminate number, until we arrive at or very near the top. And only there, at the pinnacle of the monolith, might we encounter aesthetic and economic idiosyncrasies, whether they be the spires or antennas that typically cap needle skyscrapers, the function of which has often been chiefly to break height records, or the observation platforms that, from an early stage in the evolution of the tall modern building, became a customary feature.

I therefore would like, as a segue to further argument, to supplement my first provocation: in its formal essence, the skyscraper is *an ascendable monolith with a view*. This might seem about as blankly theoretical and ahistorical a claim about architectural form as one is likely to encounter. I wish to suggest that it is not so blank, that the ascendable monolith with a view has both a history and a continuing material-cultural life. For the purposes of elucidating that history and life, I first direct attention back approximately 230 years.

Cartographical Vision

In 1791, the new US president, George Washington, formed a commission to develop the "Territory of Columbia," a ten-square-mile region along the Potomac River in Maryland.[9] At the same time, Washington appointed the French-born architect and civil engineer Pierre Charles L'Enfant, who had been working in New York City since the Revolutionary War, to draw plans for a new "Federal City" on the Potomac's north bank. L'Enfant traveled to Georgetown, Maryland, in early March of 1791, and by the end of that month had produced his famously grand scheme, titled "Plan of the City Intended for the Permanent Seat of the Government of t[he] United States."[10] L'Enfant's design, to some degree following patterns familiar in Enlightenment city planning in Europe, superimposes a pair of highly regular but disparate street grids: first, an orthogonal matrix dividing the city into residential-scale blocks, and second, an axial array of much broader avenues cutting through the orthogonal grid and linked at large nodes or circuses intended to contain major public buildings and monuments. On his drawing, L'Enfant indicates the most significant of these axial nodes with capital letters and, in a brief "references" section, specifies the structures intended to be located at each.

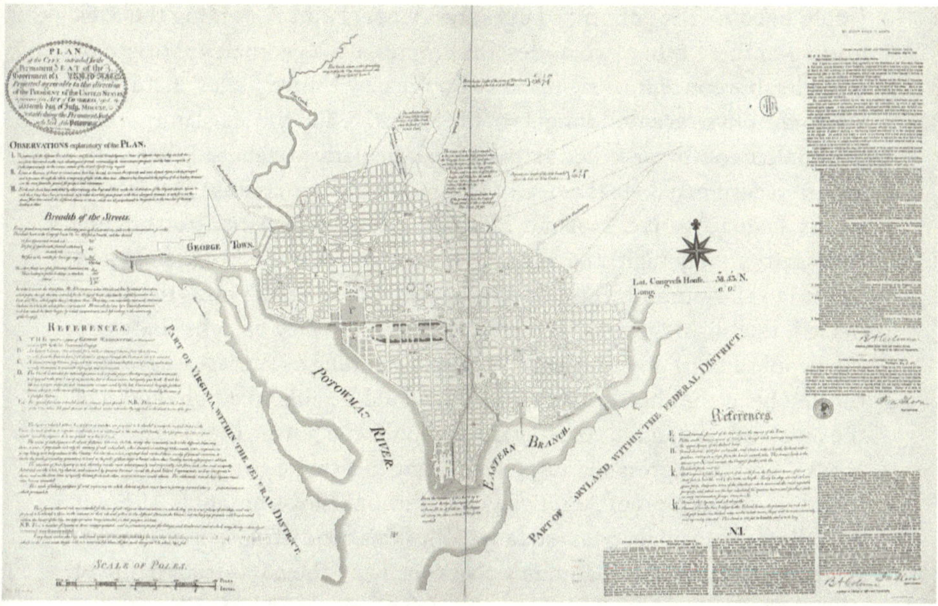

FIGURE 8.3 Pierre Charles L'Enfant, plan for Washington, DC, 1791 (Library of Congress)

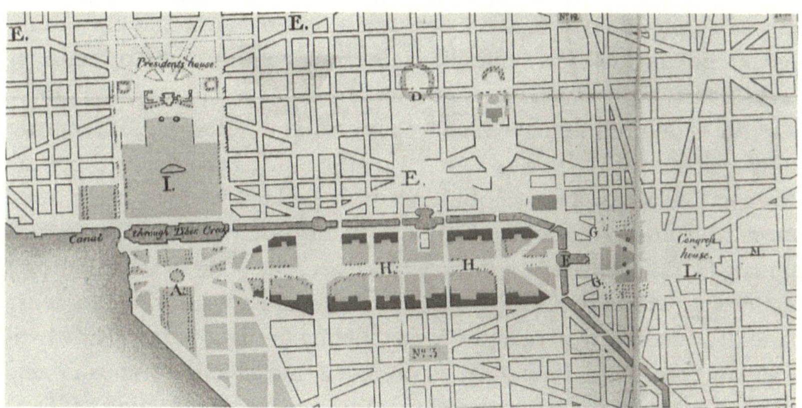

FIGURE 8.4 Pierre Charles L'Enfant, plan for Washington, DC, 1791: detail (Library of Congress)

The node labeled "Point A" is a crucial juncture in L'Enfant's plan, the right-angle corner of an immense Pythagorean triangle, at the other two points of which are located "Congress's House," a new Capitol Building atop Jenkins Hill, positioned at "Longitude 0.0" in order to establish a prime meridian for the new nation, and the "President's House," which would become the country's largest residence. Point A, joining the axes leading to these other two nodes, thus represents a geometrical origin of considerable conceptual significance for the new United States, a site from which the physical embodiments of the executive and the legislature could be simultaneously surveilled across perpendicularly juxtaposed allées, and in turn reconnected via the nearly two-mile-long hypotenuse that is now Pennsylvania Avenue. Nor did L'Enfant intend this geometrical figure to remain merely tacit; the allées in his plan were to be broadened and cleared to allow uninterrupted views between the distant points they connected, establishing what L'Enfant calls a "reciprocity of sight" between the people and its government.[11] A citizen standing at Point A, merely by turning his or her head ninety degrees, would be able to adjoin views of the outstanding symbols of federal and republican power, the "President's House" and "Congress's House," reenacting in a single sweeping gaze the founding calculation of American constitutional government.[12] At Point A itself, the principal vertex, so to speak, of this geometrical, political, and metaphysical calculus, L'Enfant's plan specifies "The equestrian figure of GEORGE WASHINGTON, a Monument voted in 1783, by the late Continental Congress."

A variety of environmental and bureaucratic circumstances conspired to prevent the installation of a statue of George Washington at Point A, as well as a good portion of the network of streets that would have established the practical and symbolic connections of this node to the larger city. In fact, the vast avenue that L'Enfant envisioned between Point A and the Capitol Building, which we now call the National Mall, was not fully realized until the 1930s, nearly a century and a half after its proposal. Even at that stage, a series of intractable problems necessitated several more revisions to the siting of Point A. In the 1901 McMillan Plan, which updated L'Enfant's scheme via the influence of the "City Beautiful" movement popularized by Chicago's 1893 Columbian Exposition, an immense landfill was added west of Point A, completing the figure of a roughly two-mile-long cross, like a vast open-air cathedral, and effectively repositioning Point A itself at the transept crossing.[13] The now-iconic reflecting pool was installed in the landfill west of Point A and, at the pool's far end, near the substantially reshaped bank of the Potomac, the new "apse" was dedicated to the Lincoln Memorial.[14] The familiar modern layout of Washington, DC, in which the central position of Point A is decisively marked by the Washington Monument, did not clearly emerge until the 1920s, and even then continued to evolve in fits and starts.

As late as the mid-1800s, fully half a century after L'Enfant's original drawing, construction on any scale befitting either L'Enfant's vision or

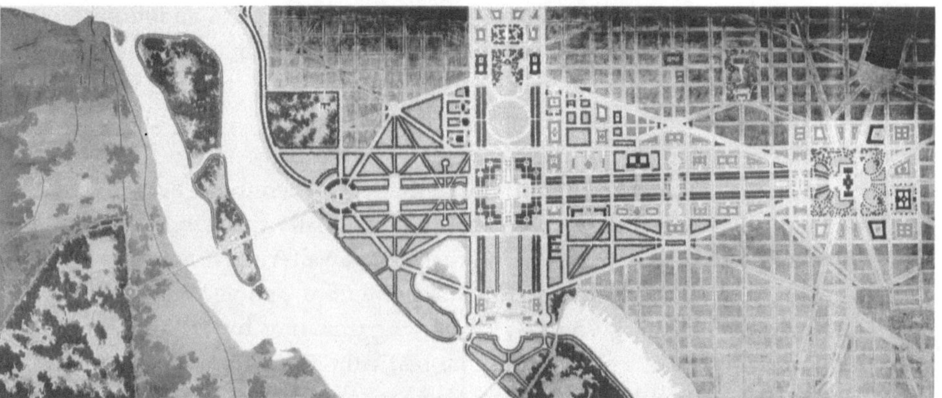

FIGURE 8.5 McMillan Plan for Washington, DC, 1901 (US Senate Park Commission; Library of Congress)

the lavishness of the forthcoming McMillan plan would have appeared improbable or even absurd. In lieu of the equestrian statue of George Washington that L'Enfant had desired at Point A, other monuments to Washington were sometimes placed elsewhere in the city through the 1840s, although none near the site L'Enfant had originally designated. The reason no statues were erected anywhere near Point A would have been obvious to anyone venturing in that direction from the Capitol. To get to Point A, one would have had to traverse a mile of "'waste ground' . . . where people dumped trash and tended their own vegetable gardens," occasionally "'patrolled by outlaws and outcasts,'" and only then would one have arrived at the swampy glade that occupied the far end of L'Enfant's still wholly hypothetical allée.[15] As Kirk Savage writes, "for most of the nineteenth century, Point A was merely a scraggly spot on a riverbank" and "probably under water for at least some period of the year"—in terms of urban development, "purely a geometrical fancy."[16] Even a commemorative stone that Thomas Jefferson had ordered placed at Point A in 1804 to mark the city's new prime meridian "was used to moor boats in Tiber Creek."[17]

In short, the nodes and axes of L'Enfant's scheme remained for many decades a mere cartographical hypothesis about politics, geometrical order, and "reciprocity of sight," rather than any realistic proposal for configuring the land.[18] Especially ignominiously, by the 1840s, the "grand avenue" that is now the Mall was known as a route for the district's slave trade. The city's main slave market was located at Seventh Street on the Mall's edge, a site from which "slave coffles—groups of slaves chained together—shuffled across the Mall's 'waste' on their way to loading docks on the river."[19] Facts such as these were frequently cited in abolitionist literature to highlight the disparity between the capital's architectural ambitions as a symbol of democracy and the bleak facts of its real political economy. The bigness of L'Enfant's aspirations to monumentality and visibility persisted chiefly in the guise of historical irony.

In 1848, a confluence of political, aesthetic, and economic pressures, not entirely dissimilar to those that had originally thwarted the full development of L'Enfant's scheme, furnished an alternative solution to the twin problems of constructing a monument to George Washington and properly utilizing Point A. Employing drawings by the architect Robert Mills, from a competition he had won several years earlier, a group of wealthy citizens proposed a new monument, clearly cognizant of the significance of L'Enfant's nascent Pythagorean juncture.[20] The first Mills design for Point A is a hodge-podge of federalist and imperialist imagery on an immense scale. An Egyptian-styled obelisk rises to a height of six hundred feet, surrounded by a colonnade of Doric columns and ornamented sculptural groupings: Washington himself riding a Roman-style chariot, an accompanying pantheon of Revolutionary War heroes, and so on. Although the new Washington Monument was to be funded through private subscription, the federal government donated the public land surrounding Point A for the project, relocating the exact site about four hundred feet farther east of Tiber Creek in order to provide a viable foundation for such a massive stone edifice. When completed, the monument would be the tallest human-made structure in the world by a considerable margin; moreover, for the first time since 1311, the world's tallest structure would be something other than a cathedral spire.[21]

Even amid the ornamental excesses of the first Mills design, one perceives a conceptual shift in the monument's most basic function, from an iconographic object on display for the public gaze, like an equestrian statue of a national hero, to something like a universal focal point for the overall design of a modern city, embracing the holistic ambition of L'Enfant's axes and nodes. The new Washington Monument generates a unique and supervisory geometrical viewpoint, befitting the singularity of the hero it commemorates, even as the immensely tall design supplants, or perhaps condenses or distills, the miscellaneous symbols originally intended to celebrate him. Indeed, the abstract bigness of Mills's obelisk, immediately its most identifiable characteristic, starkly differentiates the vertical portion of the monument from the fussy Doric colonnade and statuary at its base. In any case, nearly all of that ornamentation would soon be eliminated from the design. Savage suggests that the intention of

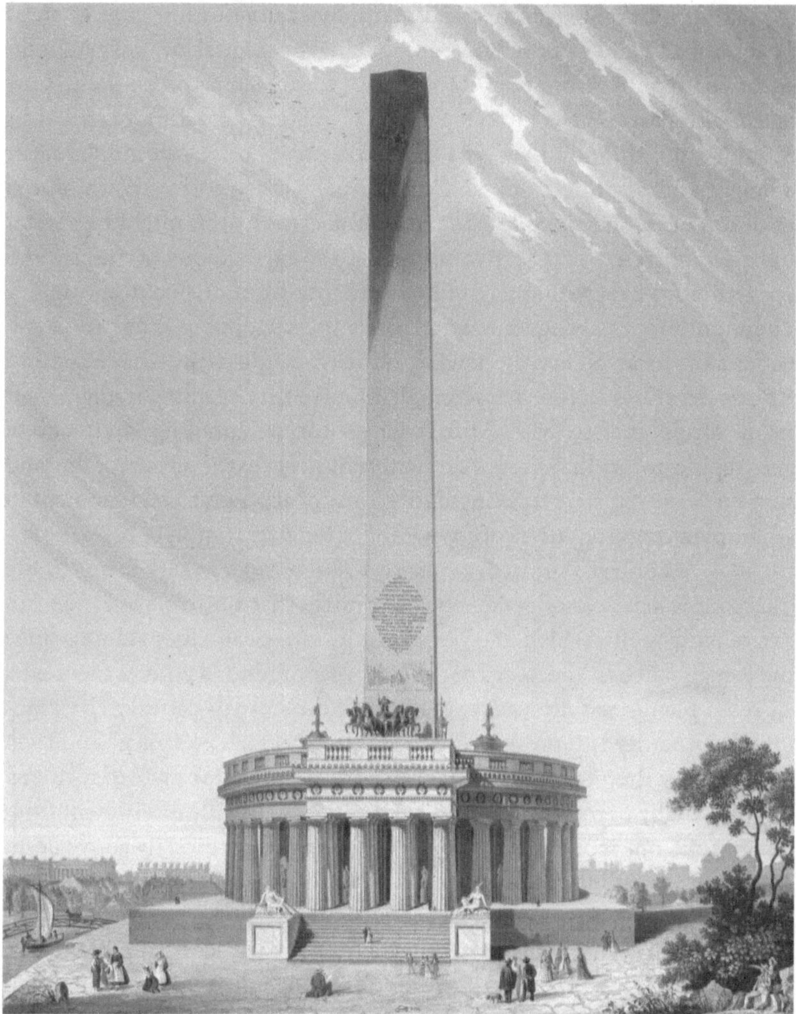

FIGURE 8.6 Robert Mills's first design for Washington Monument, 1836 (Library of Congress)

this new monument was to refocus attention away from the republican Capitol Building and back toward federal structures and iconography—it "did everything humanly possible to steal the Capitol's thunder," serving as an "affront to Republican restraint."[22] In this sense, quite aside from specific iconography, what is created through Mills's design is essentially a singular viewpoint in and from the sky, high atop the vertical axis of a three-dimensional Cartesian grid, the origin of which the obelisk simultaneously marks and occupies.

Taking L'Enfant's geometrical-metaphysical ambition several steps beyond itself, and in broader keeping with techniques of universal perspective inherited from post-Renaissance European art, with their "Cartesian emphasis on the knowing subject," the configuration of the Mills monument fashions a new type of *citizen*, positioning that individual at a height and position from which potentially the whole of Washington, DC, and even, in principle, the entire objective world, might be seen.[23] In brief, subjective perspective comprises the cartography of the city and (potentially) everything beyond it, radiating from one central origin.[24] The monument's change in status from a merely opaque effigy to something akin to a subjective viewing position aligns with what Rosalind Krauss describes as the characteristic nineteenth-century paradigm shift from "landscape" to "view," the latter prototype entailing "an image of geographic order" that Krauss explicitly connects to the advent of the land survey: "*view* registers this singularity, this focal point, as one moment in a complex representation of the world, a kind of complete topographical atlas."[25] Hubert Damisch, explicitly linking modern city forms to the burgeoning sciences of perspective, proposes that a bird's-eye view of an entire metropolis, which had been tacit in European city planning since the Renaissance—"the image of the city . . . confounded with its maquette, its relief plan"—is fully conceptualized in nineteenth-century city planning.[26] Urbanity is represented as a single "spectacle, a scene," and then filled out by the proliferation of architectural sites from which a citizen might actually perceive it.[27] Thus, gazing up at the Mills monument from the ground, one would see at the top, far up in the sky directly above Point A, no mere symbol of the government or its most famous founder, but rather, from an uncannily literal yet proxied position, the *city plan itself*, the very matrix that, now in geometric rather than iconographic terms, lends to the interconnected nodes of L'Enfant's plan their political and metaphysical significance.

According to Savage, almost immediately following Mills's proposal for the new Washington Monument, artists began rendering perspectives of Washington, DC, that tied together the projected obelisk, the Capitol Building, and other major civic centers such as the Smithsonian Museum, at the same time expunging inconvenient natural or political details, all the messy history on the ground. "The managers of the monument society," as Savage remarks, "had set into motion a powerful fantasy—a new way to project the nation's image from an alternative center."[28] In essence, this "new civic scheme" renders in perspective an erstwhile hypothetical extrapolation of L'Enfant's original synthesis, which for the first time seems achievable in stone and mortar.[29] The task of democratizing viewpoint is lent an ironic hubris appropriate to the "biggest building in the world": *everyone* could potentially ascend the monument and view the "map" or "maquette" of Washington laid out before him or her. Such a "powerful fantasy" literalizes the quasi-Cartesian metaphysics of infinite observation, still nascent in L'Enfant's plan, by constructing an empirical viewpoint over the city, but at the same time it paradoxically strives to "decorporealize vision" by elevating that viewpoint so far above the surface that its quotidian embodiment is all but sublimated away.[30] In fact, what is achieved by the individual visitor looking out from the top is less a vision than a "visual" of Washington, DC, transcending the squalid minutiae of the landscape—the sludge, the woodland scrub, the garbage, humidity, and mosquitoes, the meandering public, the petty commerce, the slavery.

Here, then, is finally an object that might exemplify the aspirations to bigness and visibility that motivated L'Enfant's design, while at the same time effectively rendering the city as a single object, the literal manifestation of its original *partis pris*. The architectural bigness of the city is realized at the same moment that, in effect, its entirety is condensed into the overview of a single person, as it might later be on a postcard or stereoscope slide, or, more recognizably today, in a Metro map or tourist pamphlet. The Mills obelisk seems to make such a "system of knowledge" possible, and not only as an eventual rendering or representation of Washington, but through the agency of a physical position in space, undergirded by the literal infrastructure of the big built object.[31] In this light, we might note that Mills considered it crucial to include a "rail system" to convey passengers to an observation deck or portal at the peak of his obelisk. The details of the proposed machinery were vague, and it is unclear whether Mills or anyone else knew exactly how it would work. The important thing seems to have been the sheer potential of the infrastructure to relocate actual humans to the monument's apex, providing a physical site from which the maplike layout of the city would be available to the gaze of any citizen, who now becomes the civic equivalent of the master architect objectively surveying a plan or model. We may consider the notional elevator and observation deck of Mills's design as among those modern "technical inventions through which all earthly space has become small and close at hand," in Hannah Arendt's words.[32]

The possibility of a literalization of cartographical vision is dependent not only upon what Krauss identifies as the emergence of "view," but upon what Jonathan Crary calls a "vast hegemonic organization of the visual" during the nineteenth century, as well as an "autonomy and abstraction of vision" that characterizes a "new kind of subject or individual" arising with the development of nineteenth-century capitalist economies.[33] Such an observer achieves "a more comprehensive vision of the city," inhabiting, as it were, the *entire* city in something like the same sense in which, for Foucault, a hypothetical observing subject abides at the focal point of the panopticon, or in which, for Benjamin, the flâneur successively occupies the potentially infinite vantages upon the "phantasmagorias of space" comprising the modern cityscape of Paris.[34] Damisch suggests that "all views of the city current in our own time are tributaries, in one way or another, of the perspective configuration—perspective being essentially constructive, if not urban."[35] In perspective, all is seen in its (ostensibly) real scalar geometry, every object and distance properly sited at their uniformly apportioned coordinates. As Damisch observes, "it is as though, at the moment when the great city, the metropolis, the *Großstadt*, was beginning to call for an image of agglomeration other than a strictly architectural one, it seemed indispensable to preserve its visibility or, to evoke a Freudian problematic, its *representability*."[36] The viewpoint constructed by the Mills monument realizes or reifies a potentially infinite surveillance of the abstractly mappable universe, the sublime too-bigness of the natural world (but first, of the evolving city, the quasi-natural cosmopolis) rendered in miniature so as to become merely *big*.[37] Thus, too, Washington, DC, is reduced; it becomes *small*, a single object representable on a carte or tourist brochure, at the very moment its single biggest architectural gesture is becoming achievable. In this sense, L'Enfant's fantasy of Washington as a city unified by viewpoints had already implied the very skyscraper that would consummate its geometrical aspiration at Point A, long before such a thing was capable of construction.[38]

The literal yet decorporealized viewpoint high in the air fulfills a rationalist fantasy of the completed city interconnected by lines of sight, through a neoclassical conception of what Crary calls "a body that . . . [is] a neutral or invisible term in vision."[39] Even if, as Crary argues, such a body was already obsolete in the post-Kantian shift to critiques of the perceptual subject occupying the nineteenth-century scientific imaginary, still its remnants persist up to the present moment as the ghost of a Cartesian subject's abstracted cartographical vision, the making-small of the city's bigness in grandiose gestures of metaphysical reduction, in turn empirically instantiated in mundane acts of inhabitation, navigation, tourism, and the marketing of urban identity.[40] The modern commercial and civic city emerges organized or reified in the guise of a singular object, and its simultaneously empirical and decorporeal icon—the skyscraper, the tallest structure at its physical and ideological heart—composes a single urban "world picture" for the subject who might at any time (even if he or she doesn't actually) climb it:

> His elevation transforms him into a voyeur. It puts him at a distance. It transforms the bewitching world by which one was "possessed" into a text that lies before one's eyes. It allows one to read it, to be a solar Eye, looking down like a god. The exaltation of the scopic and gnostic drive: the fiction of knowledge is related to this lust to be a viewpoint and nothing more.[41]

This is the democratized modern city, having no distinctive iconographic form, no identifiable hierarchy in its superstructure, however thoroughly stratified its economic base, but nonetheless unified via the hypothesis of a single, godlike "reader," the parameters of whose gaze are at once fashioned and exhausted by the three coordinates of a geometrical point. That point is supplied at the apex of the monolith, a literally elevated site of cartographical vision and the single most visible position in the city, the one place most easily *seen* and most blatantly *seen from*. The monument, like the cathedral it supplants, is thus an ideological structure par excellence, the modern building in which the economic "base" is paradigmatically concealed by and within the fantasy of radically visible "overstructure."

The Value of Monotony

In 1909, at a moment when the new architectural type that Louis Sullivan called "the tall office building" had already begun to rise to heights of hundreds rather than dozens of feet, *Life* magazine printed a sketch that depicts, as Rem Koolhaas describes it, a "theorem" about what the skyscraper might eventually become.[42] Uniformly stacked within a huge framework is a series of individual homesteads, each isolated on its respective floor as discretely as parcels of private land might be segregated by fences or hedges. On the left side of the drawing, along the vertical edge of the framework, numbered elevator signs identify the floors we are currently viewing, specifically eighty through eighty-four, implying an overall height for this building that, in 1909, would have been colossal even for an imaginary structure. Sporadic clouds, interrupting the rise of the frame's structural columns like the break lines of an engineer's drawing, suggest that the stacked floors might proliferate indefinitely into the sky. The caption proposes, with coy understatement: "Buy a cozy cottage . . . less than a mile above Broadway."

The *Life* drawing represents a decisively modern formula for living in a big city, even a "utopian device," as Koolhaas suggests.[43] In essence, human habitation is reoriented ninety degrees along the vertical axis. The artist emphasizes the novelty of such verticality by highlighting a pair of

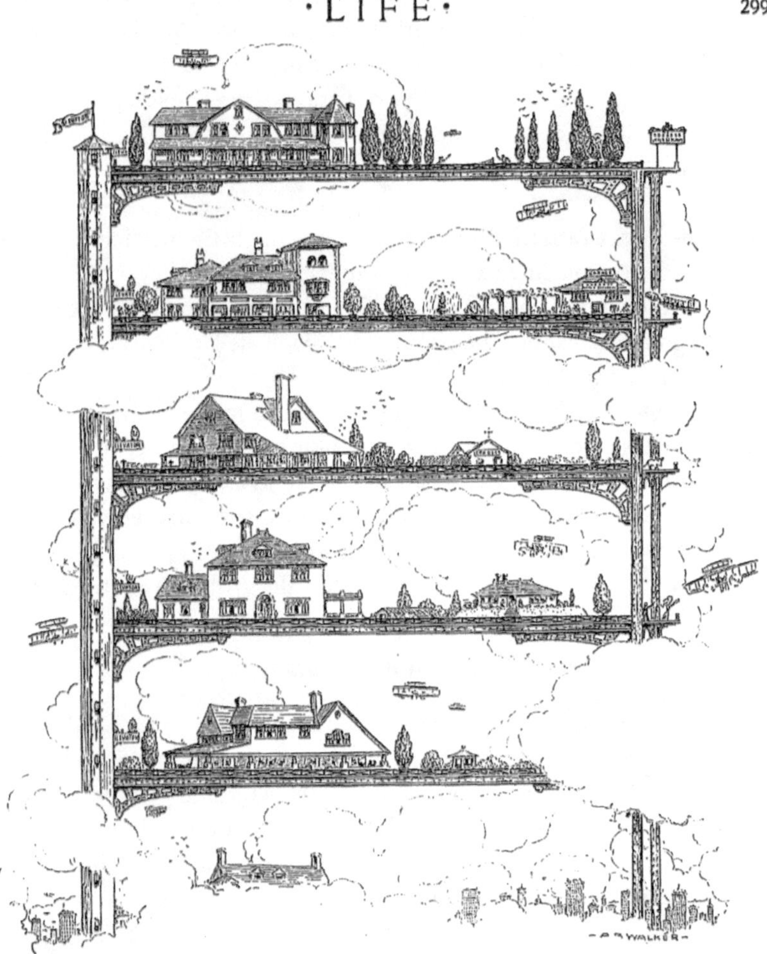

FIGURE 8.7 "Buy a Cozy Cottage," illustration from *Life* magazine (*Life*, vol. 53, issue 1375 [March 4, 1909]: 299)

additional technological innovations allowing access to the modern sky: the elevator and the airplane. A third invention, one typically concealed by the very architectural forms it enables, is also foregrounded here: the steel frame, which, along with the elevator, is generally understood to be a primal technological catalyst for modern architectural bigness.

Of course, the persistence of gravity makes vertical architecture inhabitable only in peculiar ways. The portions of the "theorem" building in (or on) which humans actually reside, once they step off the infrastructure of steel frame and elevator, comprise incongruous, even slightly absurd individual properties that remain resolutely horizontal, as both physics and the ergonomics of human anatomy require. This discrepancy between the idiosyncratic horizontality of the old-fashioned houses and the homogenizing verticality of the larger frame suggests a reactionary retrofit rather than a truly new, utopian concept. In effect, an arbitrary number of "choice lots," in the caption writer's words, have been summarily extracted from the pastoral landscape, like pieces of cut sod, and dropped intact onto the platforms of their respective levels. Each level then provides "all the comforts of the country," as the caption (dubiously) declares, "with none of its disadvantages"[44]—each floor is a "virgin site" or "fully private realm," and the skyscraper therefore becomes what Koolhaas calls "a stack of individual privacies."[45]

It is possible to perceive, in the *Life* theorem's halfhearted advocacy of a vertical modernity, a certain imaginative failure, as though only the form but not yet the content or the complete tableau of habitation along a *z*-axis could be conceived. More to the point, the *Life* drawing makes explicit a basic ambivalence within a certain classic description of the skyscraper that architects, developers, and critics have continually embraced, and to which I have already alluded, the "self-contained city" or "city-within-a-city."[46] The holistic ambition of such a figuration implies a faith that architecture will simultaneously ground and fulfill human living, as though the full range of geographical features and phenomenological experiences of urban (or even country) life could be incorporated into the synthetic form of a single tall building. This would be "total architecture," as the prolific skyscraper developer William Starrett calls such an ideal in his 1906 proposal for a hundred-story "City within Itself": "a mammoth structure, towering into the clouds and containing within its walls the cultural, commercial, and industrial activities of a great city."[47] A theological penchant infuses such architectural holism, and Koolhaas suggests that programs like Starrett's are grounded in neoclassical or Neoplatonic theorizations of architectural self-containment previously represented by images of the "globe," the "cosmopolis," or the building as a "reproduction of the world."[48]

Unsurprisingly, the utopianism of the city-within-a-city remains in continual tension with long-standing critical complaints that both the colossal scale of skyscrapers and the vast economic forces required to construct them render them essentially inhumane—"phantom cities, colossal piles, . . . silent Towers of Babel," or "monsters of the mere market."[49] Architectural bigness exhibits, or is continually assumed to exhibit, hints of menace and oppression, and the overconstruction of industrial modernity provides an especially convenient target for critical attacks on such an evil. In my discussion of Kevin Roche and John Dinkeloo's Oakland Museum in the opening chapter, I observed such ambivalence in discussions of museum architecture, an abiding feeling among both architects and critics that citizens are victimized by monumentality or that bigness is opposed to "the comfort, convenience, and psychological needs" of the public.[50] Discourses around the skyscraper exhibit similar qualms that bigness may be amoral or even violent, in short, that skyscrapers are *too big*. From "the top of a high building," O. Henry suggests, "man . . . appears to be a creeping, contemptible beetle" and "the city itself becomes degraded to an unintelligible mass"; Lewis Mumford complains that "the obdurate, overwhelming masses" of skyscrapers "take away from the little people who walk in their shadows any semblance of dignity as human beings."[51] The force of such critiques is bolstered by their resonance with reasonable misgivings that any utopianism surrounding skyscrapers—the rhetoric of their "economic height," as Koolhaas says, or what he calls "the alibi of 'business'"[52]—is convenient propaganda for commercial and political interests that cheerfully indulge in overdevelopment at the expense of a city's inhabitants.

I wish to tarry on the level of form, not in order to sidestep the considerable economic and political implications of commercial skyscraper development, but rather more directly to understand how an architecture's inherent tendencies emerge through its built iterations. Once the advent of steel frame and elevator effectively abolishes structural limitations on the height of commercial buildings, what tends to take precedence—and, incidentally, what the *Life* theorem half-wittingly struggles against—is the "sheer multiplication" of floors, or what could be called the skyscraper's strictly quantitative aspect, by which virtually all qualitative attributes are subsumed, and which also suits the skyscraper's function as both profit generator and locus of propaganda.[53] Architecture becomes, in a way it arguably never had been fully before, sheer magnitude.

Louis Sullivan describes this propensity with startling prescience in 1896, at a moment when the world's tallest buildings (aside from cathedral spires or towers such as the Washington Monument or the Eiffel Tower) were still a mere twenty stories high:

> Above [the second story], throughout the indefinite number of typical office tiers, we take our cue from the individual cell, which requires a window with its separating pier, its sill and lintel, and we, without more ado, make them all look alike because they are all alike.[54]

Homogeneity in the building's vertical surfaces, an effect Sullivan gleefully labels "bald" and "heartless," abandons any iconography of accumulated "privacies" upon its structurally identical floors.[55] Indeed, Sullivan explicitly rejects the sentimental hybridity that animates the *Life* theorem: "the sixteen-story building must not consist of sixteen separate, distinct and unrelated buildings piled one upon the other until the top of the pile is reached."[56] It is not that Sullivan altogether discards the concept of a city-within-a-city. Rather, he shrewdly foresees, and then exalts the domination of, structural tendency over functional variety or capacity, the propensity of the tall building to coalesce into a single monolithic object and therefore to become increasingly blank and unidimensional in both its exterior elevations and its modular interior spaces, regardless of the diverse economic, social, and infrastructural demands that may still prompt its planning. Seeking a "simple straightforward naturalness," Sullivan insists that we "heed the imperative voice of emotion" (by which he appears to mean sheer form):

> It demands of us, what is the chief characteristic of the tall office building? And at once we answer, it is lofty. . . . It must be tall, every inch of it tall. The force and power of altitude must be in it, the glory and pride of exaltation must be in it. It must be every inch a proud and soaring thing, rising in sheer exultation that from bottom to top it is a unit without a single dissenting line.[57]

Thus Sullivan sees the tall building as a hyperfactical *reduction*, unabashedly flaunting its predominant attribute, height. His own ideal tall buildings hew very close to the sheer monolith of the Washington Monument, blank magnitudes in the vertical dimension (at least up to a certain point, as I will discuss shortly). The fact that office buildings, unlike monuments, also contain "occupants or patrons" seems beside the point. With the bravado of a Taylor or Ford, Sullivan casually purges the buildings' machine-like interiors of human personality: "an office [is] similar to a cell in a honey-comb, merely a compartment, nothing more."[58]

With Sullivan, what Koolhaas called the "automatic architecture" of the skyscraper distills itself into a metaphysical formula, "meaningless and anarchical," the paradox of which Sullivan comprehends better than nearly any designer or theorist following him: *the bigger a building becomes, the less space it contains.*[59] Like the obelisk, the logic of the skyscraper leans toward the unidimensionality of the needle, "a building without an interior."[60] Comprehending this tendency, Sullivan dismisses the significance of interior design as brutally as he purges human choice or fancy: "Only in rare instances does the floor or plan arrangement of the tall office building take on an aesthetic value."[61] We are back to the sculptural silhouettes of Hugh Ferriss's renderings of setbacks: solid magnitudes with regularized articulations only on their surfaces. Ironically, though not surprisingly, Sullivan's peremptory disdain for interiors largely agrees with the criticisms of the skyscraper's enemies, for instance, Lewis Mumford, who jokes that the skyscraper "has no accommodating grace or perfection in its interior furnishing, beyond its excellent lavatories."[62] The rhetorics of both champions and foes concur that horizontality, the space of human living, is violently sacrificed to verticality, the non-space of sheer infrastructure. As Michael Tavel Clarke notes, "photographs, illustrations, and written descriptions of skyscrapers in popular magazines, books, art exhibits, and postcards unfailingly pictured the buildings from outside in order to emphasize their defining characteristic: height."[63] Thus, at its formal heart, and alongside its ambivalence toward the "city-within-a-city," the skyscraper continually belies one of the central dogmas of modernist design, that the exterior appearance of a work of architecture is the effect or expression of (interior) usage, ironically a variant of Louis Sullivan's own enduring maxim that "form ever follows function."[64]

By 1900, office buildings in New York City had begun to approach the 554-foot height of the Washington Monument. In 1908, the Singer Building surpassed that height, the first time a commercial building had become the world's tallest structure. By this time, skyscrapers had long since been explicitly imitating towers instead of traditionally massed public or commercial buildings, their shapes self-consciously verging on monoliths, both something new in the urban fabric and a throwback to premodern types of monumentality. For example, the Singer Building achieves its record-breaking height not over the entire floor plan but solely with a thin tower rising out of a portion of the lower, more traditionally massed office block. In 1909, the skyscraper that replaces the Singer as the world's tallest, the Metropolitan Life Tower, consists of a campanile-like tower perched atop a broader existing building, even more self-consciously modeled like a monolithic needle rather than like conventional commercial architecture. By the time the 792-foot Woolworth Building is completed in 1913, the prototype of the needle has become the standard mode for achieving great height in skyscrapers, and will remain so until at least the end of the twentieth century.

The chief characteristic of a needle, following but also exaggerating Louis Sullivan's guidance for tall office buildings, is the extreme formal

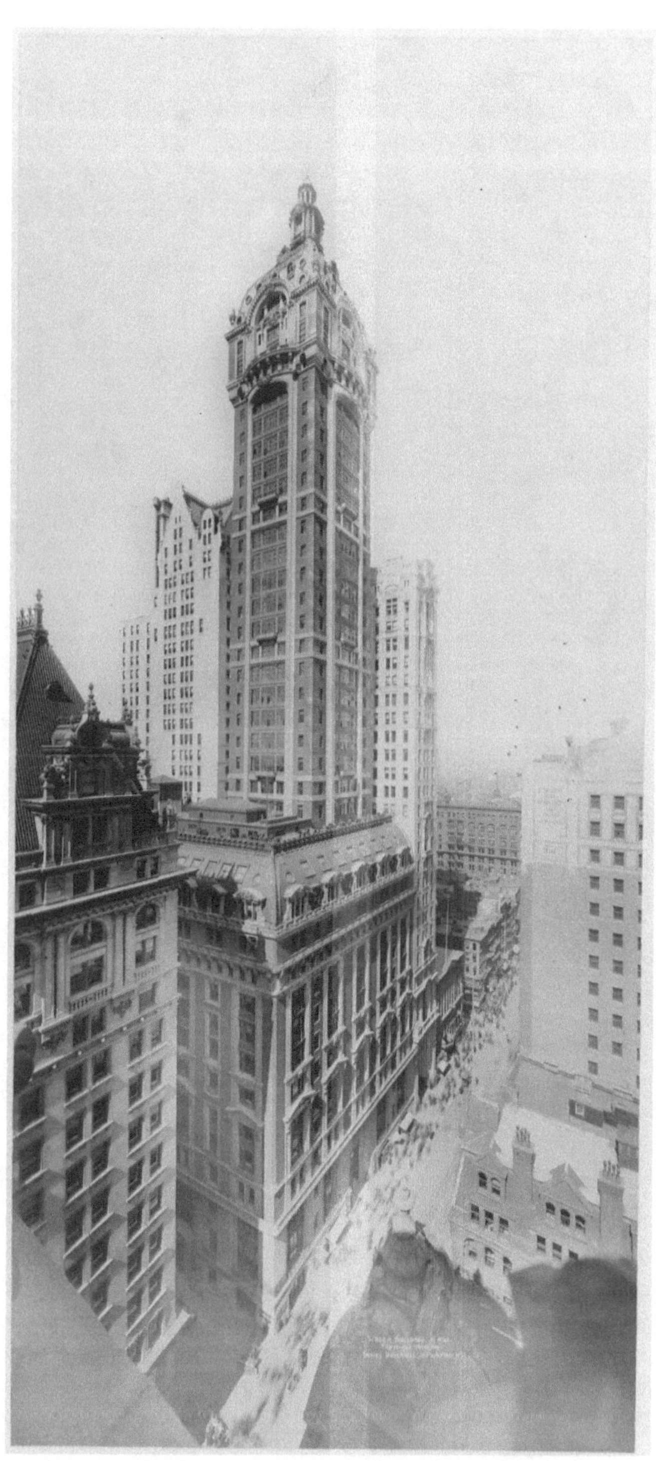

FIGURE 8.8 Singer Building, New York, 1908 (photo 1908; Library of Congress)

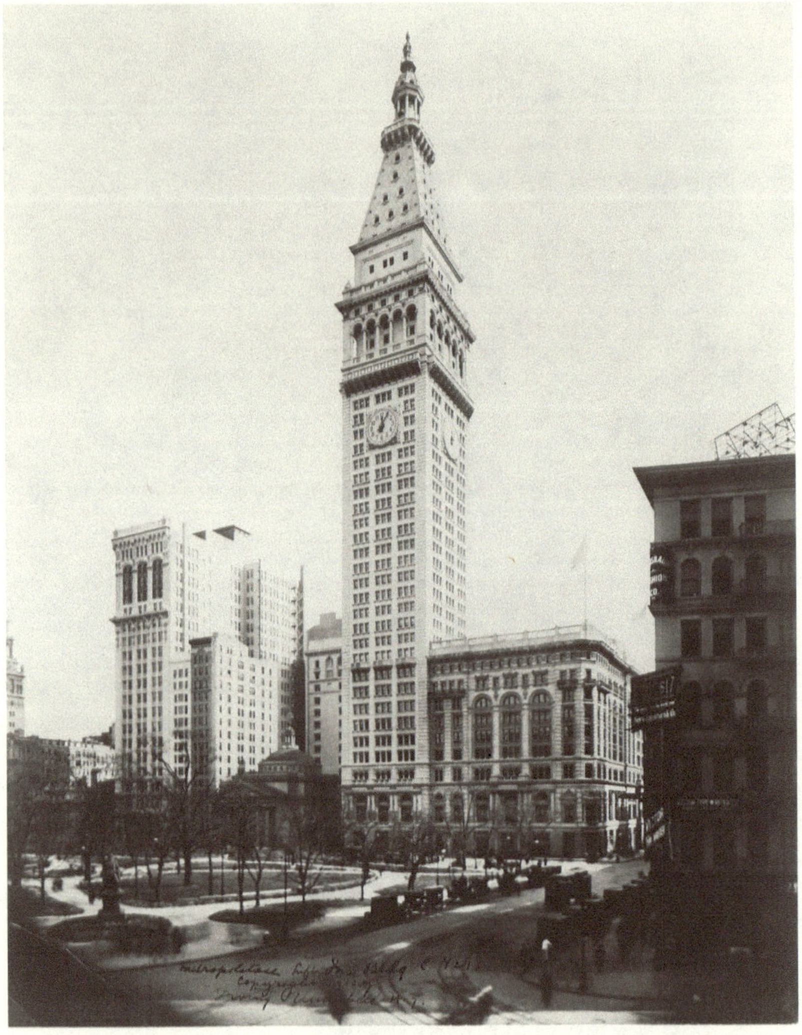

FIGURE 8.9 Metropolitan Life Building, New York, 1909 (photo 1913; Library of Congress)

minimalism of its vertical magnitude. The blanker the building's surface, the more effectively its height is emphasized. Such exteriors reflect, as Montgomery Schuyler writes, echoing Sullivan, "facts that everyone knows," namely, "that the rentable stories of an office building are all identical in function and equal in dignity."[65] But Schuyler goes even further than Sullivan, rejecting nearly every traditionalist tendency. Too often, Schuyler laments, the skyscraper remains tied to a neoclassical "triple

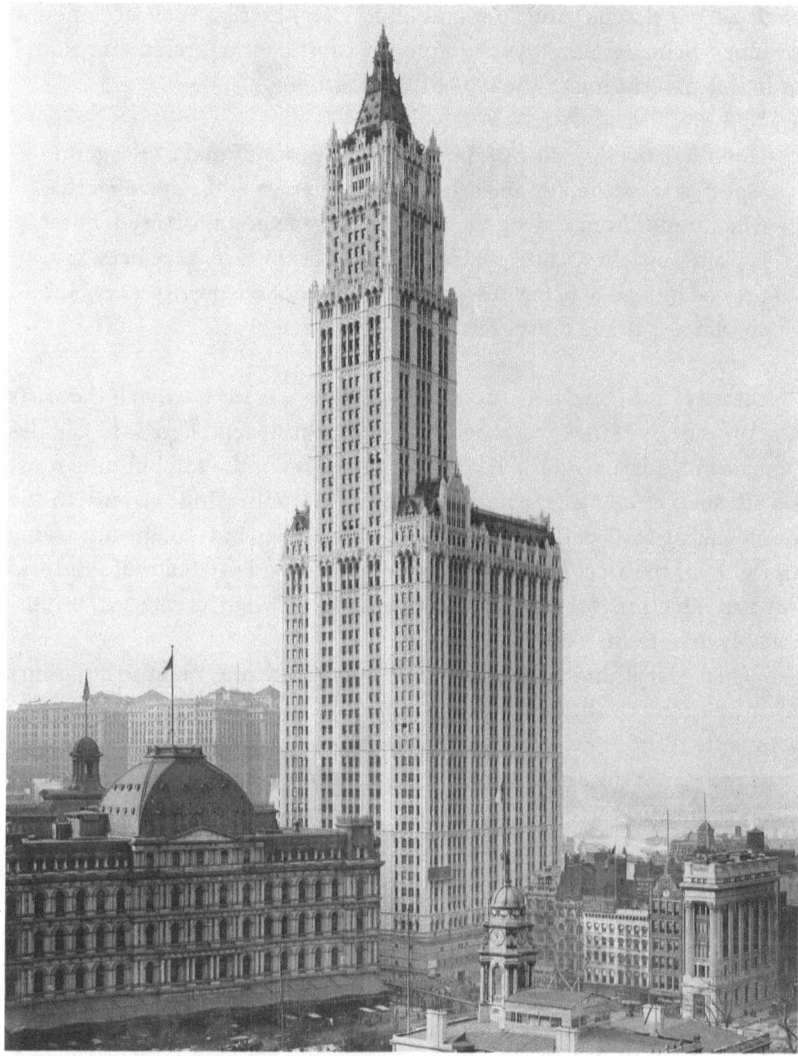

FIGURE 8.10 Woolworth Building, New York, 1913 (photo circa 1913; Library of Congress)

division" based on the classical column (base, shaft, capital), an "inheritance of three thousand years" that even the modernist Sullivan, still reliant on "inherited notions of proportion" in his ornamentation, was not ready to abandon.[66] Polemically opposed to this legacy of quasi-theological aestheticism, Schuyler emphasizes the "high architectural value of monotony," characterizing any and all differentiation along a skyscraper's vertical shaft as "capricious" and "dissembling."[67] To describe such ornamental residues, Schuyler employs the superbly caustic term "architecturesque," as in this description of the 1898 St. Paul Building:

> Doubtless the doubling of the stories "gives scale," and a swaggering aspect to the structure, and avoids the squareness of the openings that would result from leaving the actual arrangement undisguised. But it is plain from the architecturesque parts, that the facts have been suppressed instead of being expressed. . . . "I do not see the necessity," the spectator may and must exclaim.[68]

"Necessity" is Schuyler's crucial term, just as it is for nearly all theorists and promoters of the skyscraper from Le Corbusier and Ferriss to Charles Jencks and Adrian Smith. The tendentious rise of the tall building must be affirmed at all costs, even to the point of "adher[ing] strictly to the unpromising facts of the steel cage."[69] For Schuyler, indeed, the unvarying uprights of the steel frame are a "primary fact" of the tall building, and such architecture is therefore praiseworthy only when its exterior "unmistakably denotes its skeleton."[70]

When everything architecturesque is stripped away and the building's form reduced to the redundant expression of its own height, the skyscraper tends ever more literally to embody what I have suggested was its proto-metaphysical function in the modern representation of urbanity, the positing of a cartographical focal point, a singular perspective that sees from far above and in turn is seen (seeing) from far below. Thus, breaking with his own penchant for "monotony," Schuyler suggests that it is only the architect's "crowning member" that "give[s] any form or comeliness to the skyline of his building."[71] Apparently without irony, Schuyler avows a special fondness for the ornate roofs of the recent Washington Life Building (1898) and Bayard Building (1899), the latter designed by Sullivan and Lyndon P. Smith. Yet, in the end, Schuyler's odd preference for ornate tops or crowns is not inconsistent with his reductionism. The higher skyscrapers grow, and the more distilled and indistinct their central shafts become, the more powerfully their significance is concentrated and then exhibited at the apex. Hence the abiding importance, in terms both of iconography and of real estate marketing, of the skyscraper's topmost features—spires, antennas, airship mooring posts, spotlights, or other visible elements—but above all, the observation deck. The raison d'être of the skyscraper, like the modern obelisk that heralds it, is to posit such a platform for viewing high in space, even if the particular citizen never visits it. As Koolhaas finally declares, "only at the top is there symbolism,"[72] and what that symbol

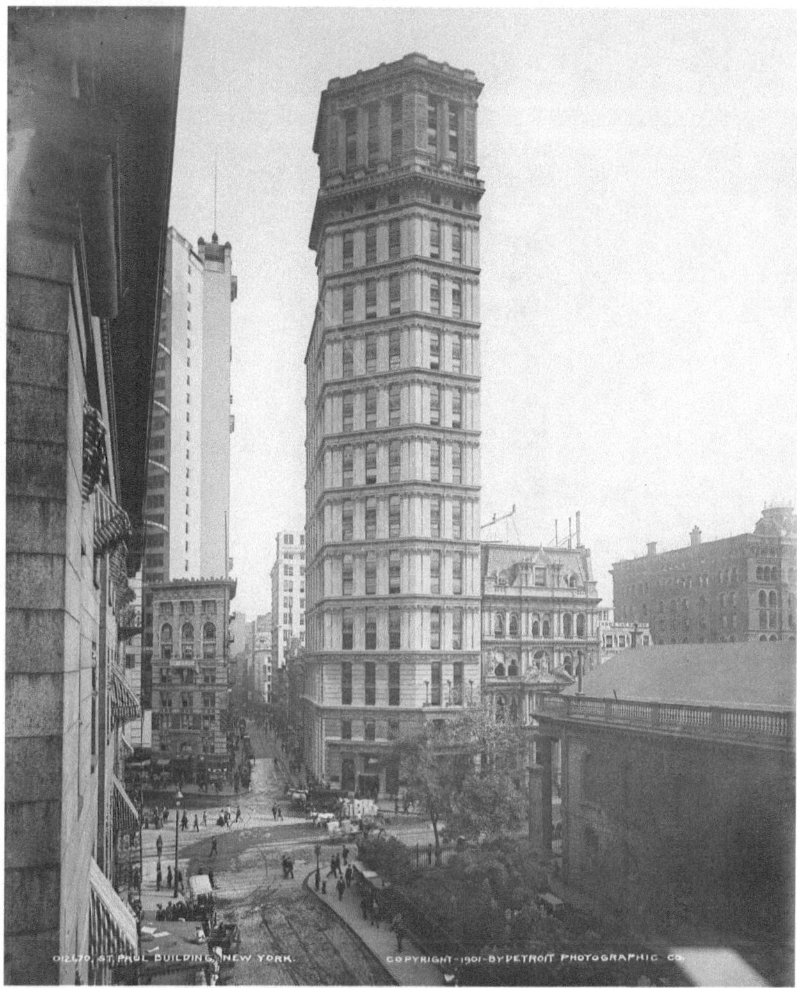

FIGURE 8.11 St. Paul Building, New York, 1898 (photo 1901; Detroit Publishing Co. Photograph Collection, Library of Congress)

at the skyscraper's top designates is the manifestly physical location of a viewpoint high along the *z*-axis of the Cartesian city grid.

Speaking in 1913 of his admiration for the Metropolitan Life Tower, and again contradicting his own recommendations for strict reduction and "monotony," Schuyler comments on both the high "visibility" of "its steeply sloping roof" and the "justification" of its small terrace "as a 'belvedere'": "We believe it has actually made money as an 'outlook,'" he suggests; "If not, it evidently might do so."[73] The 1913 Woolworth Building, which remained the world's tallest until 1930, has a similar peaked

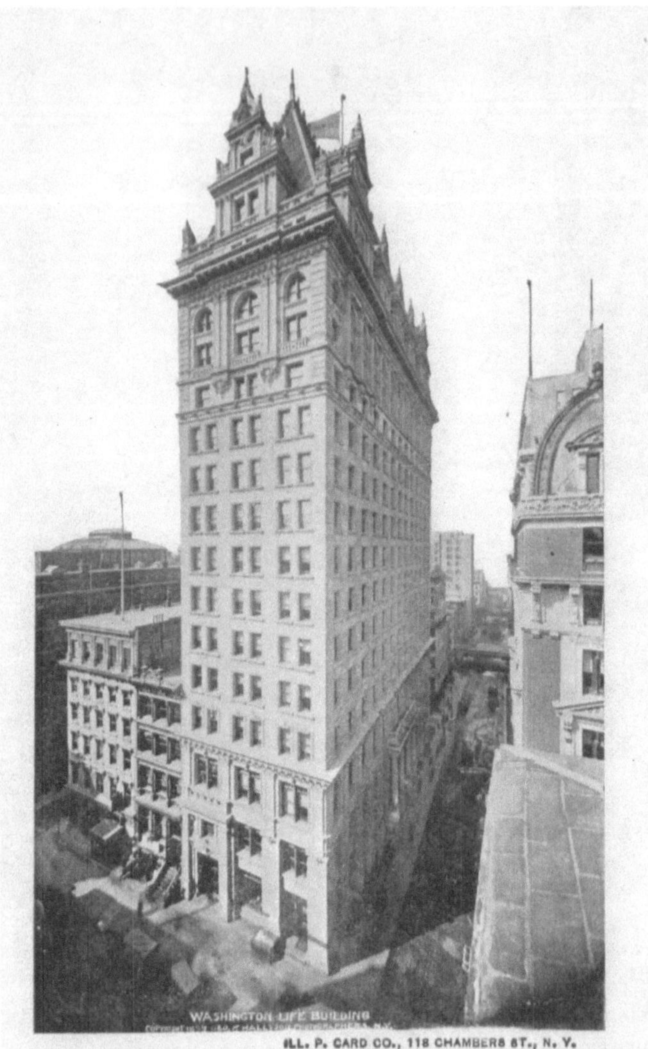

FIGURE 8.12 Washington Life Building, New York, 1998 (postcard)

campanile-style roof and belvedere, and was eventually to become among the first skyscrapers in New York to add a public observation deck. As Schuyler's remarks about the Metropolitan Life Tower's "outlook" imply, long before citizens and tourists could regularly ascend to the tops of skyscrapers to view the city from observation decks, as they were able to do in the Washington Monument, the Eiffel Tower, or the Statue of Liberty, the presence of a visible viewpoint at the building's top was vital to the skyscraper's role in the urban fabric.[74]

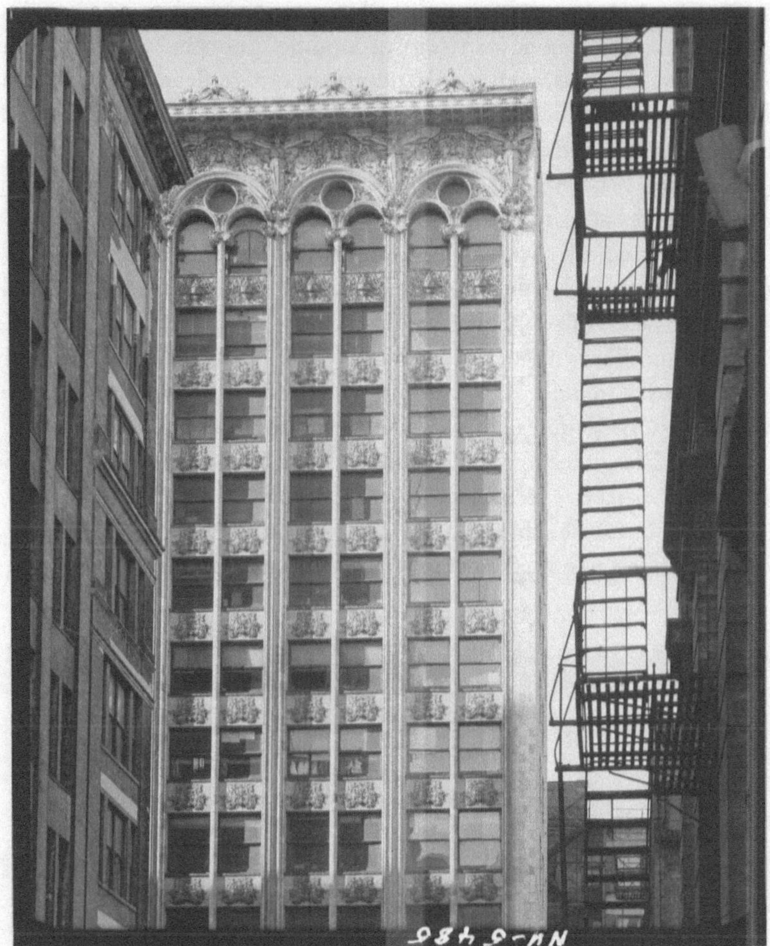

FIGURE 8.13 Bayard Building, New York, 1899 (photo by Cervin Robinson, 1970; Library of Congress)

By the 1930s, when zoning regulations, especially in New York, had consolidated the "setback" model for skyscraper design and prompted construction of the most unalloyed and visible needles, such as the Chrysler Building and Empire State Building, virtually every skyscraper included an observation deck. The observation deck is the literalization of a camera-like site from which a cinematographic tableau of urbanity is "shot," a tableau at once intensely subjective and wholly abstract and public, "both within and outside the scene" of the city.[75] The citizen's ascent to the observation deck thus fulfills the tendentious formal legacy inherent, from the start, in "the ideal-type longitudinal building."[76] In a quasi-geometrical operation, the elevator transports a visitor directly along the z-axis from ground to apex, scorning the phenomenology of "middle" floors bustling with their anonymous business, up to the building's only significant juncture: that crown, ornamented with window openings, decks, or balustrades, which that same visitor had espied from the ground moments before.

Recall the Washington Monument, the only significant modulation of which emerges at its top, in the convergence of its four sides to form the Egyptianesque peak of the obelisk. This variation in the otherwise sheer vertical surfaces is detailed with small pairs of viewing windows on each of the four faces, the only openings in the entire structure aside from the single ground-floor entrance in the east elevation.[77] The windows effectively materialize the geometric point from which the cartographical vision of Washington, DC, equivalently viewable from four cardinal directions out of the four faces of the pyramid, is made available as a single, diagrammatic object in perspective. A subject (neither exactly "I" nor "we" nor "they," necessarily, but *some* subject, as "a viewpoint and nothing more") sees *out* of those windows, and therefore sees the entire city as its map or maquette.[78]

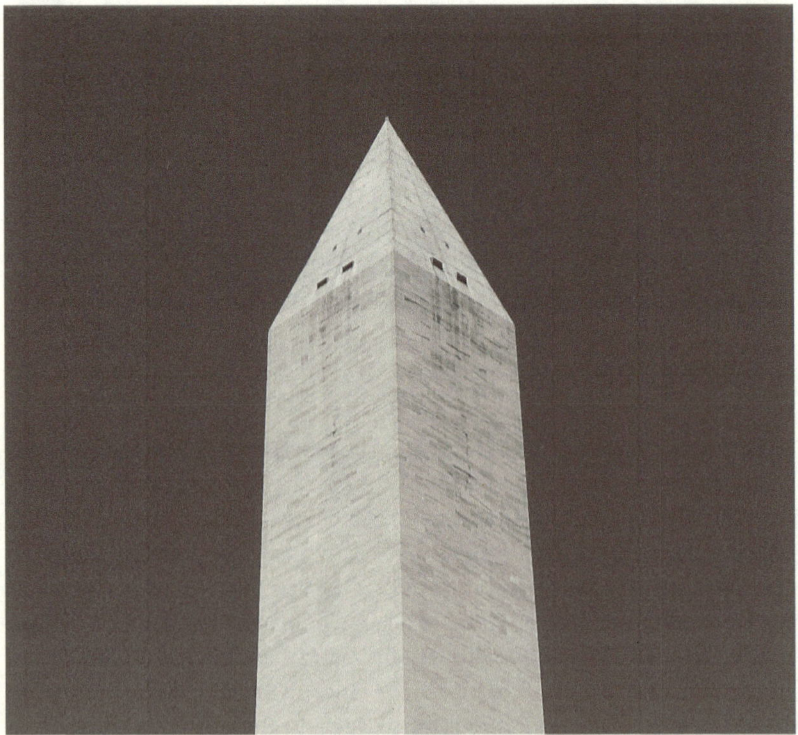

FIGURE 8.14 Washington Monument, Washington, DC: detail (photo by Carol M. Highsmith, 2007; Library of Congress)

Weapon

Positioning a visible viewpoint high in space, the skyscraper rearranges the landscape into an idealized object of aerial surveillance, designating itself the city's unique synecdoche. In this way, the skyscraper also constructs a gaze of extreme condescension, as critics of skyscrapers perpetually remark. Madelon Vriesendorp, in a playful apotheosis of such criticism, describes the 30 St. Mary Axe Building in London as "a brain, phallus, screw, bullet, finger, missile."[79] Vriesendorp's list cycles from the commonplace notion of the skyscraper as masculinist overcompensation to the specific equation of the building with weaponry, a figuration of violence and war that critics at their most zealous have frequently attached to skyscrapers: "brutal," "urbicidal," "mercenary," "tyrannical," "utterly barbaric."[80] Not at variance with such critical vehemence, the strident formal tendency of the skyscraper itself, especially the more it evolves into the needle, is to redeploy surveillance functions previously consigned to military technology. Paul Virilio links acts of viewing from the tops of towers to the kinds of telemetry that transform an individual sightline into a generalized apparatus of mass destruction: "From the original watch-tower through the anchored balloon to the reconnaissance aircraft and remote-sensing satellites, one and the same function has been indefinitely repeated, the eye's function being the function of a weapon."[81] The continuum Virilio proposes between towers, anchored balloons, and (eventually) airplanes and satellites is not simply an update of the visual architectonics of the guard tower, or even a material fulfillment of the fantasy of a hawk's eye or god's eye overseeing the ground. The aeronautically lifted perspective, for example, in the balloon floating at sufficient height to survey a broad swath of the landscape, shares its architectonic with the skyscraper: a cartographical vision untethered from the ground or, in short, a physically realized viewpoint with no space underneath, furnishing the absolute minimum infrastructure required to position an eye or lens high above the earth.[82] Here is a more primal sense of the standard modernist trope connecting architecture to aeronautics, most famously articulated by Le Corbusier.[83] The skyscraper is aeronautical in something like a literal rather than merely formal or allegorical sense. It is a device for conveying passengers into the sky; the cartographical adventure for which it provides transport is conspicuously akin to that of the balloon, plane, or satellite.

Of course, military engineering has frequently been a component of the planning of cities, which, if they did not emerge quasi-organically from the accretions of villages or hamlets, were almost inevitably laid out as fortifications.[84] The modern city, arising in a military-aeronautical epoch that has rendered ground-level fortification superfluous, still inherits

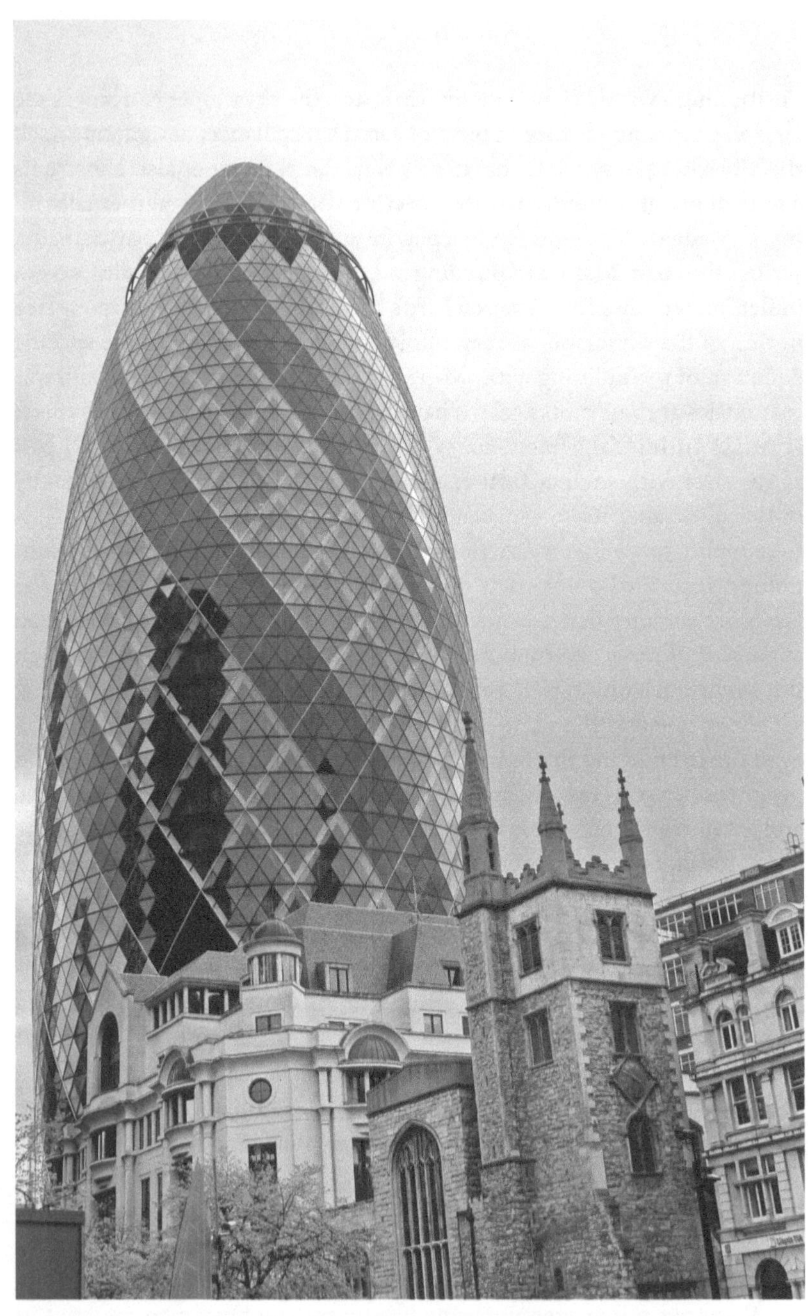

FIGURE 8.15 30 St. Mary Axe Building, London, 2003 (photo by Maria Guilia, 2012; Wikimedia Commons)

a paranoia perhaps inherent in urban cartography itself, the impulse to concatenate the city into an administered object. What Virilio calls the "tactical necessities of cartography" align with the motives of urban planners who must accurately survey lines and distances. The city is inherently "defensible," if you will, with minimized logistic, strategic, or aesthetic weak points. The centralized (but ironically therefore decentered) urban plan exemplifies "a technicians' version of an all-seeing Divinity" in the guise of a "general system of illumination," in which all sites in the landscape are rendered equally homogeneous and available for surveillance, an aesthetic extrapolation of a military tactician's fantasy of general bombardability.[85] Yet, the individual subject is also for the first time—excepting those church, royal, or military officials who might have been privileged to climb to the tops of towers prior to the late nineteenth century—in a position literally to perceive the city as a single entity. Modern cartographical vision is thus decoupled from (some of its) institutional and class affiliations and becomes a generalized or disembodied eye, the touristic rather than the militaristic "aerostatic view," whose telemetry is metaphysically omnipotent even if politically impotent within the Cartesian space it surveils.[86] Automatic and entirely profane, surveillance of the city is made available, like the view of the carceral panopticon or through the gunsight of the bomber—but also like the view for sale to the tourist through public binoculars atop the observation deck—to any real eye that happens to be manning the device.

And with this we may sum up the elements of a decisive theory of the skyscraper, accounting for both its contingent infrastructural legacies and its inherent formal ambitions. First, the skyscraper is essentially homogenous in the vertical, as Sullivan and other early theorists staunchly declare, and therefore always of strictly indeterminate height or bigness. Second, the significance of the skyscraper is concentrated at the top, where its primary function is to posit a visible viewpoint at great height. Third, the skyscraper, very much like the balloon with which it shares its metaphysical shape, contains *no space* beneath its peak, or its tendency is to reduce such space—the horizontality of everyday life, work, commerce, and social interaction—asymptotically to nothing. Fourth, in positing a visible viewpoint, the skyscraper consolidates the cartography of the city into a single object of visual surveillance; in essence, the skyscraper renders the city a map or maquette, and, precisely in this sense, the big city becomes *small*. And fifth, the skyscraper fashions the urban citizen as a decorporealized Cartesian subject, distinct at once from its own body and from any quotidian habitation that such a body (of course) requires. The generic citizen at the peak of the skyscraper, peering out over the uncannily miniaturized cartography of the city, is like a glorified yet thoroughly depoliticized avatar of the federal republic, empowered to overlook or repress, via the indeterminate magnitude of his or her vertical remove, the dankness, disorder, and oppression below.

Barad-dûr

In J. R. R. Tolkien's *The Return of the King,* as Frodo and Sam prepare to ascend the slope of Mount Doom, Frodo first glimpses Mordor's most infamous work of big architecture:

> Then he saw, rising black, blacker and darker than the vast shades amid which it stood, the cruel pinnacles and iron crown of the topmost tower of Barad-dûr. One moment only it stared out, but as from some great window immeasurably high there stabbed northward a flame of red, the flicker of a piercing Eye.[87]

This description of Barad-dûr, the Dark Tower of Sauron, gives us an epitome of the skyscraper, or a précis of its metaphysics: the singular, colossal monolith atop which is positioned the "Window of the Eye," simultaneously the most visible and the farthest-seeing point in Middle Earth, and thus its malevolent authoritarian center—perhaps Tolkien's ideological symbol of overrationalized modernity.[88]

Can we observe such a "monstrous caricature of futurism" in a less fictional or mystical guise?[89] In January 2010, the Burj Khalifa, a 160-story needle skyscraper designed for the city of Dubai, United Arab Emirates,

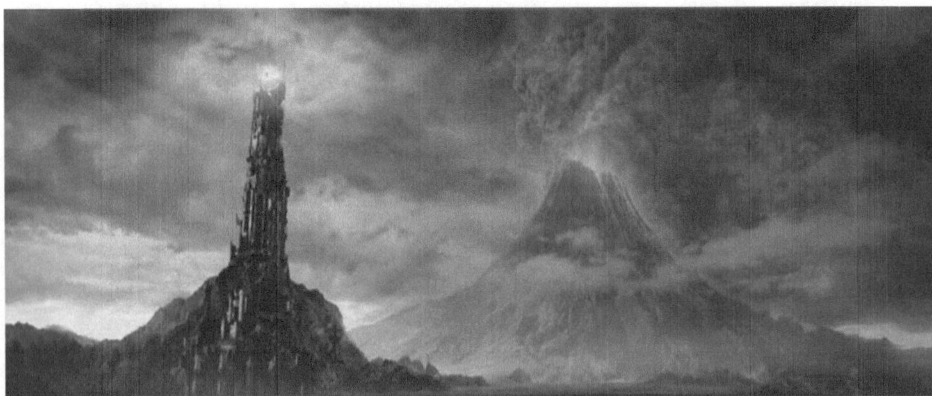

FIGURE 8.16 *The Lord of the Rings: The Return of the King* (2003): Barad-dûr

by Adrian Smith of Skidmore, Owings & Merrill, opened for business. The 828-meter-high building, considerably taller than its nearest competitor in Shanghai, contained an aspirational mix of capacities and functions, including over one thousand private apartments, fifty floors of office suites, a large hotel, and a variety of public and retail spaces. The Burj Khalifa also had several observation decks, the topmost of which was the highest in the world and set the visitor back about a hundred dollars to visit. The observation deck and its expensive touristic function were the most overt indicator of the building's role as the centerpiece of a vast redevelopment of the city of Dubai, even the lynchpin of a long-term effort to install Dubai as a global hub for travel and business, reviving the region's past role as a waypoint for commerce, exploration, and colonial expansion.

Such aspiration reflects the UAE's optimism during the economic boom of the mid-2000s and, with the hindsight of the post-2008 recession, some considerable overreach.[90] Within a year or two of the Burj Khalifa's opening, news reports frequently speculated, sometimes with thinly veiled schadenfreude, that the building would devolve into a permanent symbol of economic and political hubris. The Burj Khalifa's occupancy rate remained dismal for several years, by some estimates as low as 10 percent in the residential apartments. Its rents fell precipitously; the Emaar Holding Company that financed its construction continued to leak money, and in general the entire project of redeveloping Dubai remained a shaky proposition. Both the city's and the building's prospects somewhat recovered after 2011, along with the general welfare of the region, although the Burj Khalifa's position in the economy of Dubai remained, and in fact still remains today, ambiguous or confounding.[91]

Some of these ambiguities are echoed by internal tensions in the propaganda offered by the Burj Khalifa's managers, tensions that reflect the ambivalence around tall architecture still lingering from its late nineteenth- and early twentieth-century inception. A 2009 press release describes the Burj Khalifa (then called the Burj Dubai) as "the world's first 'vertical city,'" a metaphor repeated obsessively in pamphlets and websites promoting its commercial and touristic appeal.[92] However, the chief business of the Burj Khalifa is simply to be *very big*. Rising nearly twice the height of the Empire State Building, the Burj Khalifa overtook its nearest competitor by between 230 and 300 meters, depending on the basis for comparison. The building's publicists make no bones about the importance of this single metric: "Highest observation deck in the world," proclaim the Burj Khalifa's "Promotions" pages, numerous times.[93] On the same website, the link titled "Vision" continues the theme: "World's tallest building. A living wonder. Stunning work of art. Incomparable feat of engineering. Burj Khalifa is all that. In concept and execution, Burj Khalifa has no peer."[94] A second link, "Facts and Figures," offers the following list under the heading "World's Records":

- Tallest building in the world
- Tallest free-standing structure in the world
- Highest number of stories in the world
- Highest occupied floor in the world
- Highest outdoor observation deck in the world
- Elevator with the longest travel distance in the world
- Tallest service elevator in the world[95]

Thus, in a fashion so blatant that it seems to leapfrog any opportunity for critical scrutiny, a single external aspect, height, supersedes the building's numerous other attributes or potentials. This supersession dominates the discourse surrounding the Burj Khalifa to such a degree that to the present day it can be difficult to locate even rudimentary pictures or plans of the building's interior spaces, although those spaces remain very decidedly for rent. Overemphasis on a single exterior metric achieves a kind of apotheosis with this extremely big building, which distends so aggressively in one dimension that it effectively suppresses its own considerable repertoire of other qualities. In the Burj Khalifa's presentation—or more precisely, in its sheer, hyperfactical presence, as well as in the propagandistic reinforcement of that presence—its business is simply *to be,* a kind of blank evidentiary substrate for the hyperbolic terms that attach to it: "highest," "tallest," "finest," or generally, "superlative in every respect."

I have argued that the skyscraper's peculiar technique of vision consolidates a cartography of the city even as the physical structure enabling such a perspective slims and evanesces, becoming a needle with (essentially) no interior space.[96] The bigness of the modern city miniaturizes to the same degree that the skyscraper gains altitude and diminishes in substance, asymptotically approaching the monolith with an "eye" at its peak, the Barad-dûr. And therefore the city—and even the larger Cartesian world to which it belongs, seen from this place in the sky—is what David Nye, slightly mystically but nevertheless appropriately, calls a "concrete abstraction."[97]

In Dubai, the abstraction of a Barad-dûr is indeed concretized. Look west from the observation deck of the Burj Khalifa, out over the Persian Gulf, and what you will see is an enormous archipelago of three hundred artificial islands called "The World," which literally reproduces a map of the earth in the form of real estate plots sellable to commercial developers. This artificial world picture is visible only from high in the air, which is to say, discounting satellites or coincidentally passing airplanes, it is visible only as a "world" at all from an aerial viewpoint such as the one at the top of the Burj Khalifa.

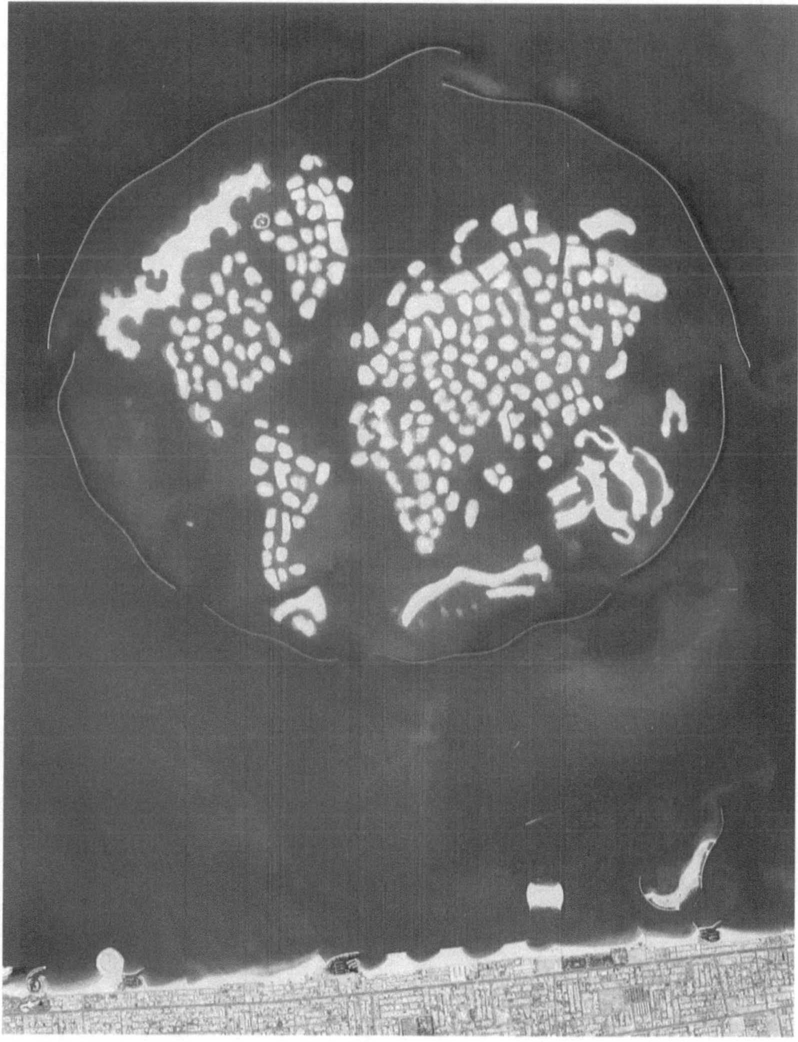

FIGURE 8.17 "World" archipelago, Dubai (image courtesy of the Earth Science and Remote Sensing Unit, NASA Johnson Space Center; photo source: ISS022-E-24940, eol.jsc.nasa.gov)

So: one pays one's ticket price, boards the elevator at sea level, rides the *z*-axis, and steps out onto the observation deck, having insensibly traveled straight through nearly a kilometer of space-less vertical structure. And there at the top, if it is a clear day and one squints sufficiently, the extreme abstraction of *big culture* is reduced to the concrete *smallness* of a single cartographical image, a nine-kilometer-wide map of the earth observable by an "eye" physically placed at the highest built point upon the actual planet it represents. Possibly nothing on earth could be bigger or smaller at the same time.

✷ 9 ✷
Disaster

THE *TITANIC*

Live News

Late Sunday night, April 14, 1912, the White Star ocean liner *Titanic,* having departed Southampton, England, five days before, collided with an iceberg in the Atlantic about 1,300 miles from its destination in New York City. Within a few hours, newspapers were composing stories for their Monday morning editions, even as details of the event remained sparse and inconsistent. The editor of *The New York Times,* Carr Van Anda, having guessed the real magnitude of the disaster, scooped most of the other New York papers by running the headline shown in figure 9.1 on the morning of April 15th. The *Times* identifies its news source as a wireless message from a Marconi radio station at Cape Race, Newfoundland. Some other American newspapers, taking their cues from the same Cape Race dispatch, accurately report that the ship is in serious trouble: "Titanic, Biggest Ship Afloat, Sinking; Hundreds of Passengers May Be Lost" (*Chicago Tribune*); "Largest Vessel Afloat Sinking Off Newfoundland" (*Washington Post*); "Titanic, Ocean Liner Probably Sinks with Thirteen Hundred Passengers" (*Charlotte Daily Observer*). The inclusion of qualifiers—"may," "probably," and even the *Times*' own adjective, "blurred"—conveys editors' uneasiness about the paltriness of the wireless reports, perhaps alongside a perennial suspicion on the part of print journalists toward newfangled technology.[1]

A number of other newspapers, whether warier of midnight wireless dispatches or more sanguine about the buoyancy of modern ships, hedge their bets by offering reassurances of impending rescue: "Passengers Were Taken Off by Other Steamers: Hero Boat Was at Hand" (*Kansas City Star*); "Virginian Speeds to Aid: Women Being Taken Off in Lifeboats" (*Washington Post*). It was generally believed that several vessels were in the *Titanic*'s vicinity and would be able to assist her, a notion

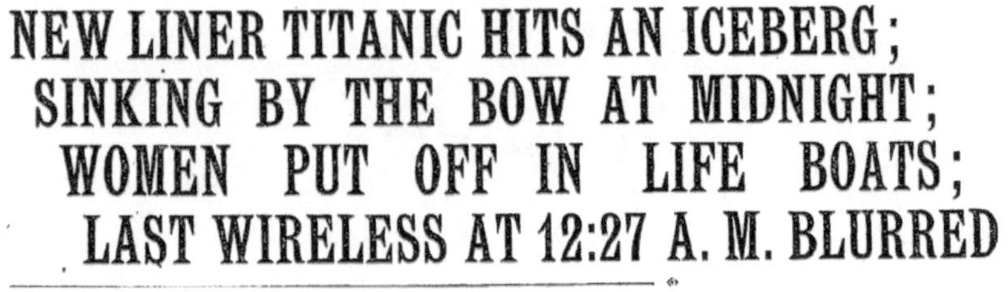

NEW LINER TITANIC HITS AN ICEBERG; SINKING BY THE BOW AT MIDNIGHT; WOMEN PUT OFF IN LIFE BOATS; LAST WIRELESS AT 12:27 A. M. BLURRED

FIGURE 9.1 Headline (*New York Times*, April 15, 1912)

supported by a faulty Associate Press report of additional wireless messages relayed through Halifax from potential rescue ships such as the *Olympic* and the *Carpathia*. Trusting these clues, some newspapers get the story utterly wrong: "Passengers on Giant Liner Titanic Transferred Safely" (*Fort Worth Star-Telegram*); "Liner Titanic Kept Afloat by Water-Tight Compartments" (*Washington Times*); "All Passengers Safely Taken Off by Lifeboats" (*London Evening News*); "Passengers Finally Saved After Thrilling Experiences" (*Columbus [GA] Ledger*). Most notoriously, William Randolph Hearst's *New York Sun*, a chief rival of *The New York Times*, declares "All Safe on Titanic," adding that the ship is currently under tow to Halifax.[2] Such upbeat accounts were bolstered throughout the day of Monday, April 15, by the insistence of White Star bureaucrats, in particular a senior executive named Phillip Franklin, that the *Titanic* was still afloat, its passengers safe, and damage to the ship minor.[3] As *The New York Times* declares a day later, White Star's officials had been "optimistic in the extreme," and the *Times*' writers do not refrain from mockery in their Tuesday subheadline: "Franklin Hopeful All Day: Manager of the Line Insisted Titanic Was Unsinkable Even After She Had Gone Down."[4]

In the days following the disaster, newspapers shift their focus to the imminent arrival of the *Carpathia* in New York, carrying the survivors. Papers that had misreported the *Titanic* safe and afloat now print their mea culpas. More significantly, journalists begin to amass a litany of questions about corporate accountability, technological hubris, class and ethnic discrimination, and gender chivalry or inequality that, for the rest of the twentieth century and beyond, will dominate what Stephen Biel calls the "conventional narrative" of the *Titanic* disaster—the event is quickly elevated to an epochal cultural fable.[5] But it is worth dwelling longer on the messier details of those first few days, especially on the manner in which the news story emerged out of a mix of new media and generic melodrama. From this narrower vantage, certain ancillary narratives appear, some arguably more influential than the "defining catastrophe" or "transformative event" of the actual sinking.[6] One such ancillary narrative is the rise to prominence of *The New York Times* itself, which, prior to this moment, had been one among a large number of dailies in New York City. After April 1912, and capitalizing on its scoop of the rival Hearst papers, the *Times* emerges as the Western Hemisphere's preeminent journalistic organ, a status it maintains until the end of the twentieth century, if perhaps not beyond. Another ancillary narrative concerns the impetus that revelations about the *Titanic*'s poor hull design and lack of safety provisions lent to the legal struggle to improve maritime and other industrial safeguards. In particular, the travesty of the *Titanic*'s lifeboat shortage became a catalyst for legislation; Stephen Biel goes as far as to suggest that "the disaster changed nothing except shipping regulations."[7]

However, the particular ancillary narrative on which I wish to dwell is that of wireless communication. Wireless was a new technology in 1912, one that the *Titanic* disaster thrust into public view both for its role in summoning potential rescue ships and, more vitally, for the extraordinarily rapid reporting it enabled. Arguably, the contribution of the Marconi wireless relay stations on the Atlantic coast of North America, even more than the sheer magnitude or character of the disaster itself, established *Titanic* as a paradigmatic object or symbol of big culture in the century to follow, perhaps second in notoriety only to the atomic bomb.

I noted that *The New York Times* inserts a brief qualification about electronic messaging in its April 15 headline—"Last Wireless at 12:27 A.M. blurred"—in effect treating the mode of transmission as a crucial element of the event. Many other papers make similar interjections about media, whether to bolster the vérité of a given report or as an interesting item in itself. The *Los Angeles Times* says, "Last Message from the Wireless Operator, Blurred and Indistinct, Tells of Women Being Put Off in Lifeboats"; Hearst's *New York Sun*, amid its egregiously wrong account, declares "Baltic, Virginian, Olympic and Other Ships Summoned by Urgent Wireless Calls"; *The Christian Science Monitor* has, "Wireless Dispatches Immediately Sent Out That Vessel Is Sinking." Even the distant *Times of India*, getting its information a full day late through Reuters, conveys the news under the banner headline, "Latest Telegrams." Journalists were plainly excited by the prospect of conducting, via electronic signals, what must have seemed an almost instantaneous transmission of events happening hundreds of miles away in the middle of the ocean. The wireless medium enables headline writers freely to indulge the gerund to indicate a story still in process: "Sinking by the Bow at Midnight"; "Titanic, Biggest Ship Afloat, Sinking"; "Steamer Titanic Near Sinking"; "Unloading Passengers."[8] The present-tense style of this reportage prompts a counterintuitive theoretical claim: the *Titanic* disaster is something like the first major "live" news event of the modern era, a story inextricable from the instantaneous electronic media through which it is relayed. In a mode now so habitual for television and internet journalism that it has long since buried its novelty, this is a story fundamentally about the technological means of its own reportage, akin to what Daniel Boorstin famously calls a "pseudo-event" or "media event."[9] In this sense, at least, Slavoj Žižek is right to compare the sinking of the *Titanic* to the attacks of September 11, 2001, an instantaneous spectacle executed by media-savvy al-Qaeda planners in tacit collusion with the TV and internet venues that would first carry the action live and then continually replay it.[10] The basis for Žižek's comparison ought not to be that both the 9/11 attacks and the *Titanic* disaster are allegories of technological or political hubris, a cliché that tends to preoccupy accounts of both events, including Žižek's own. Rather, in epistemological terms, both *Titanic* and the 9/11 attacks are quintessentially *actual* constructions of nonfictional imagery, and in turn, stories about how electronic media narratives are produced in their unfolding moments—how events are constructed to emerge or to appear "live."[11]

What the newspapers fabricate or fabulate, quite regardless of the nonpictorial nature of both wireless communication and most early twentieth-century print journalism, is a transpiring *visual* image of the *Titanic*. Such visual imagery is generated from the very first hours of the disaster, certainly long before any eyewitnesses return to furnish firsthand descriptions. Indeed, by the time the witnesses do arrive ashore, they themselves, complying with the reporters on hand to record their accounts, largely follow the press's lead in composing the elements of their tableaux. Such elements, presumably because they are prejudicially selected or "premeditated," tend to be drawn from a stock repertoire—an almost imperceptible jolt as the ship first strikes the iceberg; the crew running about, warning or reassuring the passengers; the decks listing and water rising; the entire ship tilting up in the water, especially as seen from the boats several hundred yards away; the ship's electric lights still ablaze, then blinking out just before she founders; the ship rearing and splitting in two before vanishing beneath the water; and so on.[12] A litany of supplementary incidents of uncertain provenance embellishes this generic scenography, inflected with the racial, gender, ethnic, and national stereotypes typical of such fodder—the women and children off-loaded; the immigrant steerage passengers storming or bullying the crew; the band remaining to finish playing "Nearer My God to Thee"; the craven J. Bruce Ismay, chairman of the White Star Line, sneaking onto a lifeboat possibly disguised as a woman; the stoic John Jacob Astor remaining on deck dressed in his suit, calmly smoking cigarettes; Ida Straus refusing to board a lifeboat without her husband, Isador; and so on.

But it is the Marconi wireless dispatches, prior to the advent of any eyewitness narratives, that enable the fantasy that *someone* is seeing the event as it unfolds, just as a film or video camera might capture what it sees "live" even when an audience reviews what has happened only later. Everything transpires before the eye of a proxy apparatus, the "view" of which one now receives in what is given to be an unmediated mode.[13] The *Titanic* disaster is thus, paradigmatically as well as ironically, a *moving* picture, or rather a moving image (technologically) frozen into a tableau, for the sake of a putatively instantaneous view, in effect, a cinematic or even a videomatic *still*. Wireless, despite its inherent invisibility, serves as "mechanical witness" to a preeminently unfolding—which is to say, a live, visual, and moving—event, nonetheless "snapped" in order to display a singular object.[14]

The "spectacular drawing" printed on the front page of *The New York Herald* on April 16 is a case in point.[15] Extrapolating freely, the drawing constructs the event as an action shot seen from a specific distance, so as to contain the entire huge ship in the act of listing on the way to its demise. As Paul Heyer notes, the *Herald*'s artist is uncredited, since "to cite the person would of course detract from the realism implied in the

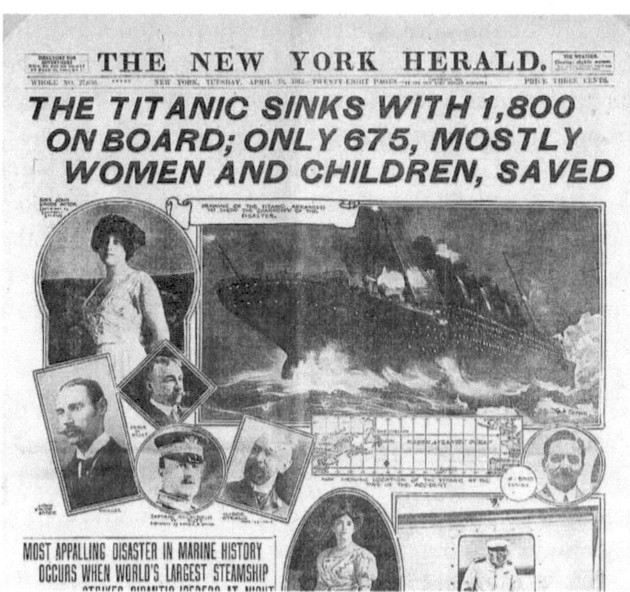

THE NEW YORK HERALD.

THE TITANIC SINKS WITH 1,800 ON BOARD; ONLY 675, MOSTLY WOMEN AND CHILDREN, SAVED

MOST APPALLING DISASTER IN MARINE HISTORY OCCURS WHEN WORLD'S LARGEST STEAMSHIP

FIGURE 9.2 *New York Herald*, front page, April 16, 1912 (Library of Congress)

illustration."[16] Here, reliant wholly on speculations based on the sparse wireless reports of the night before, we have one of the first depictions of the *Titanic* disaster as big culture, a precedent for a century of imagery about to come.

Now begins the history of pictures standing in lieu of the historical record, a history composed of a canon of clichés that Linda Maria Koldau, going further than Biel's "conventional narrative," bluntly calls "the *Titanic* code."[17] Arguably the core of conventional myths about the *Titanic,* quite aside from whatever historical facts were recoverable or interpretable in the data it bequeathed, is a collection of action shots, foremost among which is that medium-distance view of the ship tilting or sinking, as though seen by a survivor in a lifeboat, the tableau reproduced both after and before the fact by *The New York Herald*. But in a sense, the *Herald*'s printed picture is as extraneous to the general construction of the moving image—to its epistemological shaping, so to speak—as any hypothetical "live" portraits of the sinking. Such imaginary photographs are already immanent to the event itself, to its liveness, and to its eventual shape as big culture. Consider the following text, a eulogy given by Shan Bullock for the *Titanic*'s architect, Thomas Andrews, that captures in an entirely typical way both the still, spectacular framing of the climactic moment and the sense of an unfolding narrative paused for the benefit of a view—in effect, the ship not simply still but *bestilled*:

> Well, all was done now that could be done, and the time remaining was short. The forecastle head was under water. All around, out on the sea, so calm under those wonderful stars, the boats were scattered, some near, some a mile away or more, the eyes of most of them turned back upon the doomed ship as one by one her port lights, that still burnt row above row in dreadful sloping lines, sank slowly into darkness. Soon the lines would tilt upright, then flash out and flash bright again; then, as the engines crashed down through the bulkheads, go out once more, and leave that awful form standing up against the sky, motionless, black, preparing for the final plunge.[18]

The sense of deliberate stoppage is palpable—"all was done now that could be done"—and Bullock goes as far as to call the ship "motionless," dialectically alluding to the action we feel we are perceiving through the description. Such assertions are what Bernard Shaw calls "outrageous romantic lying."[19] At this exact moment, hundreds of people were still alive on the ship's decks or in the water trying to climb into lifeboats, a fact frequently given as proof of the villainous indifference either of the White Star Line or of those passengers fortunate enough already to be in the boats, and who, to save themselves from potential swamping, failed or declined to pull more victims from the water.

Bullock's melodramatic eulogy, like *The New York Herald* picture, is a thoroughly mystified revision or distillation of disaster into a singular, sublime object. For one thing, each such image dogmatically retains the well-framed viewpoint required of such tableaux: far enough away to take in the ship as a whole, and therefore also far enough away to disregard the viewpoints of the many individuals already dead or about to drown. We saw such logic both in the dreadful middle distance of Hiroshima victims such as Toyofumi Ogura and in the abstracted "cartographical" overview of visitors (actual or potential) to the tops of skyscrapers. The temporal stoppage that each such view posits colludes with its specific spatial distance: a moment of narrative suspension in which the spectacular image is not merely static but "motionless," in Bullock's incongruous term. The prime pathos of early *Titanic* narratives is therefore not the ship's symbolic significance, per Žižek, or some fable of technological hubris or class or gender prejudice, per the usual tales—although certainly each of these contributes to the construction of its aura—but rather, ultimately thanks to the wireless, the bald but ironic fact that we (believe we) view the singular big thing destroyed. Every other big-cultural spectacle of the next century, from the *Hindenburg* crash to 9/11, will share this structure of active immobilization, so to speak, which is also duplicated in the disaster film: the big object fully present, destroyed, but ultimately *seen*, as "catastrophic time stands still."[20]

In essence, the wireless prefigures what Laura Marks will describe as the special domain of cinema, and by dint of a similar ostensibly built-in realism: "Cinema is not merely a transmitter of signs; it bears witness to an object and transfers the presence of that object to viewers."[21] Marks's insight is derived from phenomenological theories of vision, which often seem like film theory before the fact. Speaking of how we represent temporal events to ourselves, Maurice Merleau-Ponty writes that in every imagination of an event, we "are tacitly assuming the existence of a witness tied to a certain spot in the world . . . there are no events without someone to whom they happen and whose finite perspective is the basis of their individuality."[22] The putative instantaneity of wireless, implying a "live" recording of its "view," borrows on credit, so to speak, from video. Thus, in its long afterlife as paradigmatic big culture, the *Titanic* disaster survives foremost as a proto-videomatic tableau, in essence a reconstructed "clip" about itself, presented first as a photographic "still" and eventually as a discrete cinematic scene. And because this "clip" is necessarily an ex post facto revision, understanding it requires, perversely, *not* the historicist reconstruction of the events themselves but instead a revisionist look backward through the fantasmatic lens of a fictional film or video camera. Indeed, from the start, the *Titanic* disaster is an event transpiring *backward*, re-viewed through its later fabulations. This was true even on its first day.

Expenditure Spectacle

On April 18, a mere three days after the *Titanic* had sunk, *The New York Times* carried the small advertisement shown in figure 9.3, wedged among notices such as “Blanche Ring in The Wall Street Girl, A New Musical Comedy, with Harry Gilfoil” and the “Miner’s 8th Ave.” variety theater, offering attractions such as “Amateurs Friday,” “Broadway Gaiety Girls,” and “Wrestling To-Night.”[23] In this unassuming way, on the back pages of the same newspaper still speculating on the nature of the actual event, a history of *Titanic* disaster films begins. This history accompanies the development of narrative cinema itself. Arguably no single event more persistently occupies the attention of producers of popular visual culture, both in its direct entrée into the content of films and as a prototype for many other instances of disaster footage, both fictional and nonfictional.[24] At least a hundred films about the *Titanic* were made during the subsequent century.[25]

About a half hour into the most extravagant of all narrative versions of the disaster, James Cameron’s 1997 film, *Titanic*, Jack Dawson (Leonardo

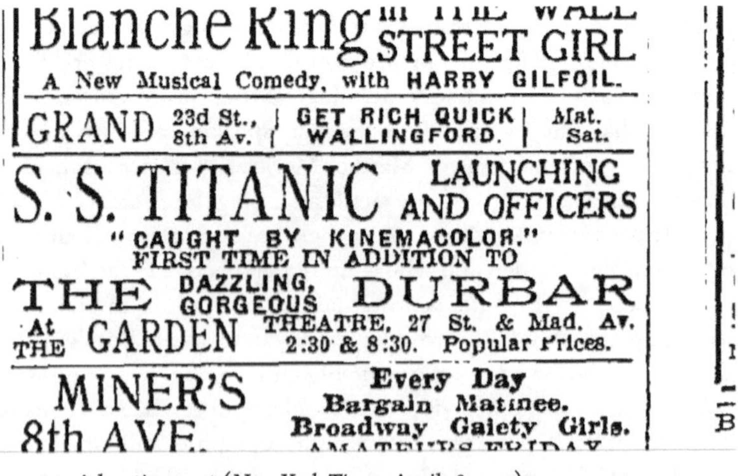

Blanche Ring STREET GIRL
A New Musical Comedy, with HARRY GILFOIL.
GRAND 23d St., 8th Av. | GET RICH QUICK WALLINGFORD. | Mat. Sat.
S. S. TITANIC LAUNCHING AND OFFICERS
"CAUGHT BY KINEMACOLOR."
FIRST TIME IN ADDITION TO
THE DAZZLING, GORGEOUS DURBAR
At THE GARDEN THEATRE, 27 St. & Mad. Av. 2:30 & 8:30. Popular Prices.
MINER'S 8th AVE.
Every Day Bargain Matinee. Broadway Gaiety Girls.

FIGURE 9.3 Advertisement (*New York Times*, April 18, 1912)

DiCaprio) and his friend Fabrizio (Danny Nucci) lean over the ship's bow as it steams ahead into the Atlantic; Jack yells a much-repeatable tagline accompanied by some fist pumps and mannish screams. The camera then pulls back, commencing a lavish crane shot over the full ship from bow to stern, revealing minutiae of design and machinery, the labor of stewards, the leisure of passengers strolling on the decks, and in general the vastness and meticulous detail of this cinematic reconstruction of the *Titanic*, accompanied by stately music and slightly incongruous wave sounds. The tempo of the shot gives it the feel of a dream sequence, a fabulation of what might have been seen but never will be. Eventually, the whole of the ship is encompassed by the frame, its name (and the film's) visible on the stern as the camera comes to rest near the water, watching the *Titanic* recede into the open ocean.[26] The camera takes a full forty seconds to complete this luxurious reveal, at which point, having arrived at the long shot of the entire ship, we segue to a fancy dinner party on board. A brief j-cut interjects a fragment of conversation just before the change of scene; with the whole of the *Titanic* still in our sight, the infamous White Star Chairman J. Bruce Ismay (Jonathan Hyde) delivers this rather overwritten line: "She's the largest moving object ever made by the hand of man in all history."

Cameron's *Titanic*, drawing from the long agglomeration of cultural myths that precede it, offers the usual fare of big-budget Hollywood melodrama: a love story, a lineup of legibly good and evil characters, some rudimentary class conflict, some famous actors, and so on. Arguably the film's chief rationale, quite aside from its perfunctory interpretation of the "*Titanic* code," is simply to *show* us the enormous ship itself, as in the long reveal I have described, or perhaps to display the technical virtuosity with

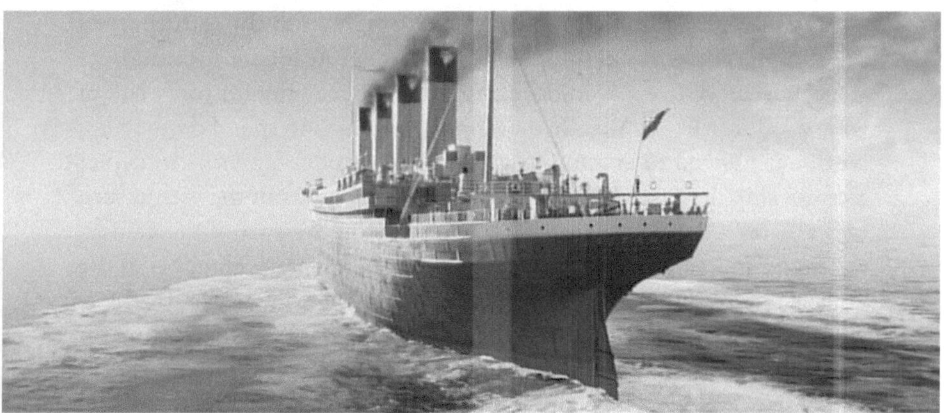

FIGURE 9.4 *Titanic* (1997): shot of full ship

which such a cinematic artifact may, at stupendous cost, be constructed for view. At other moments, and with a similar obsessiveness, the camera scans specific parts of the vessel: engines, propellors, dining halls, leisure decks, staterooms, the famous grand staircase, and finally and most lovingly of all, the ship's huge hull tilting vertically into the air just before going down, while dozens of passengers fall spectacularly to their deaths. These last shots are the film's special-effects coup, the moment when the great object and the great violence of its destruction merge into a paroxysm of excessive bigness—climactic for the plot, to be sure, but more primally in terms of the sheer magnitude of demolition earlier foreshadowed by the mere presence of big things and now baldly exhibited. In other words, this spectacularly gruesome and yet weirdly dispassionate climax gratifies both the narrative expectations of the melodramatic storyline and the psychological expectations of the viewed object's intrinsic death drive, proportional to the stridency with which both its bigness and the lavish parsing of its details were previously offered. Above all, the spectacle is again one of *expenditure*. Whatever capital—narratological, cultural, film-historical, or bluntly monetary—had been invested to construct this hyperfactical object on screen is now fully spent in its destruction, and the fetish that it comprises is the sheer size and (therefore) the sheer cost of that big image and its annihilation.

Cameron's *Titanic* was in its time the most expensive film ever produced, as well as containing the most expensive single movie set ever constructed, a 90 percent scale model of the ship itself. We might observe the significance of the expenditure spectacle—more precisely, the difference made in the visual form of mainstream cinema by the sheer cost of objects depicted—by contrasting a scene similar in content yet very different in cost. Consider *The Poseidon Adventure*, directed by Ronald Neame in 1972, a film that, perhaps surprisingly from the retrospect of the summer-blockbuster and CGI eras, won an Academy Award for its visual effects. With a scaled-back budget of about $5 million, only half of what producer Irwin Allen had originally intended to spend on the film, Neame is obliged to employ relatively cheap models and sets to depict a cruise ship destroyed by a tsunami. The chintziness of the sets in turn necessitates a constant, subtle dissimulation on the part of the camera operators and editors.[27] We get sporadic or fragmentary glimpses of the objects we are supposed to see: the ship itself, the wide ocean, the huge wave, and eventually the upended dining hall that is our chief setting for the climactic moment when the ship keels over and swamps.

The latter set is especially telling. The dining hall scene takes several minutes to unfold in all its detail, certainly more than the real time

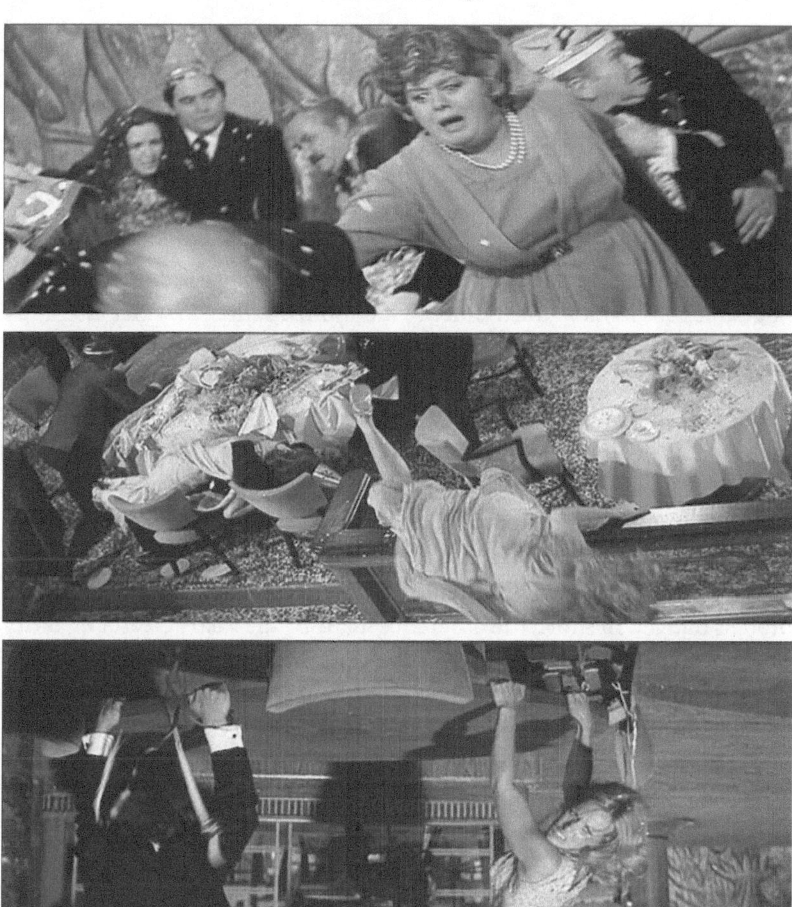

FIGURE 9.5 *The Poseidon Adventure* (1972): sequence of ship overturning in tsunami

required diegetically to upend the ship. Most of our attention is on the disorientation of the passengers, who fall in fast and close motion in and out of the camera frame. In some sense, of course, we are meant to feel as if we, too, are falling, and so the cutting between passengers tumbling and the whole ship foundering is rapid and utilitarian. This is the most traditional form of montage, fundamentally narrative in its intention, what Bazin calls "parallel montage,"[28] a straightforward arrangement of images to convey the unfolding of simultaneous events. But in order to convey this unfolding efficiently, and to maintain a modicum of the delicate realism that is constantly threatened by the cheapness of the sets and models, Neame's cameras *must* cut away quickly and frequently. Objects on screen do not warrant sustained observation, but can, so to speak, serve only as signifiers of what they are meant to depict: a grand vessel, humanity beset, an overwhelming force of nature, and so on. The overall effect is one of carefully delimited chaos, an entirely comprehensible sort of incomprehensibility. Suffering is observed at close hand but also framed by a rational temporal sequence amid the chaos: the passengers upright, the ship upright, a gigantic wave, the ship turning over, passengers falling, ship overturned, and so on.

Compare this to something like the equivalent scene in Cameron's huge-budget *Titanic*—the moment I mentioned earlier, in which the ship's hull rears up vertically before finally sinking beneath the water. Everything here differs by degree; but exactly what sort of difference does that make? First of all, Cameron now dwells on his object at great length, even dotingly, an extension or distension of view enabled by the huge quantities of money lavished on the objects we are invited to observe with such care. The camera roams apparently with perfect formal confidence, freely deploying shots from a variety of distances, whereas in *Poseidon Adventure*, the range from which the ship is shot is carefully constrained by the models budget. In short, the difference made by the vastly greater quantity of money spent on *Titanic* is decisively qualitative: the eye now attains the structural freedom promised by the cinematic apparatus, appearing to gaze infinitely and at will over the objects and events at hand. In the lower-budget film, any such freedom remains merely potential, reined in by the material indistinctness, and ultimately therefore by the cost, of sets and visual technologies.

Monad

"What montage does," writes Deleuze, improvising on Vertov, "is to carry perception into things, to put perception into matter, so that any point whatsoever in space itself perceives all the points on which it acts, or which act on it."[29] The facets of bigness that may be seen, or more precisely, the number of points in space *from which* bigness is seen, depend on how much money gets spent on them, as well as on how many "cameras" (very loosely construed, in the CGI era) are available to shoot them. In essence, the big object is a filmed monad, to draw both from Marx and Leibniz, reflecting all possible views upon it from its universe. But this monadic state is a mere dialectical idea until explicitly paid for and manufactured. And what is paid for must be both the object and its many points of perceivability—for Leibniz these would be essentially equivalent. Since the monad is a "perceiving" entity, in that in relating itself to others' perceptions it "represents a multitude within a unity," Leibniz describes the specific character of any given monad's interrelations within the whole of the perceivable universe in terms of a relative "distinctness" of its perception:[30]

> [because] a monad is representative in its nature, nothing could restrict it to representing only a part of things; although it is true that this representation of the details of the whole universe is confused, and can only be distinct with respect to a small part of things, that is to say, those that are either closest or largest in relation to each of the monads. . . . [Monads] all reach confusedly to infinity, to everything; but they are limited and differentiated by their degrees of distinct perception.[31]

In a big-budget disaster film, the infinite perceivability of an object, or the indeterminate magnitude of the "multitude" of its distinct views, is proportional to budget. Provided the money is well and fully spent, nothing ought to remain "confused."

Thus, where the budget has quantitatively increased, the act of viewing becomes qualitatively different. It is now not merely possible but required that we see the full spectacle of the ship and (eventually) its destruction. Big money places a premium on visibility, and it must be prolonged to the point of fulfillment or exhaustion. Often, therefore, viewing is abetted by slow motion, repetition, redundant camera angles, and so on, if not simply by the temporal extension of the diegetic action. In *The Wild Bunch*, a rare slow-motion shot is used to prolong the film's most expensive scene, the dynamiting of the bridge over the Rio Grande. In *Independence Day*, the obliterations of the Empire State Building, the White House, and other grandiose architecture are greatly distended, resisting both close-ups and montage (say, in order to juxtapose the largeness of the destruction with its impact on individual persons or objects) in order to display the full, costly production of the violence. We spend long stretches of time watching Elizabeth Taylor enter Rome in *Cleopatra*, or watching throngs of extras and animals cross the Red Sea in *The Ten Commandments*, or gawking at the remarkably pellucid sinking of the USS *Oklahoma* in *Pearl Harbor*, unimpeded by smoke or jitter. Moreover, through previews, posters, press packets, television spots, and so on, the consumers of each of these films would already be expecting to encounter these expensively produced scenes and objects, in some sense independent of the story being narrated through and around them. For the benefit of big culture, the narrative halts and something verging on a still life is offered, so that slow motion, excessive temporal dilation, effortlessly roving cameras, and so on, in no way detract from the ostensible realism of the story, which waits patiently on the shore, so to speak, for the big object to be shown and the big money to be spent.

When the ship does finally go down in Cameron's *Titanic,* the emphases furnished by montage are almost exactly the reverse of those in the corresponding scene in *Poseidon Adventure.* Here, the film doesn't cut between views of the object in order to convey action and suffering, but instead only to place action and suffering in the service of getting the *object* fully viewed. Indeed, most of our attention remains carefully focused on the sheer act of viewing itself, whether we or the actors in the scene are performing it. The camera follows passengers sliding down the decks, steps back to watch them tumbling over the rails, pans smoothly around throngs of tiny figures in the water, and finally dwells on the faces of those in the lifeboats who see the ship sink along with us. The delimited chaos of the lower-budget film will not do here: any excessive movement or too-quick cutting would interfere with the scene's primary affect. It would be inconceivable in *Titanic* to have the passengers fall *past* our viewpoint, rapidly in and out of the frame, as they do in *Poseidon Adventure;* the effect and its budget would then have been wasted. In short, it is not merely an aesthetic choice but a structural necessity that the camera be wholly free to return to its longer views to observe, say, a body sliding all the way down the ship, or another falling all the way into the water. And "wholly free" means, here, unconstrained by the narrative itself, which politely pauses until the expenditure spectacle has been bought and paid for.

The big thing has become, to redeploy Shan Bullock's term, "motionless." Despite all the commotion, nothing is really happening in this scene in *Titanic* except money being spent to *see.* The purpose of montage in *Titanic* is thus exactly the reverse of *Poseidon Adventure,* or, more properly speaking, there is no montage here at all, no time or narrative elapsing, only a deliciously, monstrously detailed, but ultimately static (monadic) tableau of the big object, a kind of animated movie poster of *Titanic*-the-film. Therefore, also, the verisimilitude of the scene is enabled not by our absorption in it but by our abstraction out of it. We must be able fully to watch it producing itself, in all its technological glory, and be able to ask, within the act of viewing, such questions as, How did they do that? How did they get that guy to bounce off the propeller on his way down? How did they get all that water in there? Are the actors actually freezing? How did they get the ship to look so damn big? The more "realistic" the scene appears, ironically, the more we observe and admire it as a brilliantly produced artifice, something expensively manufactured. We watch, not exactly the narrative or characters in (the experience of) the action, but the "they" who bought, built, displayed, and sold it to us.

We might sum up by suggesting straightforwardly that *Poseidon Adventure* is a "phenomenological" movie, whereas *Titanic* is a "monadic" one. In the earlier, less expensive film, we are offered a directly sensuous experience through phenomenal attributes (surfaces, color, texture, movement, disorder and din) of a sinking ship that is essentially noumenal, a *Ding-an-sich* that can never fully appear, but which we must reconstruct as best we (or the filmmakers) can, through whatever attributes we (can afford to) view. In the later, far more expensive film, the ship completely and even presumptuously *appears*—no noumenal reserve remains, so to speak, but there is only a hyperfactical object expending itself in immoderately costly presence. Therefore no movement, no disorder, no sensuous commotion or din is needed. In a sense, there is no phenomenal experience of the ship sinking in Cameron's *Titanic* at all, since every act of viewing required to complete the scene and its object is already contained within the film itself, exemplified by those lifeboat observers just beyond middle distance whose gazes are proxy for our view through the camera lens. Our own observation is oddly superfluous; the monad itself, as a perceiving thing, has always already accomplished whatever viewing may be required of its presence.[32] *Titanic* is a Barad-dûr, a great, blank thing with an "eye" that (already) sees us seeing it. Its spectacular motionlessness is, in effect, the metonymy of the nullity of our own viewing practice. The hyperfacticity of the big thing renders our perception irrelevant even as we pay to perform that perception, a phenomenological analog of the inconsequentiality haunting the consumer's infinitesimal contribution, in purchasing the theater ticket or DVD, to the capitalization of such prodigiously big culture.

Monstrous Day Residue

In an article posted online shortly after September 11, 2001, Slavoj Žižek compares the World Trade Center attacks to the sinking of the *Titanic*:

> When we hear how the bombings were a totally unexpected shock, how the unimaginable Impossible happened, one should recall the other defining catastrophe from the beginning of the XXth century, that of *Titanic*: it was also a shock, but the space for it was already prepared in ideological fantasizing, since *Titanic* was the symbol of the might of the XIXth century industrial civilization.[33]

Given the differences between these two disasters—for one thing, the *Titanic* was destroyed by a natural phenomenon whereas the World Trade Center towers were obviously brought down by very human means—one suspects that this now common comparison between the two events that are said to frame the twentieth century is a highly fantasmatic construction of its own. But whose fantasy is it? The basis for such a comparison is certainly not the aptness of analogies between September 11, 2001, and April 15, 1912, but rather, as Žižek points out, the "ideological fantasizing" that prepares a "space" for the symbolization each of these events appears to warrant. If we take the term "space" seriously, we begin to understand more precisely its literalness in this context, a simultaneously physical and theoretical region that must, in order to be effective for ideological fantasizing, be *filled* by an object.

Why, for instance, isn't a World War I gas attack a more apt comparison to 9/11; or the Johnstown flood, the Galveston hurricane, or the Triangle Shirtwaist fire (to mention only disasters in the American context)? Precisely because only the single big object—the ship, the building—can fill the "space" of the event. What renders the *Titanic* an exemplary symbol is therefore not its putative aptness as a sign of transition from a (nineteenth-century) industrial to a (twentieth-century) postindustrial economy or culture. We can easily find other moments far more apt as epochal metaphors, which is to say, figures based in the shared attributes of an event and its larger historical tendency. But to bluntly paraphrase the deconstructionist usage of tropology in which Žižek is well versed, the *Titanic* is *not* a metaphor or a synecdoche but rather a metonymy. Its size, its presence, or, in rhetorical terms, its sheer and tendentious *proximity* to view, is primarily what furnishes its exemplary value, and what subsequently enables it to be made an object of symbolic contemplation or edification. In short, the *Titanic* is a "day residue," a monstrous one, to be sure. We may then find surprisingly apt the cliché that only events that produce their own easily circulated media images—something like their own day residues—will have lasting power in the popular imaginary. The visibly large object may fill the space of fantasy, but does so *literally*, as actual (or at least re-imaged) mass and volume, something containing the *real* in a curiously insistent way, something hyperfactical.

We might finally glance at Žižek's illuminating analysis of Robert Ballard's 1985–86 documentary videos of the *Titanic*'s wreckage, a collection of footage shot with remote submersible cameras, and from which James Cameron liberally cribbed for the opening of his own film.[34] Žižek first reminds us of some standard symbolisms: vast technological achievement laid waste by mere dumb ice, social classes rendered equal in suffering or death, overweening pride castigated, and so on: "the wreck of the *Titanic* was a form in which society lived the experience of its own death."[35] "But," as Žižek immediately goes on to add, "all these are commonplaces."[36] As critics, it is far too easy to explain the symbolic overdetermination that confers on the *Titanic* its cultural weight. "The problem," Žižek continues, "is that this is not all."[37]

"This is not all"—that must be right. But what else is there? Why would the *Titanic,* real or fictionalized, remain an object of interest to us and of use to producers and investors, perhaps even among those who scoff at the abjectly generic quality of the narratives that have always surrounded this ship and its fate? Žižek does not exactly avoid the question, but he gives a rather conventional response, drawing on those physiological terms of the sublime commonly borrowed from Kant, who in turn borrows them from Burke: "a pleasant thrill . . . , a certain tranquility mixed with terror."[38] Žižek thus speaks of a "terrifying power of fascination" and "fascinating power," and, as he repeats several times, the "terrifying impact," or "terrifying, impossible *jouissance*" created by Ballard's pictures of the sunken *Titanic.*[39] This is an "impact" or "terror" in the face of the blank and excessive material *thing,* and one that Žižek even suggests we might be attempting to "escape" by creating symbols out of the story.

Having no specific quarrel with Žižek's description of the ostensible qualities of either the *Titanic* story or Ballard's pictures of the wreck, I am nonetheless more interested in the *quantitative* aspects inhabiting Žižek's descriptions, the hyperbole with which he quite drastically and yet still conventionally characterizes the "terrifying" experience of a supposedly "impossible" object. We need only direct our attention to the contexts in which Ballard's videos of the ship were shown—National Geographic television documentaries—to realize that terms such as "terror," "jouissance," even "fascination" are vast exaggerations to anyone but those who might have been either aboard the ship in 1914 or back in England, France, Ireland, or New York awaiting news of their stricken relatives. Intriguing, interesting, possibly titillating—even perhaps creepy or curious or embarrassing—these might be better adjectives to attach to our far more distanced viewing, but of course very poor critical fodder. The truth is, our pleasure in these images probably arises from rather minor emotional cathexes, at best, a "safe" encounter with the supposedly terrifying object fully mediated via the taxidermy of popular narrative film or television documentary. Indeed, we know very well how minor our responses to such pictures generally are, because we are able to distinguish from them our reactions to a different kind of imagery that unequivocally *does* act upon our bodies, or achieves the emotional movement or affect that the sublime object was supposed to have achieved: namely, pornography (broadly construed here; for instance, possibly also the "pornographic" violence or "terror" of a horror film). But isn't "terror" or "jouissance," outside the context of the strictly pornographic, merely a typical and quite vague descriptor of the *magnitude* of our response to objects and images? Isn't such a term merely the sign that there is a *degree* or *amount* of response to the bigness of the thing, or even that there is a "more" or a "too" somewhere in it, which, as competent formalists, we still don't have proper critical terms to describe, and which we therefore render only through the poor metonymy of "terror"? In other words, don't we, as critics, simply borrow hyperbole from other languages in order to signify metonymically that bigness is present, without being able exactly to qualify it?

✷ 10 ✷

Living with Bigness

KAZUO SHINOHARA

Against Comfort

In a modern apartment, one sometimes encounters a concrete structural column in the middle of the space, often in a haphazard or inconvenient spot. The apartment cannot do without the column, which belongs to the load-bearing structure of the high-rise building, upon which all the individual flats depend to remain fixed in the sky. Architects and interior designers may be tasked with lessening the intrusiveness of such columns, a problem especially pressing in a city apartment, where space is precious in proportion to the likelihood that oversized pieces of structure will obstruct it. But generally options are limited; the resident must learn to live *around* the column, or the designer attempt to integrate or camouflage it with finishes, decorations, or some cunning adaptation into a "feature."

If we eschew the circumspection of designers and residents and look directly at the column, we may discover traces of an elemental tension in the ideological configuration of the modern city, or even of modernity itself. Two incompatible scales of social life collide here: that of the domestic sphere, at which the apartment mimics with greater or lesser candor the deportment of a privately owned house, and the scale of urban infrastructure, at which the residential unit is reckoned only as a module within much larger structural and economic schemes. The column, being essential to the infrastructural scale but inimical to the domestic, pierces the apartment from the outside, so to speak, allied with regimes of sociopolitical exchange indifferent or even hostile to the inhabitation of individual dwellings. Set in place well before the "home" is configured, but lingering ever after, the column is perpetually in the way. Moreover, the resident only ever perceives a portion of the column as it ascends through the flat on its passage from the foundation up through the successive floors. In aesthetic or ideological terms, we might therefore think

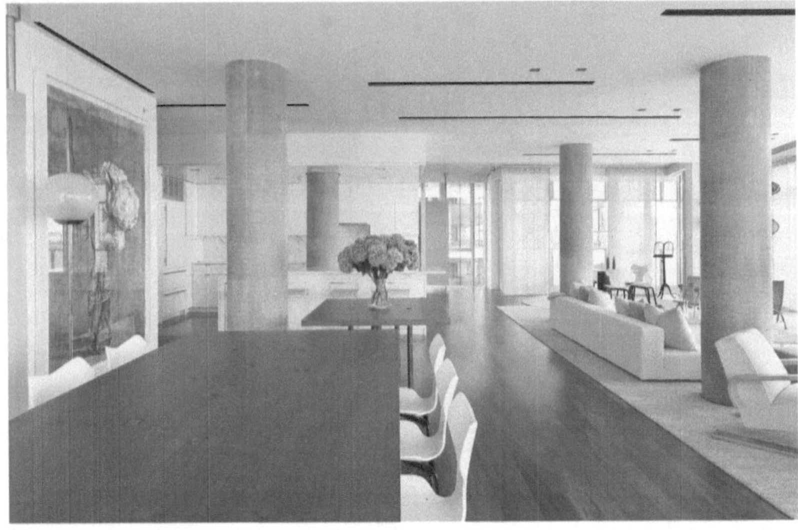

FIGURE 10.1 Hudson River Pier Residence, New York (Lee F. Mindel, architect; photo by Michael Moran/OTTO)

of the column as a symptom of the infrastructural unconscious, formed and controlled by preexisting forces out of sight, always an alien intrusion in the domicile—indeed, *unheimlich* in an unnervingly literal sense, penetrating the space of everyday life from above and beneath. Like any symptom, whether conceptual or material (or both), the column is too dense or opaque ever to be wholly lived with or wholly worked through.

But it may be theorized. I would like to do so by looking at some buildings by an architect whose confrontation with this sort of infrastructural unconscious leads to negotiations quite different than, for instance, the polite dissimulations of my hypothetical interior designer or resident. The architect is Kazuo Shinohara, who designed a series of small houses in Japan in the 1960s and 1970s, and whose work is frequently lauded by both architects and critics for its unusual blend of Japanese tradition and avant-garde provocation. I begin at a moment somewhat late in Shinohara's career, with a building he calls "a starting point for a new direction in my design," the House in Uehara (1977), located in the outskirts of Tokyo.[1] This house rather ferociously merges a series of polemical tendencies already implicit in Shinohara's earlier house designs, a few of which I will refer back to.

The plan of the House in Uehara is based on a simple square divided into apartment-like areas. In the interior of the second floor, photographs show an open-planned living space: to the left, a kitchen and dining area;

in the background, an opening from the central staircase; to the right, a smaller stair leading to an upper floor. But all subtlety and detail are overwhelmed by the "monumental presence," directly in the middle of the room, of a massive concrete column articulated with two forty-five-degree braces.[2] It is difficult to see this column is anything but a strident,

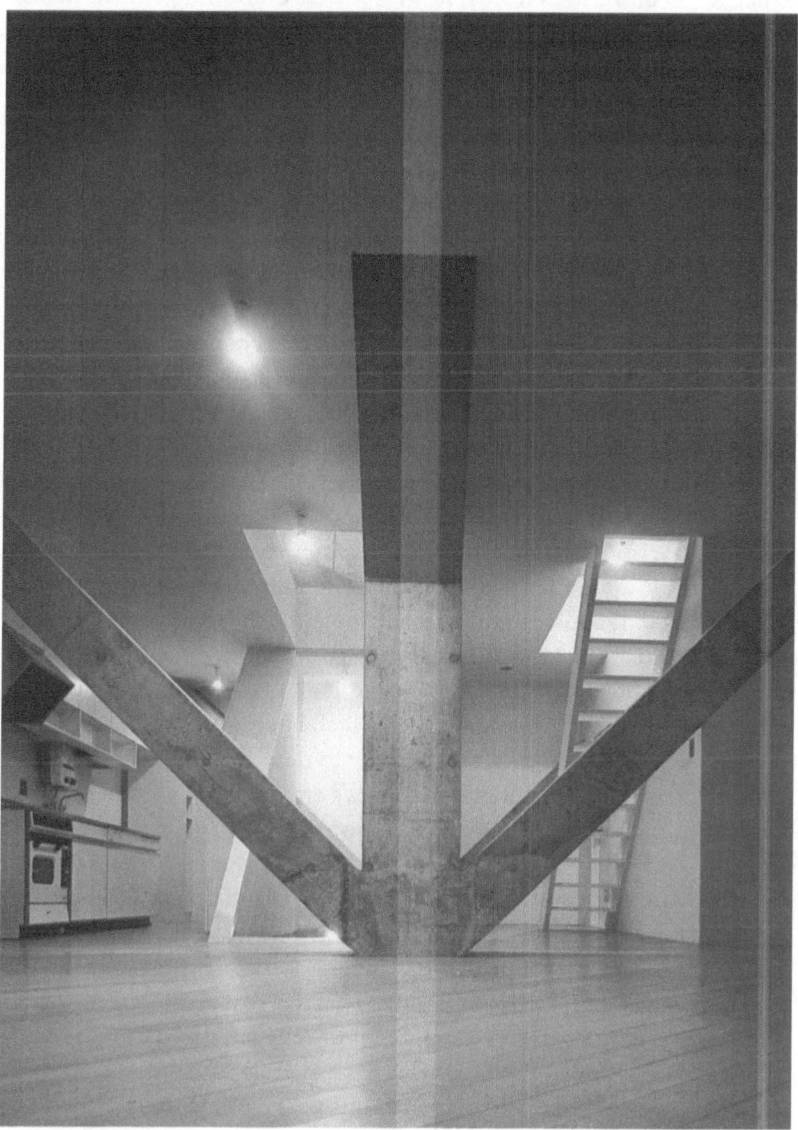

FIGURE 10.2 House in Uehara, Tokyo, 1976: interior living space (Kazuo Shinohara, architect; photo by Masao Arai, from *Japan Architect* 239 [February 1977]: 71), courtesy of *The Japan Architect*/Shinkenchiku-sha

even hostile interference with the circulation pattern of the multifunction living space in such a small house. Its discordant size is augmented by the materials Shinohara employs, the industrial concrete of post and limbs directly abutting the polished wood of the floor and the smooth plastered surface of the walls and ceiling. The column is "starkly confrontational, obstructive," in one critic's words; it "overpowers everything," in another's.[3] Presumably most people entering this space would inevitably perceive the column as simply *too big* for this room.[4]

Oddly, outside views of the house belie the confrontation within. The exterior elevation reveals that the same column seen up close in the living area helps form the upper portion of a two-story bracing system supporting a heavy concrete floor and roof slabs. From this perspective, the column's bigness diminishes considerably in proportion to the comprehensible assemblage of which it is a part. Speaking in formal terms available only to this somewhat abstracted view—the elevation framed in a snapshot from a medium distance—the asymmetrical arrangement of posts and diagonals, considerably larger on the left side of the house than the right, is warranted by the mass of the cantilevered carport, a balance of forces that Shinohara accentuates by exposing the outline of the truss-like structure in the house's facade, like a parody of Tudor half-timbering. Yet it is precisely these same structural elements, seemingly rational and apposite when viewed in the exterior elevation, that emerge as so disproportionately massive inside, "imping[ing]" upon the space or even "contradict[ing]" its overall logic.[5] In the interior, it appears as if parts of some much larger commercial or industrial building had infiltrated a small urban apartment, initiating a skirmish between public and private spheres, like an especially hostile version of the intrusive high-rise column with which I began.[6]

I use such rapacious figures advisedly to describe this interference of form, structure, and material. Shinohara's employment of contrasts has sometimes been characterized more tranquilly or quasi-metaphorically, for instance, by Koji Taki, who uses the dialectical term "opposition" to describe what he sees as Shinohara's eccentric adaptation of Japanese tradition.[7] It is true that the Uehara House invokes certain traditional elements: Shinohara likely borrows the general shape of his braces from the trusswork of Japanese farmhouse roofs, even if in that prototype diagonals would never have been foregrounded, but only appeared as temporary or concealed support features.[8] It is thus at least possible to interpret Shinohara's use of posts and diagonals at Uehara, particularly given their dominating size, as a kind of vexed revisionism: possibly a metonymical reference to the peaked roofs of traditional Japanese building types like *minka*; possibly also an oblique importation of a typically Western-style

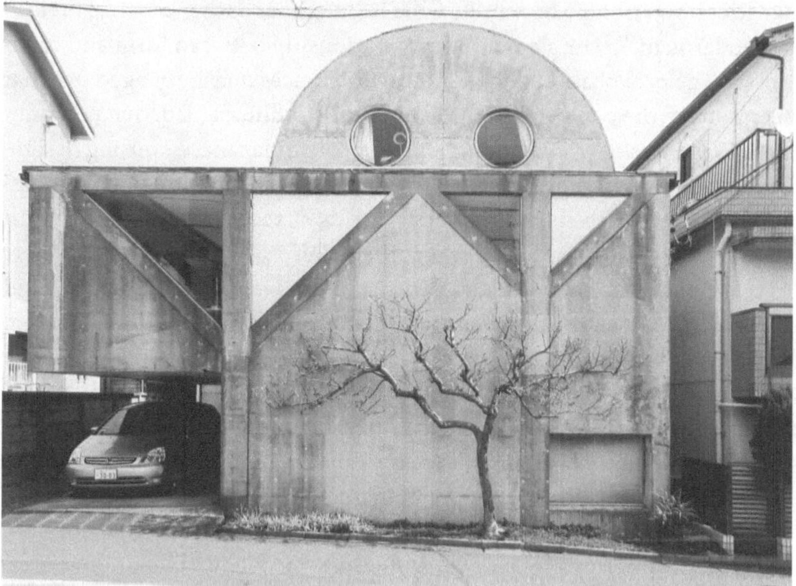

FIGURE 10.3 House in Uehara, Tokyo, 1976: exterior (Kazuo Shinohara, architect; photo 2012 by Carlo Fumarola)

truss, introduced to Japan in the 1860s; possibly an exposure or updating of auxiliary components of ancient Japanese carpentry, for instance, diagonal elements that are concealed so as not to disclose the structural shortfalls of the usual rectilinear joinery of traditional Japanese roofs.[9] Each of these readings proposes a dialectical "opposition," in Taki's language, comprehensible as a response to existing forms and histories. Yet each reading tends to overlook the experiential rigor of this big column in the small living space of the Uehara House, its sheer imposition or its feel of belonging to a structural order altogether distinct from the room. In short, dialectic, such as Taki's terminology of "opposition," seems too weak a mode to describe the architectural deportment at Uehara. One might respond to Taki that to be "opposed" to its container, a structural column would first have to abide in some mutual relationship with it—as Heidegger suggests in a passing explication of dialectic, "only those [things] which are related to one another can be opposed to one another."[10] Shinohara's column resolutely declines to enter into such a relationship, or fails to furnish a conceptual basis for "opposition" between form and structure. The column is just too bluntly *in the way*.

The House in Uehara gives an indication of the forcefulness of Shinohara's critique of both architectural scale and space itself, along with a sense of how strongly he rebuffs what he identifies as the "classical theme" of modernism, "a simple rectilinear relationship between form and function."[11] The provocation of his column and braces may be gauged by what seems, from the perspective of the modernist utilitarianism that pervades both Western and (more ambiguously) postwar Japanese housing design, a gesture so vehemently opposed to either form or function that it is plausible to label it, given the perversity of its sheer inconvenience within such a small home, as altogether "anti-spatial."[12] Shinohara himself refers to the House in Uehara as "a violent structure" and a "savage space," and Yasumitsu Matsunaga suggests that "it stands clearly beyond the limits of any classical definition of normative aesthetics."[13] In brief, bigness inside this house is no *concept*, and *a fortiori* no mere dialectical "opposition" to some other aspect of form. Or rather, bigness emerges as altogether thinglike, an imposition of an excessive materiality upon the human occupant, an intimation of possibly-being-crushed. The big thing *consumes* space—supplants or overfills or even destroys it—this is what we have consistently intended by naming something *too big*.

The idiosyncratic or perverse conflict between thing and space is hardly alleviated by Shinohara's own explanations of his design process. In accounts of the Uehara House, he declines to offer either formal or metaphysical reconciliations between space and occupant, instead insisting on "factual" exigencies that seem wholly to discount human participation:

> Because of a building restriction, the height of the street façade was limited to 5m, but use of a beamless slab enabled the provision of adequate ceiling heights. At the same time, the braces needed for the roof slab created problems in the floor plan, and particularly in the area around the freestanding central post, where a massive 45-degree brace runs directly in between the top of the entrance stairway and the living room.[14]

This ostensibly humble designer-builder's sentiment, which Shinohara also calls "a direct recognition of fact," should not obscure the sheer radicality of the description of architectural practice offered here.[15] His almost doctrinaire rationale treats conditions of engineering and construction—for instance, "the minimum anti-seismic structural regulations in the greater Tokyo region" and the sheer weight of the volume ostensibly needed to cantilever the carport—as though they were fully deterministic causes.[16] In short, despite what seems like a resolute pragmatism, or possibly *because* it seems that way, we ought to treat these proclamations as full-scale theory, even as metaphysics. Virtually in the guise of a transcendental condition, Shinohara blocks the architect's capacity to modify either the specific formal expression of material conditions or the manner in which they interact with tradition, architectural convention, context, or the resident's comfort or convenience. Yet in actual practice, a variety of compromises with site and codes would have been possible at Uehara, and, in terms either of formal expression or of hands-on execution, nothing strictly demands the singular combination of concrete slabs, cantilever, and braces chosen by Shinohara. This house is after all not an apartment in a big city building, and does not require what amounts to high-rise infrastructure, "run[ning] directly between the top of the entrance stairway and the living room," as Shinohara asserts, and imposing throughout the interior of the house a "giant forest-like order."[17] Yet Shinohara makes no effort to finesse the conflict between materiality and space, even underscoring its perversity: "The large braces, thrusting upward directly from the floor, obstruct traffic from the entrance to the second-floor."[18]

In short, the metaphysical ambition of Shinohara's pseudo-pragmatism may be measured by the extent of its arbitrariness. His disingenuously humble deference to "objective" conditions or "facts" ironically casts an aura of inevitability (or what Shinohara blithely calls "the eternal") over what are not merely contingent but decidedly idiosyncratic design choices. Despite the passive tone of his self-descriptions, Shinohara's Uehara House represents a complex and aggressive philosophy of space itself, perhaps a veritable manifesto of architectural antimodernism. Thus, in the folksy tone he tends to employ to express his most radical positions, Shinohara provides explanations that are anathematic within conventional parameters of either a modernist or neoclassical approach to form and function: "I solved the problem of this brace simply by according a detour around it. This should not be regarded as a compromise, but rather a direct recognition of fact."[19] An architect who sets out to "solve the problem" of form by "according a detour around" such an arbitrary and imposing feature has relinquished the designer's role in reconciling structure with inhabitation to a degree tantamount to virtual capitulation. David Stewart goes as far as to describe the "precedence" of "structure over human requirements" in the House in Uehara as "unfamiliar in the architecture of advanced civilizations."[20]

Form does not follow function here, nor even "oppose" it, in Taki's term. Rather, there is a radical disconnection between form and function, and therefore an intractable defiance of synthesis, a methodological stance against the dialectical interplay of structure and everyday life toward which all modernisms, and even most classicisms that precede and ground it—perhaps even the entire Platonic and Aristotelian aesthetic traditions undergirding these architectures—strive. We might more appropriately call Shinohara's ironically modest capitulation to "fact" a deeply perverse *sacrifice* of design practice itself, virtually a Satanic (in the Miltonian sense) refusal to play by the rules of architectural and ergonomic proportionality, even as it evokes *some* traditional Japanese obstructions such as the *nijiriguchi* (crawling door) of a teahouse or the precisely delimited views of a stroll garden.[21] The column, properly speaking, is not *in* the space at all, but rather *amid* or even *through* it, much in the same way the high-rise structural column arbitrarily pierces the volume of the individual apartment, necessitating the "direct recognition of fact" that one lives up in the sky, not down on the ground.

Against Space

I have so far ignored what I believe is the inscrutable beauty of the column in the House in Uehara, a beauty surely connected to its excessive singularity. Such a quality is as difficult to describe critically as it is to give precise conceptual or phenomenological terms for the column's hyperfacticity in the space. A comparison with other Shinohara designs may help. The House Beneath High Voltage Lines (1981) displays a revisionist attitude toward "fact" that parallels Shinohara's statements about Uehara.[22] Interpreting with blithe literalness a building regulation that prohibited construction near high tension cables passing over the site, Shinohara sculpts the massing of the house to conform to the "code-defined envelope" imputed by the law, thereby "unabashedly adopting the multiple circumference of the easement line as the precise contour of the roof."[23] From the exterior, the roof shape thereby acknowledges, in a kind of deadpan parody of Hugh Ferriss, the scale of powerful but indifferent infrastructural forces, carving into negative physical space an otherwise insensible zone of electromagnetism. The result is a "strangely unexpected" form, as one critic laconically describes it; "awkwardly trimmed," in the words of another; even a "large-scale practical joke."[24]

Inside the house, the effect is more dramatic: here, the inverse barrel of the roof encroaches upon the space with all its static bulk and mass. In effect, Shinohara has thrust the entire "deform[ed]" roof, with its literal but inscrutable echo of the city's regulation, directly into an otherwise conventionally dimensioned vestibule and bedroom.[25] Thus, we have a series of embodied contradictions: on the one hand, the massive scale of public utility infrastructure invades the diminutive space of the upstairs of a small house, impinging upon the finite scale of private life, while, on the other hand, the thinnest of infrastructural elements, a high tension cable encircled by an invisible cylinder of electromagnetic energy, produces a

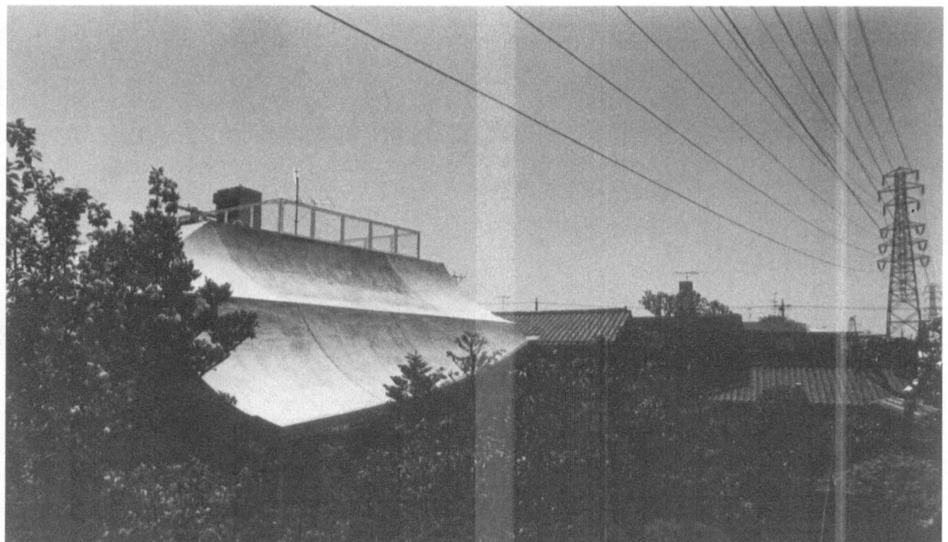

FIGURE 10.4 House Beneath High Voltage Lines, Tokyo, 1981: exterior (Kazuo Shinohara, architect; photo by Tomio Ohashi)

massively solid ceiling, seemingly less overhead than *on* one's head, an impression augmented by the oversized, dark-blue-painted column and rafters supporting it. The result is an exquisitely conflicted response to the "beauty of chaos" of greater Tokyo, a reaction to industrial and commercial modernity that Shinohara describes as "articulated ambivalence-and-coexistence" or as "progressive anarchy."[26]

As at Uehara, any potential dialectical connection between interior and exterior, private and public, urban and domestic, or form and function, remains profoundly inscrutable from inside the building. Matsunaga rightly describes the House Beneath High Voltage Lines as "a work of architecture that resists interpretation" and, in a brief but careful reading, discusses its "*Sachlichkeit*," a "unique quality" creating "an almost erotic sensation" that Matsunaga compares to the ambiguous pleasures indulged by the Marquis de Sade.[27] In a 1961 article titled "Wasted Space," Shinohara had already rejected the architectural commonplace that dimensions and scale should be made "appropriate" to plan or program, dismissing a neoclassical proportionality he perceives as dogma shared by both modernist architects and traditionalists. In 1979, just prior to designing the House Beneath High Voltage Lines, he recalls his earlier position: "I could not abandon the idea that, in houses, the bigger the better," a stance he immediately labels as "anti-rational."[28] Such stark rejection of the "theoretical framework" of Western modernism, the widespread adoption of which coincided with

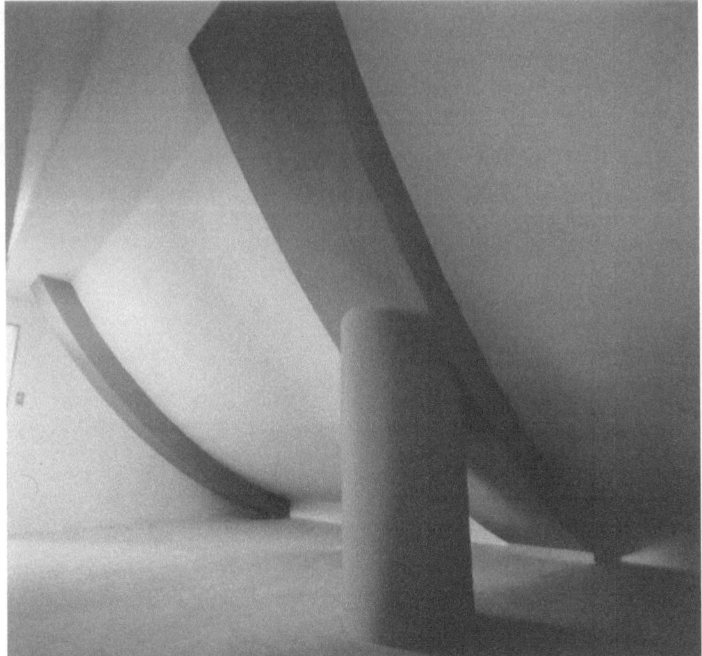

FIGURE 10.5 House Beneath High Voltage Lines, Tokyo, 1981: interior (Kazuo Shinohara, architect; photo by Masao Arai, from *Japan Architect* 293 [September 1981]: 28–29), courtesy of *The Japan Architect*/Shinkenchiku-sha

rapid industrialization and construction in postwar Japan, is attenuated, in Shinohara's characteristically folksy tone, by a half-articulated empathy with the individual resident who is dwarfed by the new scale of the postwar Japanese city. "Instinctively," Shinohara asserts, aligning himself with a populist rather than a theoretical view of metropolitan political economy, "I would be happy to design a residence as grand as Versailles."[29]

Shinohara's ironic preference for grandiose private houses, even stated in this disarmingly modest or personal tone, challenges an emphasis on the *communal* bigness characterizing Japan's most significant postwar architectural movement, Metabolism. In every case, and merely by the exigencies of scale, Metabolist projects, whether of overall city plans or of concatenations of modular building types—and possibly as an inevitable result of the immense scale at which they are drawn and modeled—interpret the private residence, for political as well as aesthetic reasons, strictly as a component of much larger communal structures. For the Metabolists, this incongruity between small and big is a self-consciously dialectical interpretation of the intersecting roles of individual and society, as well as of what Shinohara will later call, explicitly against Metabolism, "the two extreme scales at which any architecture works."[30] In this sense, the constant references to mundane desire or emotion that infuse Shinohara's early prose—"interest"; "want"; "I would be happy to"—merge both uneasily and significantly with the forceful, even strident tone of his manifesto-like advocacy of the idiosyncrasies of private occupation. Looking back a decade after his 1961 "Wasted Space" article, Shinohara perceives the spirit of his designs to be in fundamental conflict with "large general buildings and urban plans," and perceives his call for houses to be "as spacious as possible" as an "exceedingly anti-social proclamation."[31]

Even as early as his 1966 House in White, Shinohara was calling his designs, despite the elegant simplicity of plans and the traditionally "Japanese-looking" materials and fixtures, "a kind of spatial creation based on a criticism of civilization."[32] Hence Taki is now correct to label Shinohara's approach to traditional Japanese architectural elements—"shoji, tatami, posts and beams, and traditional roof shapes"—profoundly "ambivalent," a word that Shinohara himself increasingly employs in the 1970s, and which fruitfully troubles Taki's own too-polite use of "opposition."[33] For the House in White, Shinohara executes a minimalist expression of "the concept of division," which he views both as "the principle of the traditional Japanese floor plan" and as directly opposed to the method of "connection" in European architecture.[34] He calls his approach "one of the simplest plans that could be imagined for a house, an abstract composition resulting from the division of a square by a single straight line."[35] The result is that "more than half its volume [is] occupied by a single large space," exemplifying the "waste" or "superflu[ity]" through which the house both distinguishes itself from and "criticizes" the presiding functionalism of the urban sphere burgeoning around it.[36] In brief, the mere existence of interior space flaunting such profligacy, given the general social utopianism of early 1960s Japanese architectural and urban design, represents an attack on ideals of rationalization, efficiency, and modernization.[37]

But on the surface this is a very quiet design. What is immediately visible in the House in White is a gentle, almost resigned objection to modernization, or else an equally ambivalent nostalgia for a Japanese teahouse tradition now permissible only in fragments or allusions amid the concrete and traffic of modern Tokyo. Everything overt here—the "Japan-ness" of the materials and details, the "wastefulness" of the two divided rooms, the disproportionate height of the ceiling, and finally, the unabashed visibility of the whole interior surface, which Shinohara calls its "frontality" but which might also be described as the design's refusal to articulate either ornamental or structural detail[38]—all these elements compose an exceedingly reserved polemic within a "subtly balanced (Japanese) form,"

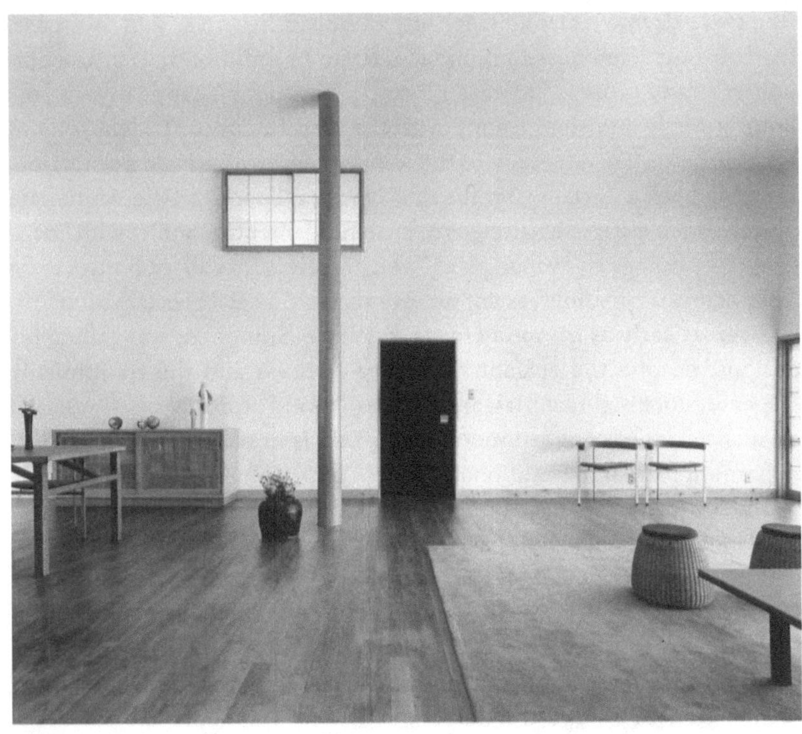

FIGURE 10.6 House in White, Tokyo, 1966: interior (Kazuo Shinohara, architect; photo by Osamu Murai, courtesy of Kumi Murai and Shinohara Archive, Tokyo Tech)

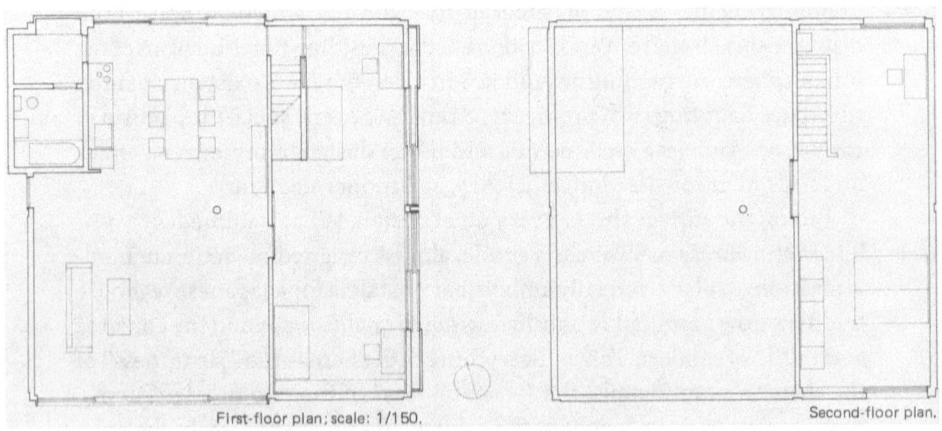

FIGURE 10.7 House in White, Tokyo, 1966: plan (Kazuo Shinohara, architect; photo by Shinohara Laboratory, courtesy of Shinohara Archive, Tokyo Tech)

seemingly far removed from the experimental "fissure" houses and oversized structural provocations Shinohara will soon start to design.[39]

Even in the House in White, however, a species of anti-spatial "*Sachlichkeit*" is imputed. Another central structural column, much thinner and more delicate than the one at Uehara, yet also rising through a seemingly arbitrary section of the space and puncturing the ceiling, introduces a hint of the "savagery" that will become pronounced in later houses.[40] In terms of the overall layout of the house, this column is perfectly centered, supporting a symmetrical peaked roof over the square plan. Performing this role, the column may be an oblique reference to Shinto architecture, echoing the "sacred pole" of well-known shrines such as Ise or Izumo, or the "ridge pole" supporting a peaked roof in the older storehouse designs on which many Shinto shrines are based.[41] But because Shinohara has also divided the floor plan into two unequal rooms, the central column now interrupts the "wasteful" larger space, confronting the interior wall of the room that now contains it in a manner that can rightly be termed arbitrary, even potentially violent. Taki notes that in the House in White, "the theme of opposition was hidden behind the theme of the large space" and that it therefore emerges "more in the section than in the plan."[42] That is to say, "opposition" emerges only when the three-dimensional interior of the house is "opened" to a human occupant who both sees (or can't see past) and encounters (or must circumvent) that column sitting "in the middle of the living room."[43] In the nondialectical terms we are obliged to employ here, we must say that the column is, by virtue of the original gesture of "wastefully" dividing the entire house asymmetrically, *accidentally* placed in the midst of the section, awkwardly out of sync with the circulation pattern implied by the doorway just behind it. In essence, Shinohara has recaptured the iconoclasm of the singular, sacred post in a Shinto shrine, but therefore, along with it, the essentially inhumane nature of the traditional spaces in which such posts are found, spaces that were designed neither to be inhabited nor appreciated primarily by people.

In short, depending on one's theoretical approach, the central column either dialectically reacts against the "superfluous" spacing of the room or simply *gets in the way*, and it is Shinohara's genius to decline to distinguish between these two modes of interference, allowing a residue of design methodology to linger in the guise of a concrete phenomenological effect: an overtly material "anti-symbol" of the inevitable clash between residential smallness and industrial bigness resulting from any effort to make a modern house "as large as possible." In this sense, against all the other ways that the House in White implies a traditionalist, even sentimental avowal of classical "Japanese-looking" aesthetics amid an explosive urban modernity outside, Shinohara's design, particularly in its section, expresses the "criticism of civilization" or the "ambivalence" inherent in his overall approach to modernism. Already, Shinohara is explicitly calling such a design, despite all immediate visual clues in either the plan or the frontal elevation, yet in line with the uneasy phenomenal uncanniness of the section, an "anti-space."[44] And to that point, Shinohara goes as far as to propose that "space has never existed in Japan, only void."[45]

Against Security

The building for which Shinohara is best known, and which most frequently appears in anthologies of architectural modernism, is the Tanikawa House (1974). Here, an interplay between space and column is again enacted with (at most) partial or problematic deference to the inhabitant. The house is located on a sloped, wooded site, and Shinohara declines to grade or finish the floor, so that what remains is the unlevel earth of the hill itself, cutting through the first story and relegating the only finished living area to a second-story loft. In some (but by no means all) ways, the Tanikawa House alludes to the traditional *minka* house with its packed-earth floor, a prototype that Shinohara had already evoked in his House with a Dirt Floor (1963) and House of Earth (1966). However, in his descriptions of the design process for Tanikawa, Shinohara eschews both traditional and revisionist terms, employing only another deceptively modest avowal of "fact": "In the case of this house, it is a simple matter of having the slope of the gently undulating land enter the house on one side and emerge on the other; but, because of this incline, the interior of the house alters considerably."[46] The resulting effect is what Shinohara calls, with evident gratification, "insecurity," a term borrowed from the account of a visitor: "A poet who visited the house spoke of the insecurity he felt in walking over the soft black soil. But it may be this very feeling of insecurity that keeps people walking."[47] Expanding upon the quirk of using "insecurity" as a compliment for domestic design, Shinohara employs a variety of odd figures to describe his "anti-space": "naked space," "Black Space," "dry Black Space," or, in his paraphrase of Gilles Deleuze's book on Proust, a "space machine."

Making inhabitants or visitors feel insecure is by no means a typical goal of residential architecture. As Shinohara says, "most people—I among them—believe that floors ought to be level," and therefore "the encounter between this slope and the artificially created space covering it produces a single architectural fact," a kind of parti pris.[48] But now we must return, as so often in Shinohara's designs, to the columns, which in the Tanikawa House seem relatively modest alongside the singular, even outrageous,

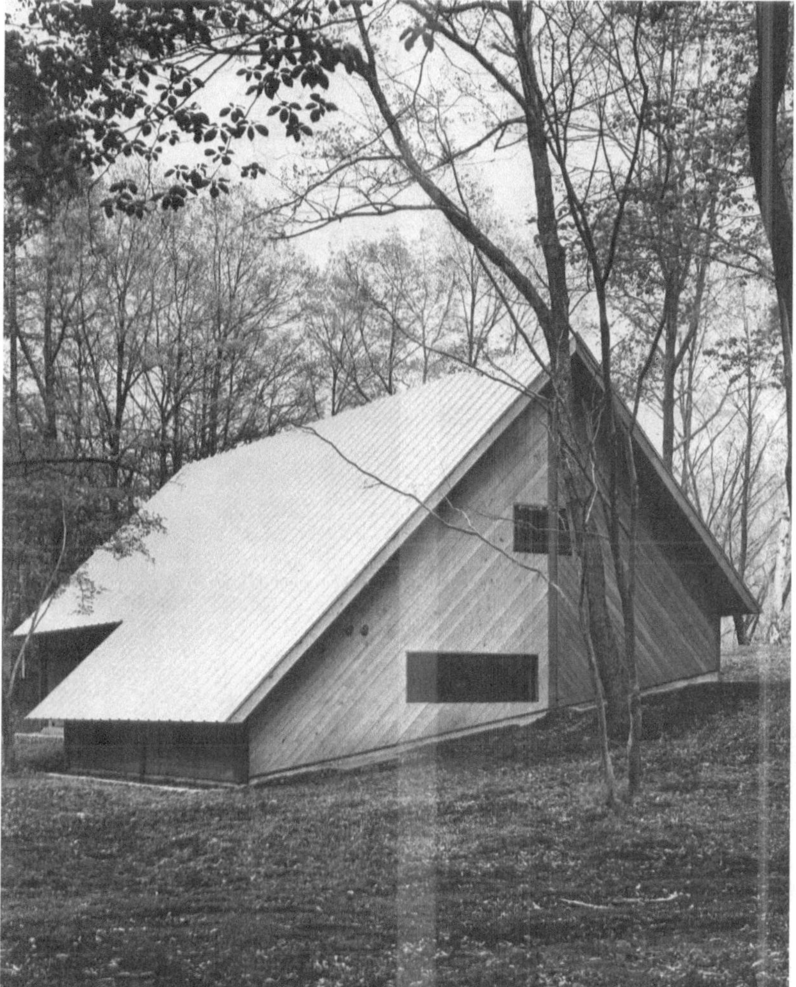

FIGURE 10.8 Tanikawa House, Nagano Prefecture, Japan, 1972: exterior (Kazuo Shinohara, architect; photo by Koji Taki, from *Japan Architect* 228 [vol. 51.2; February 1976]: 56)

gesture of the inclined dirt floor, but which nonetheless exhibit an anti-spatial polemic similar to that observed in the House in White, and which will be expressed more bluntly at Uehara and in other later designs.

In the interior photographs accompanying the essay "When Naked Space Is Traversed," Shinohara's introduction to the Tanikawa House, all the shots except one consist of somewhat claustrophobic views of people walking through the network of articulated columns that suspend the roof over the "naked" sloped floor. This is an uncharacteristic selection of photographs for Shinohara, who nearly always requires his buildings to be shot

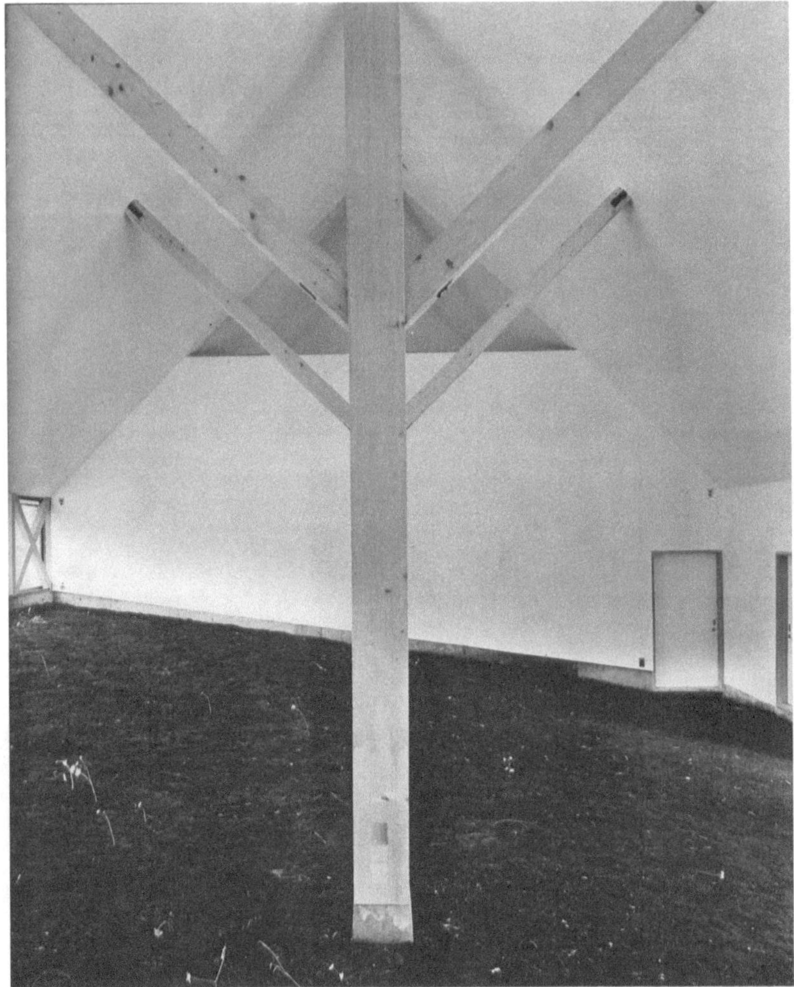

FIGURE 10.9 Tanikawa House, Nagano Prefecture, 1972: interior (Kazuo Shinohara, architect; photo by Masao Arai, from *Japan Architect* 228 [vol. 51.2; February 1976]: 57), courtesy of *The Japan Architect*/Shinkenchiku-sha

from carefully framed and static medium-distance perspectives, devoid of either people or movement. As the essay's title suggests, "traversal" is the phenomenon these photographs intend to depict, but the "insecurity" implied by both movement and the congestion it creates is enhanced by the interference of the columns, which penetrate the frames of the photos at multiple and seemingly arbitrary points. In stark contrast to later, more typical documentation of the Tanikawa House, not one of these original photographs shows the whole span of the interior either horizontally or

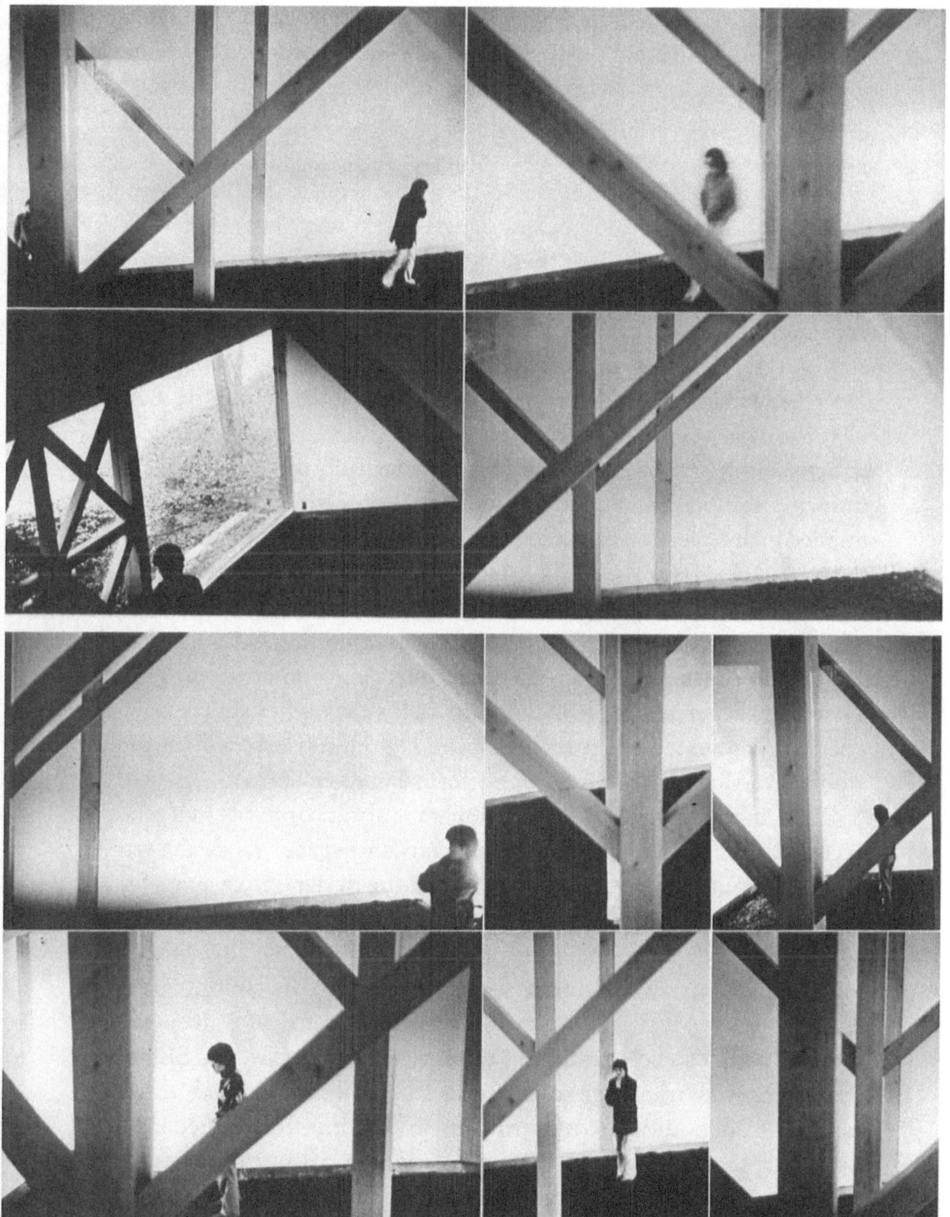

FIGURE 10.10 Tanikawa House, Nagano Prefecture, 1972: "traversal" (Kazuo Shinohara, architect; photos by Koji Taki and Shinohara Laboratory, courtesy of Shinohara Archive, Tokyo Tech)

vertically. The effect is something like a distorted evocation of a Japanese stroll garden, which famously restricts its views in order to modulate an unfolding excursion through them: the columns are intrusive, partial, and generally inexplicable, obstructing the viewer's eye and the paths of the proxy figures who cross both the room and the photographic frame.[49]

Shinohara's explanation is characteristically laconic: "The verticals of the posts and the forty-five degrees [*sic*] angles of the angle braces characterize this manmade space."[50] That these posts and braces play a more determinate role than just "characteriz[ing]" is indicated by Shinohara's typically cryptic rejection of a principle he considers central to traditional Japanese architecture, as well as to his own earlier work, "frontality": "I believe that, in a wooden house, for the first time consciously, I have given the diagonal view the same status as the frontal one."[51] The interference of architectural structure with form, initially set up as the incongruity of a "manmade" structure atop the "naked" sloped ground, but sustained by the impossibility, implied in the selection of photographs, of complete views or paths through the room, subverts any static "frontal" composure the building might otherwise achieve. The resulting "insecurity" is tantamount to the introduction of actual human bodies into a regular geometric volume, bodies that, by their nature, decline to adhere to orthogonal circulation patterns imputed by rectilinear grids or plans. Shinohara calls such bodies simply the "first person," represented by figures who move, shift, and even blur in the photos while traversing the building's highly formal mise-en-scène.

Thus, in a very strict sense, Shinohara is again correct to call what he accomplishes in the Tanikawa House an "anti-space," since the frontal view that could have potentially gathered the design into a single image is instead dissolved into "a collection of cross sections," like those that compose a walk across a city, as one inevitably stops or slows for crossings, traffic lights, stoops, other pedestrians, and so on, continually modulating one's movements to accommodate the "facts" of a given route.[52] Indeed, with a sociological bent reminiscent of de Certeau, Shinohara characterizes his transition from "frontality" to "diagonals" and "traversal" as a shift from tradition to *modernity itself*, as well as from reified image to dynamic process—a polemically cosmopolitan critique of the very sort of historicist sentiment or traditionalism frequently attributed to him by architectural historians:

> Obviously the encounter with the architectural treasures of the deep and extensive culture of Japan gives me great pleasure. But it cannot compare with the pleasure of crossing an everyday street in a large city.

> The street of a modern city clearly expresses the cultural level of the nation in which the city is located.[53]

Crucially, such cosmopolitanism is available only to the "first person" who *moves* through a space or city, never to a third person merely observing the city's static tableau, for instance, from atop a skyscraper or surveying a map. The "encounter" with culture is both a multiplied perspective ("a collection of cross sections") and a temporal succession of meetings with physical objects that inhibit, delay, and only eventually tolerate both view and movement.

At exactly this point in the essay, while still considering an anti-frontal "first person" engagement with the interior of the Tanikawa House, Shinohara abruptly turns his attention back to his earlier House in White, reevaluating its subtle self-subversion in a new light: "The single cypress log in the middle of the living room as in the House in White . . . has a meaning that surpasses its structural importance: it has the responsibility of giving meaning to the space."[54] In this (again) deceptively simple statement, Shinohara emphasizes the material properties of the thing in space alongside its formal singularity, and asserts what neither he nor any of his critics up to that point had yet said about his architectural practice: even despite the "Japanese-looking" aesthetics and resolutely symmetrical configuration of the House in White, it is only the big *thing*—redescribed by Shinohara in precise material terms rather than formal or structural ones, a "cypress log" in lieu of post or column—that "gives meaning" to the architecture:

> Nor was the design made with dynamics first and spatial meaning second in my mind. On the contrary, spatial meaning had precedence in my thinking, and the single post might be said to be the whole space.[55]

Quite right: the column, the most thinglike, nonspatial object in the house, *is* the space, or more precisely, is the "anti-space." Confirming the formal emptiness of the room precisely by intruding into it, obstructing both view and circulation, however mildly, the column imposes a severe limit upon any conceptualization of the house in terms of its abstract division of space, and in essence reveals a fundamental conflict between plan and section, which is also to say, between program and use, and between concept and experience, all discrepancies with which Shinohara feels entirely at ease: "I always observe the world around me in this kind of strong and distinctive polarization."[56]

The House Is Bigger Than the City

Returning to the House in Uehara, we may now better observe the too-big column as an especially bold assertion of the noncompliance of architectural registers in the midst of real space: a blunt interference of structure with both form and human circulation, and therefore far more visible in section than in either plan or exterior elevation. Indeed, much too visible: the room is congested with a material thing interloping, as it were, from the scale of the city.[57] While the home certainly appears all the smaller for this intrusion, in another sense the bigness of modernity itself may never be more present inside a modern house than here. The column at Uehara is like a remnant of the monumental systems of industrial and commercial environments crossing the threshold of the (premodern) domestic sphere. It is somewhat as though the massive post of some fantastical Metabolist megastructure had punctured the individual domicile, inscrutably protruding through the floor and confronting the (perhaps) obsolete privacy of the home with material-structural "facts" of urban planning and macroeconomics, the final postindustrial-age extrapolation of a "single cypress log" interfering with an otherwise well-proportioned "Japanese-looking" room. Indeed, it is plausible to read Shinohara's columns as a conjecture about what might happen inside a given residential unit of a Metabolist megastructure, were one ever built. Nearly all such utopian projects, by virtue of the immense scale at which they must be conceived, as well as the deliberate vagueness with which habitation is left free to evolve, tend to omit the actual drawing or modeling of specific residential units. In this light, Shinohara's designs may be a dystopian romance about Metabolist consequences. His houses seem to ask, where and how, very precisely and concretely, does an infrastructure intended to house thousands or millions of people penetrate the space of a single home? Precisely how imminent *is* the transformation or obliteration of individual space and life in modernity, even as we continue to live in it or with it?

Throughout the 1970s, Shinohara seeks a vocabulary, both architectural and verbal, for the fundamental noncompliance of the material thing in space. He sometimes calls his design approach "irrational" or a process of "eliminat[ing] . . . meanings" from space.[58] In his 1980s writings, he speaks of the aim of the design process as a "set of parts with zero meaning," or a kind of pure mechanism, possibly analogous to the "thoughtless" or "automatic" process of skyscraper design perceived by both advocates and critics of modernism from Sullivan to Koolhaas:

> Since what I call my second style, I have used various adjectives to describe the points I have passed: neutral, inorganic, naked, and so

> on. Tangents drawn through these points all meet in the domain of the machine.[59]

The use of "machine" as architectural method resembles (although Shinohara never states it this way except obliquely, by citing Deleuze) the radical demystification undertaken by both Marxist and psychoanalytic critique, in which conceptual meanings and metaphors are distilled back into strictly metonymical assemblages of their material parts. It is quite deliberately unlike the approach of Le Corbusier, who famously described the house as a "machine for living in":[60]

> If symbolic meanings remain, they are stripped away. Parallel with this, a check operation is performed to halt all movement in the direction of conceptual assembly. I call a machine a physical system in which objects are simply joined together in a "sachlich" manner.[61]

In the House in Uehara, the *Sachlichkeit* of the too-big column merges into Shinohara's ongoing struggle against the symbolic tendencies of space or its reduction to concept or dialectic—in a word, its frontal or photographic quality. The interference of the big "thinglike" (*sachlich*) object—anti-spatial, anti-metaphysical, hyperfactical—therefore again emerges only in section rather than plan or elevation, which is to say, in movement and penetration rather than in stasis or viewpoint. Or in other words, the object emerges only temporally, in the necessarily multiplied, fragmented, perspectival gestures and impediments of the actual practice of living, rather than in synthetic images like plans and photos: a "zero degree machine" operating with the complexity or chaos of modern life itself, like the walk across the city that Shinohara compares, with "intense excitement," to the "insecurity" of the Tanikawa House.[62]

Likewise, rejecting the hyperurbanist ambitions of the Metabolists, who necessarily work at too large a scale to intervene directly in everyday life and praxis, Shinohara insists on the importance of the single street.[63] Especially when *crossed*—that is, when traversed in discrete sections—the street "instantaneously reveals a crystallization of the distinctive culture and history of the nation in which the city is located."[64] Against the lavish "techno-rationalis[t]" anthropology of Metabolism, Shinohara retrenches himself as a sort of empiricist ethnographer, charting the vicissitudes of phenomenal movement.[65] The bigness of the city thus belongs to an immediate, concrete materiality confronting the individual pedestrian rather than to any cartographical overview. At the scale of the human body, bigness is the wholly nonsymbolic obstacle, the sheer thing-in-the-way.

But among the miscellany of modern buildings, only the *house* exists on this scale, and it is therefore the house that remains our primary encounter with both architecture and urbanism. The single house on the single street is the first site of modernistic conflict, where the pathos of the interpenetration of public and private, of infrastructural and domestic, of planning and experience, continually recurs. Only at this lived scale are "naked realities . . . available for encounters"; beyond it exists only abstraction, hence, in experiential terms, only "confusion," "disorder," "turbulence," and "chaos."[66] For Shinohara, the house is therefore also the maximal architectural unit capable of expressing *tradition*, even where it subverts or destroys it.

In short, the bigness of the modern city happens first and foremost in the *interior* of the home. That is because bigness does not consist in either space or concept; the column in a Shinohara house is never a symbol or metaphor, but always the city's real metonymy. The prime attribute of bigness is literal, hyperfactical intrusion, interruption, interjection: a post or column rising up through the floor and vanishing inexplicably into the ceiling; an oversized diagonal brace blocking circulation through a room or views out a window; the *wrong* material disrupting the "Japan-ness" of a domicile; the ineluctable heaviness of concrete instead of wood, screen, or void. In short, the bigness of architecture is the unavoidably dense and figurally opaque quality of a *thing* where there ought instead to have been *form*.

✷ 11 ✷

Perception and Illusion

Bigness Before Size

In assembling elements for an aesthetics of magnitude, I offered the following two postulates, extracted from analyses of the experience of big things: *What is big is too big; What is big is small.* The usefulness of such postulates presumably lies as much in their revealing incongruity as in any correct claim they make about objects or images. In their mutual incompatibility, they imply that, in some essential way, bigness fails to *be*, or that the big thing contravenes or negates its own undue magnitude, appearing altogether too much or too little to be quite itself. In turn, this combination of failures indexes the nonconscious, immeasurable, or unscalable registers upon which any metaphysical configuration of bigness must be sought. Bigness is an ontological impropriety, and magnitude more generally a metaphysical enigma, too great or too small to correspond to its own concept.

However, at the risk of a graceless obviousness—which may nevertheless be part and parcel of the theoretical embarrassment into which the problem of magnitude continually thrusts philosophers and theorists—I must recall that we are speaking here of what is *big*, and therefore of what is (tautologically) *obvious*. Any pursuit of theoretical obscurity or metaphysical inscrutability must pull up short at the disconcertingly blunt fact that big things overween; that what is big is more present than anything else. The metaphysics of bigness inevitably discovers an all-too-physical superfluity, uncouthly profligate, ontic, fulsome, always (more) undeniably *there*. The big thing's strange failure to *be* transpires—with profound irony—only through a gratuitous overachievement in being. Here then is the logical kernel of what I earlier analyzed as the antinomy of bigness.

I have presented the consequences of this antinomy in a number of ways: as the ambivalent "taxidermic" repression of the hyperfactical density or violence of the big thing within the visible image; as the unsublime wrongness of narratives or depictions of bigness, for instance, in accounts of atomic bomb blasts or in bodies enlarged by cinematic special effects; as conflicting demands of the relative and the absolute in everyday estimations of object size; as a euphemistic suppression of the erotic cathexis of bigness in the language of proportion and scale, for instance, in Swift's ironically prudish macrophilia; as the paroxysm of such infantile cathexes in racist fantasies of the outsized "super-predator"; as the making-small of urban bigness through the cartographical vision furnished by the skyscraper; as a compensatory violence revisited upon the image of bigness in the monadism of the cinematic "expenditure spectacle"; or as the simultaneous irruption and repression of the bigness of modernist infrastructure in the house. To conclude the book, I will turn to a final few examples to consider the overweening obviousness of bigness alongside its equivocal ontology, and in turn try to indicate what might remain unsettled, perhaps permanently, in any aesthetics of magnitude. Ultimately, I would like the examples to help reconfirm the claim I made earlier about magnitudes, that *bigness comes before size.*

Moon Illusion

"When the moon hangs low over the horizon, it looks much bigger than when it is high in the sky."[1] This apparent difference in size, usually referred to as the "celestial illusion" or "moon illusion," is discoverable in many (perhaps all) cultures, in children as well as adults, and under a variety of geographical and environmental circumstances.[2] As the behavioral physiologist James Enright suggests, the moon illusion "is probably the best known and most frequently discussed of all optical illusions, since it occurs in a natural setting, and represents a compelling, large-magnitude distortion of reality."[3] I intend to offer no new explanation for the illusion, but I wish to consider how its strange persuasiveness might prompt us to reconsider broader physiological, psychological, and metaphysical questions about size.

In an essay in 1687, the Irish natural philosopher William Molyneux gives a concise account of the illusion, employing the angular notation that astronomers conventionally use to measure the size of celestial objects: "it is well known that the mean apparent Magnitude of the Moon is 30 *m.* 30 *s.*[;] we will take it *Numero Rotundo* to be 30, that is, an Arch of a great Circle in the Heavens of 30 Minutes is covered by her Diameter."[4] Molyneux then offers a lay equivalent: the thirty minutes of arc covered by the full moon, when observed by the naked eye at the zenith of the meridian—that is, at the highest point in the sky—corresponds to a diameter of "about a Foot broad." He continues: "But the same Moon being looked upon just as she rises, she appears to be three or four Foot broad, and yet if with an Instrument we take her Diameter, both in one Posture and t'other, we shall find that still she shall be but 30 Minutes."[5] It is worth observing, as Molyneux himself does, the startling extent of this discrepancy: the moon at the horizon can appear to be several times its usual diameter, and Molyneux later comments that, on some occasions the moon has "look'd ten times more large in Diameter than ordinary."[6] Such extreme variance contributes to an enduring belief, among philosophers and astronomers as well as lay stargazers, that the moon illusion must have a physical rather than merely perceptual or psychological cause. Indeed, the illusion is so convincing that not until the eleventh century, in the *Optics* of the Arabic writer Ibn al-Ḥaytham, was it even contemplated as a strictly nonmaterial phenomenon.[7] This is despite the fact that any observer with a simple measuring device can easily confirm that the disk of the moon is *not* actually bigger—or, in more precise terms, that the arc it covers in the meridian does not actually subtend a greater angle—"when nigh the Horizon [than] when Higher elevated."[8]

Prior to Ibn al-Haytham, the moon illusion was frequently attributed to atmospheric refraction, as in Ptolemy's description of celestial objects: "the apparent increase in their sizes at the horizons is caused . . . by the exhalations of moisture surrounding the earth being interposed between the place from which we observe and the heavenly bodies, just as objects placed in water appear bigger than they are, and the lower they sink, the bigger they appear."[9] By the time Molyneux was writing in the seventeenth century, refraction theories such as Ptolemy's had been discredited, although their remnants persist well past the eighteenth century and even to the present day (as I can confirm by way of personal conversations), likely because, again, the illusion's potency tends to bias observers toward physical explanations.[10] Even in 1709, George Berkeley, although he has no truck with refraction and is well acquainted with Molyneux and other theorists of the illusion, still claims that the "far greater quantity of atmosphere" lying "between the eye and the moon, when situated at the horizon" effectively renders the moon "less strong and vivid" and therefore "bigger," a connection that we learn to draw through prior empirical observations: "faintness of appearance caused in this sort has been experienced to coexist with great magnitude."[11] Berkeley's account belongs to a subspecies of what Cornelis Plug and Helen Ross term an "aerial perspective" explanation, which is one among a wide range of models offered through several millennia of efforts to account for the illusion.[12] In fact, although theories of the moon illusion still proliferate in diverse disciplines, no conclusive interpretation, or even a consensus about the proper method for analyzing it, has ever emerged.[13] The amateur stargazer may be surprised to discover that the moon is not in fact bigger when closer to the horizon, but he or she may be even more astonished to learn that, after "so many Authors should rack their Brains for solving an Appearance," to this day neither philosophers, astronomers, nor psychologists can agree about the cause of that appearance.[14]

The moon illusion is an instance, albeit an especially intractable one, of a larger problem in both philosophy and the sciences of determining the relationship between size and distance. In turn, the size-distance problem indicates a quandary in the more general relationship between sensory data and objective attributes, a relationship at or near the core of all metaphysical inquiry. When expressed in strictly geometrical terms, the size-distance problem seems easy enough to solve. Euclid, in his treatise on optics, tells us "that those things seen within a larger angle appear larger, and those seen within a smaller angle appear smaller, and those seen within equal angles appear to be of the same size."[15] This being the case,

> Let AB and GD be equal magnitudes. Let them be unequally distant from the eye, E. Let AB be closer [to the eye than GD]. I say that AB will appear larger [than GD].[16]

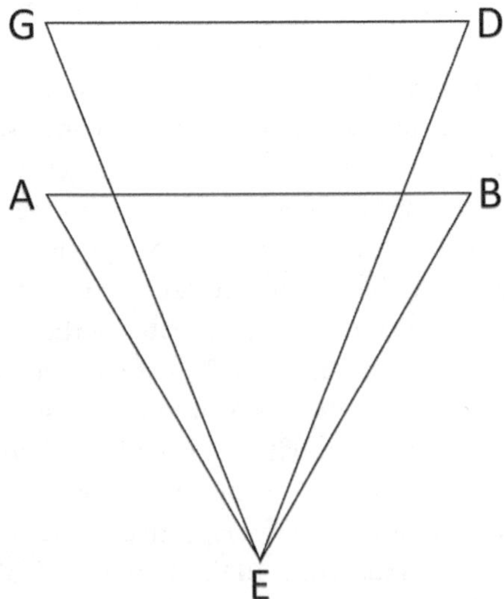

Euclid's description seems to agree with our intuitive sense of what happens when same-sized things are perceived at different distances, and therefore provides a mathematical basis for what is referred to by both psychologists and optical theorists as the "size-distance invariance hypothesis" (SDIH). The SDIH states that perceived size is inversely proportional to distance, so that the ratio of the object's magnitude to its distance from the perceiver remains constant.[17] A simplified version, employing the term "visual angle" to describe magnitude in the same manner as Molyneux and other optical theorists, is as follows:[18]

$$\text{Visual angle } (\alpha) = \frac{\text{apparent size (S)}}{\text{apparent distance (D)}}$$

For example, if a horse of height S, seen at a distance D, appears to subtend an angle of α, then as we approach the horse, the subtended angle will increase proportionally as our distance from the animal decreases. Likewise, the size of the horse (or its subtended angle) will decrease proportionally as we move away. The SDIH seems necessary if, "under normal conditions of perception," we are able to know that the *same* horse remains present despite the continual variation of its size as we (or it) move about the world.[19] Kilpatrick and Ittelson label this faith in the reliability of objective size "invariance behavior," and it belongs to the general collection of behavioral phenomena that psychologists call "subjective constancy."[20] The moon illusion, depending on how one theorizes it, would be either a "paradox" (from any perspective employing the SDIH to explain size constancy) or an exceptional case of how an SDIH—not merely in theory but in everyday perceptions of all sorts—might lead us astray.[21] Either way, such an intractable illusion indicates a potential crisis in the SDIH and, far more significantly, a crisis in the principle of size constancy itself, the epistemological underpinnings of which we are now prompted to question.

We can proceed first at a simple logical level, drawing on the Euclidean model we have outlined. The sticking point for the SDIH, and in general for any geometrical account of size constancy, lies in determining exactly how a perceiver identifies S or D in the first place, since it seems we can only reckon the distance of a particular object by knowing something about its size, yet only properly reckon that size by already having some idea of how far away it is. The SDIH can give at best a blank description of a successful (albeit elemental) aesthetics of magnitude, but it must rely on what looks like a circular argument when it tries to explain our initial perceptions of either of its variables. Thus, writers responding to Euclid or the other geometrical optical theorists nearly always begin by insisting on mental resources over and above mere observation or intuition: "The size of the angle under which an object is seen," Pecham writes, "does not suffice for the apprehension of its size"; Roger Bacon agrees that "certification of the magnitude of an object cannot depend on the size of the angle [alone]," and Desaguliers argues "that although visual resolution was dependent on visual angle, visual size was not."[22] In more recent work, Baird suggests that the geometrical approach to perception "was never satisfactory when confronted with empirical results."[23] In short, it appears that if we don't start out already familiar with the typical magnitude of, say, horses or similar animals, we are in no way able to gauge the distance of one particular horse, and therefore we lack any basis for assessing its "constant" size after the fact. The result, in "geometrical" judgments of size, even when ostensibly correct, is not categorically different than if we were simply to make an error, for instance, if we mistook the horse for a small pony or if we believed it to be an overscaled statue, as happened to me once in New York's Central Park.

Pursuing the implications of the logic that seems to underlie perceptions of constancy, it seems that we must, when perceiving a certain-sized object at a certain location, be interpreting multiple registers of sensory data rather than directly intuiting the thing's magnitude based on either its subtended angle or its apparent distance, performing spontaneous calculations that permit us to correlate its recognizable size and distance with some familiar schema or prototype. Thus, in Ibn al-Haytham's influential terms, "The magnitude of objects . . . is perceived only by judgment and inference"; or, as Roger Bacon reiterates the point, magnitude is "grasped by means of syllogism."[24] In brief, the SDIH can be neither a feature of the environment nor a transcendental condition of perception, but seemingly must belong to a complex set of phenomenological relations we discover how to intuit over time, and helpful to us only to the degree we are already acquainted with the specific magnitudes we are called upon to judge. As Hermann von Helmholtz writes in his canonical nineteenth-century treatise: "this relation between distance and size is something that can only be acquired by long experience, and so it is not surprising that children are not very proficient at it and are apt to make big mistakes."[25] However, even conceding the a posteriori nature of any reckoning of size and distance, the mechanism by which the two perceptual variables connect remains inscrutable, as does the general means of any "syllogistic" interpretation of constancy. The problem emerges even in very basic descriptions of the process. For instance, Pecham proposes that "the faculty that apprehends size [*quantitates*] considers the magnitude of the distance [*longitudinem distantie*]": here, a magnitude (size) is said to be determined by way of another magnitude (distance), a circular argument that leaves bluntly unaddressed the more general, yet nonetheless more basic and essential, question of how *any* magnitudes are comprehended at all.[26] Pecham's resignation is more than usually explicit, but it is far from uncommon. One observes a certain defeatist tone throughout the cognitive-psychological literature: "the facts of space discrimination are still poorly understood"; "there is little agreement on a general theory of visual space perception"; "many critical questions remain unanswered"; "discrepancies in experimental procedure"; "conflicting results"; "uncritical mixture of physical and psychological variables"; "unbalanced"; "very unsatisfying"; "not very satisfactory"; "the inadequacy of our knowledge for a final decision is quite apparent."[27]

Man in the Street

In response to such perpetual frustration, as well as to the epistemological conundrum at its core, Gestalt psychologists and phenomenologists immediately repudiate principles of constancy, thereby sidestepping any model of perception organized around the SDIH. The foundational Gestalt texts begin by rejecting what Bruno Petermann calls "the 'atomistic' psychology" that "tried to conceive the reality of psychic life as built up of Sensations and Feelings, of conscious elements."[28] The difficulty was always conceptualizing, as Petermann says, "how it is possible for a whole to arise out of the elements," a problem that directs Gestalt psychology's criticism, especially the standard "Wertheimer-Koffka-Köhler theory," toward the largest Western-metaphysical questions about how substantial objects are synthesized (if that is the correct term) out of the miscellany of sensible data and attributes.[29]

Gestalt theorists set out like this: both a constancy hypothesis (objective perceptions correspond to specific sensory stimuli) and a "bundle hypothesis" (objective perceptions are compiled from bundles of distinct sensations) entail a basic empiricism dividing experience dualistically into sensations and judgments—the latter are deemed accurate or not with respect to the former.[30] An optical illusion would be an obvious case of an error in judgment, in other words, a failure to properly collate the terms on either side of a dualism, or to properly grasp the "isomorphic" constancy of observed objects. But in some sense, on such an empiricist model, *all* perception is "illusory," a miscellany of ambiguous stimuli reducible or correctible according to observations that presume (fairly enough, albeit mysteriously) a constancy in the physical world and an "isomorphic" consistency over time.[31] Köhler asks us, not so much to discard this fairly natural-sounding epistemology, but rather to consider the conceptual baggage that accompanies its acceptance.[32] He offers the following illustration, which is sufficiently common in philosophical discussions of size and distance to perhaps be called canonical:

> Suppose, while standing at a street corner, we see a man approaching us. Now he is ten yards away, and presently five. What are we to say about his size at the two distances? We shall be inclined to say that at both distances his visual size was approximately the same. But such a statement, we are told, is utterly inacceptable. A simple consideration in geometrical optics shows that during the man's approach his visual height must have doubled, and the same holds for his width. His total size must therefore have become four times the area which it was at ten yards. . . .
>
> If all observations of this kind are illusions which deceive us not only as to the nature of given physical conditions, but also about our own sensory data, then some powerful factor must be at work which obscures these data.[33]

If such an exercise in "geometrical optics" implies that "all observations of this kind are illusions," to be corrected by a judgment that adjusts the sense data to yield a unified object, then, as Köhler ironically suggests, what would necessarily obscure variations in the data—"the distorting influence," Köhler calls it—"can only be *learning*."[34] Köhler names such a pseudo-synthetic model, in which perceptions get rescaled in order to reveal the invariant object, a "machine theory" of perception, perhaps analogous to Descartes's somewhat infamous "mechanical" interpretation of organic functions, in which the apparatus of our perception separates out, more or less successfully, the variations by which the subject distorts the "real" object. Here is a "syllogistic" perception in sum, still described in Köhler's ironic voice:

> Day after day, since early childhood, we have found that when we approach a distant object it proves to be much bigger than it seemed to be from a greater distance. . . . Such observations have been repeated so many times, and we have so fully learned what the real sizes, the real shapes and the real brightnesses are in each case, that gradually we have become unable to distinguish between our acquired knowledge and actual sensory facts. As a result, we now seem to *see* the constant real characteristics while the sensory facts as such which, of course, depend upon distance, orientation and illumination, are no longer recognizable.[35]

Thus we are supposed to have figured out, through long practice of "unnoticed" reduction and filtering, how to perceive the man approaching or retreating on the street as the *same* man, just as we figure out how to see the newspaper on the table under flickering sunlight as the same newspaper, and the table itself, seen here or from across the room, as the same table. "Clearly," Köhler says dryly, "this is just what we have to expect if such constancies spring from our knowledge of the physical situation, in other words, if they develop in some form of learning."[36]

Gestalt psychology replaces this "empiristic" model and its underlying "machine picture" of perception with what is now very familiar in the psychological literature, a "unitary process" in which "the organism responds to the pattern of stimuli to which it is exposed"; in turn, emergence replaces synthesis as an etiology of objects, and a holistic "world" replaces syllogism or learning as a mechanism.[37] Any situation arising subsequent to the emergence of objects in our environments—say, an ambiguity or illusion in which sensation and object must be distinguished so as to be re-collated, whether accurately or in error—is not only an exception, in pragmatic terms, but for any metaphysical exposition it represents an untenable "isolation of local facts."[38] In short, the "unitary whole" comes first, and only then the sensation and the individual object we judge (or learn to judge) as constant. The size of the man on the street, like the color of the clothes he is wearing, the degree of shadow obscuring his face, or the breed of dog walking beside him, is always already given (with)in the whole, and never, at least in its primary appearance, as an "atomistic" attribute detachable from its environs.

Merleau-Ponty later invokes the same example as Köhler, and for similar theoretical purposes:

> Is not a man *smaller* at two hundred yards than at five yards away? He becomes so if I isolate him from the perceived context and measure his apparent size. Otherwise he is neither smaller nor indeed equal in size: he is anterior to equality and inequality; he is *the same man seen from farther away.*[39]

The man, like all the objects in my (usual) perceptual environs, belongs to "a world of undistortable objects" in which I am "already involved," and in this sense the man is indistinguishable from any other object in its spatial context.[40] Thus, to compare an even more mundane example, Merleau-Ponty notes that "the apparent size of the perceived ash-tray is not a measurable size" until I specifically set out to quantify it: "by breaking up the perceptual field and isolating the ash-tray, by positing it for itself, I have caused size to appear where hitherto it had no place."[41] Similarly, "the apparent size of the table, the piano and the wall" or the "car [that] slowly climbs up towards the horizon, all the while decreasing in size," first belong to a "primordial" depth:

> More directly than the other dimensions of space, depth forces us to reject the preconceived notion of the world and rediscover the primordial experience from which it springs: it is, so to speak, the most "existential" of all dimensions, because (and here Berkeley's argument is right) it is not impressed upon the object itself, it quite clearly belongs to the perspective and not to things. Therefore it cannot either be extracted from, or even put into that perspective by consciousness. It announces a certain indissoluble link between things and myself by which I am placed in front of them.[42]

In short, apparent size and apparent distance are indissoluble "moments of a comprehensive organization of the field" we call depth, and "cannot be given as elements in a system of objective relationships."[43] To describe them, Merleau-Ponty instead employs terms radically different from the "atomistic" vocabulary of either empiricism or geometry: "they are present in the experience of depth in the way that a *motive*, even when it is not articulate and separately posited, is present in a decision."[44] We can then observe Merleau-Ponty employing these very terms to describe the moon illusion, which is now reconceived independent of (or more precisely, prior to) any question of an SDIH: "When I look quite freely and naturally, the various parts of the field interact and *motivate* this enormous moon on the horizon, this measureless size which nevertheless is a size."[45]

With such language of "total perception," Merleau-Ponty goes even farther than the Gestalt psychologists in repudiating constancy hypotheses; indeed, at a number of points he directly criticizes Köhler and Koffka for retaining an empiricist faith in the objectivity of size—essentially, an objectively based standard of judgment and correction—rather than fully elucidating the "flow of experiences" that characterizes the "natural attitude" under which perception normally takes place.[46]

Yet Merleau-Ponty himself retains a residue of an empiricism that ironically tends to flatten the perceptual world into something approaching a geometrical array of objects. We may detect that residue if we look again at the language with which Merleau-Ponty describes the objects he selects, perhaps directing some disconcertingly simple questions toward his account. The man on the road, as Merleau-Ponty writes, directly invoking and refuting Euclid's geometrical terminology, "is neither smaller nor indeed equal in size; he is anterior to equality and inequality." Indeed, the man on the road is entirely a part of the situation of "the road itself," a situation in which I am entirely "engrossed."[47] In this sense, the man belongs to the road in the same way the ashtray belongs to the table, or the table to the room, along with the wall and the piano—they are separable only when, for whatever ulterior reasons, I explicitly set out to measure them against each other. But *is* a man in fact like an ashtray or table or piano? Or to ask this even more bluntly, *is* the man on the road "*the same man*" after he has approached us, just like the ashtray is the same ashtray after I walk over and view it up close?

In geometrical terms—the Euclidian ones Merleau-Ponty so casually borrows and discards—clearly these objects are "the same," provided we retain even a minimal confidence in the effects, if not necessarily the exact etiology, of constancy. But it was precisely *not* an a posteriori geometrical judgment of who or what this object is that we have set out to parse—we must know *how* the man is the "same size" in advance, within an indissoluble "world of undistortable objects."[48] Yet I can no more presume, in advance, that the man is the *same* man than I can presume that this very big moon on the horizon is the same moon, unless I have already decided (via geometrical calculation? syllogism? learning?) that their variation in size is contingent or illusory, the very species of conclusion by way of a constancy hypothesis that both Gestalt psychology and phenomenology repudiate.

So, quite regardless of geometry for the moment, we might again ask that ingenuous and counterintuitive question: Is it the same man? Late at night, on an otherwise deserted sidewalk, in an unfamiliar part of town, I certainly might not consider this approaching man quite the same as the one I earlier saw farther down the street. What differs, obviously, is not his quantitative attributes, or even his objective identity, which I can hardly either fail or bother to acknowledge at this dicey moment, but rather his qualitative imminence, his alarming proximity, his *cathexis*. Such qualities of the nearer man are decidedly not equivalent to those of the farther one. Nor, for that matter, are they quite comparable to those of the ashtray I spotted on someone's windowsill and then meandered by, or the postered wall I paused to read, or the piano I curiously examined as I passed, or the car that drove by me. The man who has come closer is, in a word, a *bigger* man, not one who merely *appears* bigger. Indeed, he is *too big*, and in this way decisively *not* the same as the farther man, who possesses a definite size but cannot, if we might say it this way, possess a definite bigness. We can therefore conclude something like this, against the residual empiricism of even Köhler and Merleau-Ponty: insofar as objective size must be constant, that man I see is (of course) the "same" man and therefore the "same" size, but insofar as his magnitude *matters* to me here and now on the street, he has become bigger than he should be, indeed too big. Bigness is something quite other than size—it comes *before* size, in the way the unconscious comes before any specific conscious perception, or cathexis before object. Momentarily—but all bigness, we might suggest, is thus "momentary"—we must supplement phenomenology with psychoanalysis.[49]

In short, to understand, not merely the man's (putatively constant) size but his bigness, we must cease treating him like an ashtray, piano, wall, or car. Merleau-Ponty, in nearly every other part of his work, is more attentive to the rich intersubjective relationships that "motivate" my perceptions. Yet here he makes an error in phenomenological analysis so basic that we can discover it addressed more than a century earlier in Hegel's master-slave dialectic, a text with which Merleau-Ponty himself was intimately familiar, but which he perhaps now overlooks.[50] In its initial foray into sociability, the subject considers itself a self-sufficient agent, like a perceiver of mere things, a "simple being for-self," as Hegel says, for whom the others in its environment are precisely "inessential objects": ashtrays, walls, pianos, unspecified figures at various distances, and so on.[51] Everything that is not-I—"all that is *other*," as Hegel says—is an "object designated by the character of the negative."[52] Such a dialectic operates nicely right up to the point when the other who is down the street—now we can again call him the *man*—begins to move on his own and approach me, indicating that I was mistaken ever to have considered it/him an "unessential, negatively characterized object." In his new potential for excessive proximity or violence, the perceived other is no longer seen objectively. Indeed, he is now all-too-subjective, and it has become my own subjectivity, my "certainty of self," that is threatened. Therefore the phenomenological situation in which I suddenly discover myself no longer resembles the placid equanimity of an indissoluble "depth," wherein size remains objective and consistent, but rather something closer to an affective dis-integration—emergency rather than mere emergence—in which magnitude overweens, implying the violence of a possibly-being-crushed.

In such a light, we might instead opt for the uncanny quasi empiricism of Jean-Jacques Rousseau's version of that man-on-the-street example. Rousseau calls the individual who does the subjective perceiving of the other a "savage man," which, for all its problematic tinges, might be closer to the phenomenology of *cathected* bigness that we seek, a proto-psychoanalytic subject who "does not begin by reasoning but by feeling" and who therefore encounters bigness in something closer to its raw, infantile form.[53] Here is Rousseau's famous description of the first approach of the other:

> A savage man, upon meeting others, will at first be frightened. His fear will have made him see those men as bigger and stronger than himself; he will have given them the name *giants*. After many experiences, he will have recognized that, these ostensible [*prétendus*] giants being neither bigger nor stronger than him, their stature did not suit the idea he had at first attached to the word giant. He will therefore invent another name common to them and him[self], such as the name *man*, for example, and leave that of *giant* to the false object that had struck him during his illusion.[54]

As a shorthand for the difference between Merleau-Ponty's "man" and Rousseau's, we can suggest that what Rousseau shows us, once again, is that bigness comes before size. The *thing* down the road is first a giant, then perhaps another subject (a man?), and only then determinately an object or person reckonable as a certain size at this or that distance, by comparison with whom the category of "giant" turns out to have been an illusion and a fiction. Indeed, Rousseau suggests that what we do, in evolving a balanced language adequate to the less infantile or less "savage" impressions of our mature encounters, is precisely to re-cognize the violent impression of the "passions" and therefore to place that other man in his correct scalar context.

In turn, we reserve the now-superseded cathexes of primary impressions for poetry, which alone is capable of reviving "the figural word that was born before the literal word":

> The illusory image presented by passion [being] the first to show itself, the language that [cor]responded to it was likewise the first invented. It afterward became metaphorical when the enlightened mind [*l'esprit éclairé*], recognizing its first error, employed the expressions only with the same passions that had produced it.[55]

In the same ingenuous spirit in which we inquired of Merleau-Ponty and Köhler whether, truly, the closer man *is* the "same man," we can now inquire of Rousseau: *was* it truly an error to have been frightened of the bigger man, to have figured him as a giant? I could as easily have asked my child, back in the Farm-in-the-Zoo, whether they ought now to correct their "error" of being frightened by the "too big" cow. Rousseau, of course, would prefer us to grow up, to learn a suitable scalar taxidermy, to "recognize [our] first error" and correct it with an "enlightened" literalness that can perceive other men, alongside all other objects, as the sizes they properly are. Any more colorful reckoning based on "passion" is relegated to poetry, which now becomes an exceptional throwback to "a place anterior to theory and common sense," as Derrida says.[56] Both psychoanalytic theory of sublimation and Kantian theory of the sublime substantially concur with Rousseau's treatment of bigness, and *a fortiori* too-bigness, as a kind of *error*, something that should not *be*. And therefore if, in the spirit of Rousseau's proto-psychoanalytic theorization, and nonetheless contrary to the direction Rousseau ultimately wants to take it, we reconsider the moon illusion, perhaps we must suggest that the error committed by perception was never that of perceiving the horizon moon as *too big*. Rather, the error was in presuming that the correction of the illusion gives us an *actual* moon in its constant magnitude instead of merely an eviscerated silhouette, a "live" moon instead of a "stuffed" one. From any perspective of proper empirical measurement and scale, of course, the error comes first and perception is then corrected by a more adequate judgment that this too-big moon cannot *be*. Yet from another, possibly more fruitful perspective—which precisely cannot *be* a perspective, because it antecedes perspective—the too-bigness of the moon is no error, but rather the fuller reflection of our body's involvement in the environment to which it, down at the horizon rather than up in the sky, properly belongs. The bigness of the moon is a visceral echo—more like a prickle in the flesh than any objectively perceived distance and magnitude, and yet, as Merleau-Ponty says, still a "measureless size which nevertheless is a size"—of the possibly-being-crushed.

And the cow, too—or the man on the street or, for that matter (on special occasions), the ashtray or the piano or the car—if these objects can ever again be *big*, regardless of their real size constancy and scalar propriety, it can only be because things like them were once *too big* and can become so again, revivified by the cathexis they awaken in the perceiver who momentarily *feels* (rather than sees) their imposition or the threat of their proximity. Bigness came before size, just as, for Rousseau, feeling came before reasoning and, for Freud, the unconscious is the "past" of consciousness. Bigness *is not*—at least not anymore—but all the more present for (not) being so.

Acknowledgments

I would like to thank a number of people who helped me begin, improve, and complete this book: Elizabeth Branch Dyson, Michael Tavel Clarke, Hugh Cole, Jennifer Culbert, David Cunning, Melissa Deem, Doug Dowland, Lazăr Edeleanu, Frances Ferguson, Dilip Gaonkar, Naomi Greyser, Martin Harries, Virginia Jackson, Scott Krzych, Nate Kreuter, Rob Latham, Tom Lutz, Sandra Macpherson, Meredith Martin, Jay Manzo, Nina Manzo, Masaru Otsuka, Kristin Rawlings, Rebekah Sheldon, Garrett Stewart, Tracy Swedlow, Lara Trubowitz, Kyle Wagner, Richard Washbourne, Michael Witmore, and Leela Wittenberg Trubowitz. Thanks to Scott Sheldon for his work on the index, and to the anonymous reviewers at University of Chicago Press, whose detailed comments were invaluable. My abiding gratitude to Judith Butler, Jean McGarry, and Helen Tartar.

Thanks also to Carlo Fumarola, Lee F. Mindel, Michael Moran, Tomio Ohashi, and Kevin Roche and John Dinkeloo Architects, for permission to reproduce their photographs and work, and to the Shinohara Archive at Tokyo Tech and *The Japan Architect*/Shinkenchiku-sha for allowing me to reproduce photographs and plans of Kazuo Shinohara's work.

Previously Published Materials

Select portions of this manuscript first appeared in the article "Bigness as the Unconscious of Theory," *ELH* 86, no. 2 (Summer 2019). © 2019 Johns Hopkins University Press. Published with permission by Johns Hopkins University Press.

Portions of chapter 4 first appeared in "Introduction," in *Scale in Literature and Culture*, edited by Michael Tavel Clarke and David Wittenberg (New York: Palgrave Macmillan, 2017). Reproduced with permission from Springer Nature.

Notes

Chapter One

1. My visits preceded a major renovation of the museum from 2009 to 2013 by Mark Cavagnero Associates. The museum is now called the Oakland Museum of California.

2. "The Oakland Museum."

3. Before the museum has even opened, Ada Louise Huxtable writes, in a *New York Times* review, that it "may be one of the most thoughtfully revolutionary structures in the world" ("Museum Is Also Art," Huxtable, "Architecture," 40).

4. Pevsner, *History of Building Types*, 138; Eckes-Wahl, "Social History," 65.

5. Bruce Blake (executive director, Oakland Museum Association) in "Assignment Four Documentary—The Oakland Museum." James Brown III, the museum's original director, further remarks: "we seek to wipe out the feeling that museums are forbidding places and visited only by the so-called elite" ("'Quiet Revolution'").

6. "The Oakland Museum."

7. See Adorno, "Valéry Proust Museum," 175.

8. "The Oakland Museum."

9. See Kostov, *History of Architecture*, 704; see also Murphy, who comments that Jane Jacobs's work represents a reaction against large-scale planners such as Le Corbusier and Ebenezer Howard, whose followers were "inflicting . . . monstrous environments on the people" (*Last Futures*, 142). "Architectural Megalomania" is Albert Speer's own description of his work as the preeminent Nazi architect; he submits that a "love for vast proportions was . . . tied up with the totalitarian cast of Hitler's regime" (Speer, *Inside the Third Reich*, 69).

10. Roche interestingly downplays the effects of bigness in all three of these buildings: "the Ford Foundation building . . . has a tremendously large scale on 42nd Street, but I don't think you're overpowered by that at all"; "I hope that, when the Knights of Columbus and the Coliseum are finished, the whole complex will be a contained space. The Tower won't have so much of that overpowering effect any more"; "The Oakland Museum really has a very large scale if you see it from the air, and the elements which people deal with are actually very large elements. . . . It's a very bold scale. But nobody has ever noticed it or even mentioned it" ("Kevin Roche," 66–67). However, Roche not only built large structures, but was well known as "a man who treats architecture individually and monumentally," as Kenzo Tange approvingly suggests: "His scale, in extreme terms, is inhuman" (Tange and Isozaki, "Directions," 26).

Chapter Two

1. My child's exact words.

2. Kant, *Critique of Judgment*, 131. I have occasionally altered the translations of Kant.

3. Baumgarten's first use of "aesthetic" in the sense of a "science of perception" occurs toward the end of his 1735 doctoral thesis, *Meditationes philosophicae de nonnullis ad poema pertinentibus* (par. 116), in 1735 (see Baumgarten, *Reflections on Poetry*, 78). Baumgarten's fuller elaboration, *Aesthetica*, was published in two parts in 1750 and 1758, along with briefer discussions in his *Metaphysics* (see 205, 214, 219–28), the latter important for Kant's later employment of "aesthetic" in the *Critique of Judgment*. I am aware of no English translation of *Aesthetica*, but there is a complete German translation with facing Latin; see Baumgarten, *Ästhetik*.

4. Kant, *Critique of Judgment*, 134.

5. Or, to evoke a prior era during which nature might have been somewhat less readily containable, a stampede of bison or a flock of passenger pigeons. Jonathan Rosen quotes this eyewitness account of a flight of pigeons over Columbus, Ohio, in 1855: "As the watchers stared, the hum increased to a mighty throbbing. Now everyone was out of the houses and stores, looking apprehensively at the growing cloud, which was blotting out the rays of the sun. Women gathered their long skirts and hurried for the shelter of stores. Horses bolted. A few people mumbled frightened words about the approach of the millennium, and several dropped on their knees and prayed" (Rosen, "The Birds," 63, quoting Greenberg, *Feathered River*, 54).

6. Nietzsche, *Will to Power*, 282.

7. In the developmental stage occurring between the ages of seven and ten, Piaget claims, the child acquires the capacity for "operational series," including "quantification of previously [merely] ordinal magnitudes (*grandeurs*) and conservation of quantities. The overall structure specific to these various operations is what we called 'groupings' (*groupements*), types of incomplete groups (lack[ing] complete associativity) or semi-networks (with lower limits [but] without upper ones, or vice versa), and above all whose composition proceeds step by step, without combinatorics (*combinatoire*)" (*Structuralism*, 65–66). I have (sometimes considerably) altered the translations of Piaget for the sake of accuracy and clarity.

8. Hegel, *Phenomenology of Spirit*, 60.

9. Hegel, 62.

10. Hegel, 57; Marx, *Economic and Philosophic Manuscripts*, 147–57 (also see 69–84).

11. Freud, *Interpretation of Dreams*, 412.

12. Shklovsky, "Art as Technique," 11–12.

13. See Freud, *Interpretation of Dreams*, 397–98.

14. Coole and Frost, "Introducing the New Materialisms," 7.

15. Mary Ann Doane, partly quoting Philippe Dubois, writes about early films that use excessive close-ups, such as Thomas Edison's *The Kiss* (1896), James Williamson's *The Big Swallow* (1901), and the famous Lumière brothers' *L'arrivée d'un train en gare de La Ciotat* (1896): "The space of the close-up is 'absolutely heterogeneous . . . it completely escapes the anthropological references of canonical scale.' It destroys the scale of shots and 'it is this which generates fear.' As in *The Big Swallow*, the close-up is always a devouring close-up. It breaks the rule of proxemics that dictates the 'good distance'; it is *too close*" (Doane, *Bigger Than Life*, 64; see Dubois, "Le gros plan primitive," 21).

16. Piaget, *Child's Conception of Number*, 8, 12.

17. Piaget, 5, 8.

18. Piaget, 16. Piaget further notes that only the single dimension immediately present, or measured first, constitutes evidence of a magnitude, so that "as soon as the level of the column in the narrow glass L surpasses that of the liquid contained in the wide glass A, the child forgets the widths and believes that the first of these vessels contains more than the second. On the other hand, as soon as he reestablishes the equality of the levels, he is struck anew by the inequality of the widths, and so on" (16).

19. Piaget, *Judgment and Reasoning*, 163; also see 161–71.

20. Piaget, *Child's Conception of Number*, 11, 10.

21. Piaget, 11, 16.

22. The difference, of course, is that for Piaget this shift does not come in a "moment," whether construed temporally or logically. Thus Piaget, by virtue of his experimental evidence, extends the "realization" over the course of several years of childhood development, and through multiple challenges of various degrees of difficulty: "Judgment only functions precisely when perception does not suffice to provide information to the subject: discovering that a given quantity of liquid does not vary when it is transferred from a container of form A into one or two containers of form B presumes, on the part of the child, an act of intellectual comprehension that will be all the more important and all the more easily analyzable the more deceptive is the immediate perception" (*Child's Conception of Number*, 9).

23. Piaget, *Child's Conception of Number*, 13. Compare Bergson's discussion of "quality of quantity" (*Time and Free Will*, 123).

24. Piaget, *Child's Conception of Number*, 12, 13.

25. This is Bill Brown's description of "the thing," to which I owe a debt. Brown's theorization of things generally is apropos of, and can to a degree guide, the analysis of bigness more particularly: "You could imagine things . . . as what is excessive in objects, as what exceeds their mere materialization as objects or their mere utilization as objects—their force as a sensuous presence or as a metaphysical presence, the magic by which objects become values, fetishes, idols, and totems. Temporalized as the before and after of the object, thingness amounts to a latency (the not yet formed or the not yet formable) and to an excess (what remains physically or metaphysically irreducible to objects). But this temporality obscures the all-at-onceness, the simultaneity, of the object/thing dialectic and the fact that, all at once, *the thing seems to name the object just as it is even as it names something else*" (Brown, "Thing Theory," 5). See also Brown's *Other Things*, especially the first chapter, "Things in Theory," 17–47.

26. See "Mont Blanc." For a zoomable version of the Mont Blanc photo, see "In-2White." For what it is worth, other photos might compete for the title of "world's largest," depending on how size is reckoned, for instance, a photo of Kuala Lumpur from 2014 by a team at the University of Creative Technology International (846 gigapixels; see "Panaxity").

27. "London 320 Gigapixel." Note that NASA's "LROC Northern Polar Mosaic" image of the moon, constructed in 2014 using the Lunar Reconnaissance Orbiter Camera, consists of more than ten thousand images gathered over four years, and comprises 681 gigapixels, making it likely the largest "mosaic" photograph yet made (see "Northern Polar Mosaic"). For the purposes of my argument, I do not distinguish between mosaic and other image types, although arguably any image assembled

from smaller digital files taken at different times might properly be termed a "mosaic" regardless of its ultimate appearance.

28. See "365-Gigapixel Panorama."

29. The largest "seamless" print photograph in the world—that is, a single physical image not stitched together from smaller shots—is "the Great Picture," a gelatin silver halide emulsion print, taken in 2006 with a gigantic pinhole camera at US Marine Corps Air Station El Toro in Irvine, California. The print measures 111 feet wide and thirty-two feet high—in other words, only about the size of a rather large advertising billboard.

30. "Swiss Lab 'Nano Chisels'" (or see "World's Smallest Magazine Cover"); it is 11 µm by 15 µm, "nano-etched" by a microscopic silicon tip. By contrast, the world's smallest printed image, done by "quantum dot technology" (a version of ink-jet printing), is 88 µm by 115 µm; see "This Is the Tiniest Color Picture."

31. DiCaglio, *Scale Theory*, 48–49.

32. Ball, "World's Smallest Magazine."

33. Kittler, *Optical Media*, 38. Note that Zachary Horton goes further, asserting that "all media mediate scale" (Horton, *Cosmic Zoom*, 29).

34. Fried, "Art and Objecthood," 155. Laura Marks makes a point similar to Fried's in the context of film viewing: "Representation is inextricable from embodiment" (*Skin of the Film*, 142). Mary Ann Doane, discussing Robert Morris's theory of sculpture, similarly remarks that "scale is comprehended through the register of the body" (*Bigger Than Life*, 50); in general, see Doane's discussion of Morris (Doane, 49–50).

35. See note 31 above.

36. Bukatman, "Zooming Out," 248.

37. Bukatman, 248.

38. Bukatman, 248.

39. An excellent parody of this scene, comically but also critically overindulging the excessive scalar contrast that *Star Wars* works both to express and to conceal, is given in the opening sequence of Mel Brooks's *Spaceballs* (1987).

40. Elsewhere I have called this tendency the "postulate of *fabular apriority*," an inclination within both naive and critical readings to regard fictional narratives or images (or at least to speak of regarding them) as "real." It is arguably the essential postulate underlying all narrative, since without it only the *sjuzhet*, and ultimately the *text*, is visible, not the "story" within that text. See Wittenberg, *Time Travel*, 119–28.

41. Bukatman, "Zooming Out," 248. Compare Doane's detailed description of "the vehemence in the language of the discourses" concerned with "the potential of shifting scales in the early cinema," including "terms such as 'monstrous,' 'grotesque,' 'gigantic,' 'abnormal,' 'contortion,' 'degeneration,' 'irrationality,' and 'eccentricity'" (Doane, *Bigger Than Life*, 62).

42. Doane, *Bigger Than Life*, 59.

43. See Breuer and Freud, *Studies in Hysteria*, 143.

44. Bukatman, "Zooming Out," 264–65.

45. See Jay, *Downcast Eyes*, 268.

46. Doane, *Bigger Than Life*, 161.

47. Bukatman, "Zooming Out," 264.

48. Morton, *Hyperobjects*, 1. As Morton points out, the term originates for him toward the end of his earlier book, *The Ecological Thought*, 130ff.

Chapter Three

1. See Jungk, *Brighter Than a Thousand Suns*, 197; Szasz, *Day the Sun Rose*, 91; Jungk remarks that the Manhattan Project scientists regularly referred only to "the 'gadget'—the word 'bomb' was discreetly avoided."

2. See Hewlett and Anderson, *History of the Atomic Energy Commission*, 380; Jungk, *Brighter Than a Thousand Suns*, 197–202.

3. Farrell, quoted by Gen. Leslie Groves in his "Memorandum for the Secretary of War (July 18, 1945)"; see Feis, *Between War and Peace*, 169.

4. Farrell, quoted by Groves; see Feis, *Between War and Peace*, 169.

5. Farrell, quoted by Groves; see Feis, *Between War and Peace*, 169.

6. Rabi, quoted in Rhodes, *Making of the Atomic Bomb*, 672; Nye, *American Technological Sublime*, 228. See also Rhodes, *Dark Sun*, 175.

7. Rhodes, *Dark Sun*, 673.

8. Laurence, *Dawn over Zero*, 10.

9. Kiyoshi Tanimoto, quoted in Hersey, *Hiroshima*, 8. Hersey's "Hiroshima" was initially published in a single issue of *The New Yorker* (August 31, 1946). I cite the Vintage book republication.

10. Taeko Teramae, quoted in *Eyewitness Testimonies*, 110; Noriko Ueda, in *Eyewitness Testimonies*, 120; Ōta Yōko, in *Hiroshima: Three Witnesses*, 182.

11. Yoshito Matsushige, quoted in *Eyewitness Testimonies*, 72.

12. Hiroshi Sasamura, quoted in *Eyewitness Testimonies*, 84; Miyoko Watanabe and Michiko Yamaoka (both use the identical phrase), in *Eyewitness Testimonies*, 126, 141–42; John Farley (an American prisoner of war in Nagasaki), in Weller, *First into Nagasaki*, 35; Tōge Sankichi, from the poem "Season of Flames," in *Poems of the Atomic Bomb*, 307.

13. Kant, *Critique of Judgment*, 129.

14. Lippit, *Atomic Light*, 182n51.

15. Ogura, *Letters*, 15. The next several quotations are all from the first few pages of Ogura's book.

16. I am indebted to Lara Trubowitz's analysis of similar rhetoric in her discussion of the "threat" of Jewish immigration in early twentieth-century Britain. Trubowitz observes that "the figure of the Jew is . . . created by the inadequacy of a conceptual mode of thought, and yet ultimately that very inadequacy comes to signify a seemingly coherent truth about Jews" (*Civil Antisemitism*, 42).

17. Quoted in Oe, *Hiroshima Notes*, 91–92.

18. Lippit, *Atomic Light*, 100.

19. Bataille, "Concerning the Accounts," 504.

20. "From the beginning," as Ruth Leys observes, "trauma was understood as an experience that immersed the victim in the traumatic scene so profoundly that it precluded the kind of specular distance necessary for cognitive knowledge of what had happened" (*Trauma*, 9).

21. Bataille, "Concerning the Accounts," 504.

22. Nye, *American Technological Sublime*, 232.

23. Dori Laub, discussing narratives by Holocaust survivors, summarizes a recurrent feeling that "there are never enough words or the right words . . . to articulate the story that cannot be fully captured in *thought*, *memory*, and *speech*" (Laub, "Truth and Testimony," 63). I hope to imply no futile equation of atrocities, but rather only

to observe that A-bomb eyewitness accounts contend similarly with the limits of "thought, memory, and speech," and perhaps also with what Laub calls the "loss of capacity to be a witness to oneself" (67). For Laub, this loss is ontological, resulting from a qualitative distinction in the event of the Holocaust, what he calls its "inherently incomprehensible *and* deceptive psychological structure" (65). Such a qualitative distinction must also partake—in a manner extremely difficult to mark precisely, since it concerns the unrecoverable relationship between the well-known scale of the Holocaust as history and its unscalable effects upon individuals—of the quantitative distinction of the Holocaust, the sheer magnitude of the Nazis' success in eradicating any "independent frame of reference through which the event could be observed" (66).

24. Rhodes, *Dark Sun*, 710. See also, Hiroyuki, "August 6," 14; Nagai, *Bells of Nagasaki*, 11.

25. Bataille, "Concerning the Accounts," 502.

26. Bataille, 500. Michael Sherry remarks that "in Hiroshima and Nagasaki, most victims did not know what hit them, confronting personal extinction first; the survivors only later suffered the shock of communal annihilation as they crawled out of their wreckage and met the parade of the damned" (quoted by Selden, "Introduction," xvii).

27. Bataille, "Concerning the Accounts," 502.

28. Freud, "The Unconscious," 134.

29. Bataille, "Concerning the Accounts," 503.

30. Lanzmann writes, regarding his film *Shoah*: "There is an absolute obscenity in the very project of understanding. Not to understand was my iron law during all the eleven years of the production of *Shoah*. I clung to this refusal of understanding as the only possible ethical and at the same time the only possible operative attitude" (quoted in Lanzmann, "Hier ist kein Warum," 478; also in Caruth, *Trauma*, 204).

31. Kant, *Critique of Judgment*, 128.

32. A thorough collection of such documentation, horrifying both in its meticulous detail and in its statistical detachment, can be found in *Hiroshima and Nagasaki: The Physical, Medical, and Social Effects*.

33. See Nicolson, "Microscope and English Imagination," 29–30; also quoted in P. Shaw, *Sublime*, 27–28.

34. Burnet, *Sacred Theory*, 192–93.

35. Dennis, *Grounds of Criticism*, 17; *Advancement and Reformation*, 26.

36. Shaftesbury, *The Moralists*, 200, 201; Addison, *The Spectator*, no. 412, 66.

37. P. Shaw, *Sublime*, 39.

38. Addison, *The Spectator*, no. 418, 91; Kant, *Critique of Judgment*, 152.

39. Reynolds, *An Enquiry Concerning Taste*, 17; also quoted in P. Shaw, *Sublime*, 46.

40. Hertz, *End of the Line*, 44.

41. Burke, *Philosophical Enquiry*, 67, 123, 36–37.

42. Kant, *Critique of Judgment*, 144.

43. Kant, 129.

44. Kant, 129.

45. Kant, 134.

46. Kant, 129. See Derrida, *Truth in Painting*, 131.

47. Kant, *Critique of Judgment*, 130.

48. Kant, 144.

49. Kant, 135–36.

50. Kant, 129.
51. Kant, 136.
52. Kant, 144.
53. Kant, 141.
54. Horton, *Cosmic Zoom*, 11.
55. Ogura, *Letters*, 15–16.
56. Ogura, 21.
57. Ogura, 16.
58. Ogura, 16.
59. Ogura, 16–17.
60. Kant, *Critique of Judgment*, 134. Kant emphasizes the entire sentence.
61. Ogura, *Letters*, 27.
62. Ogura, 37; Scarry, *Body in Pain*, 29.
63. Heidegger, *Nietzsche*, 1:147.
64. Ogura, *Letters*, 54.
65. Ogura, 16, 19, 21, 31, 34, 41.
66. Ogura, 53.
67. Ogura, 61, 104, 70–71, 85.
68. "Nuclear Test Film—Trinity Shot."
69. There are several (slightly) better-quality documentary films available, although the film cited is the one included or excerpted in the usual Department of Energy films of the history of the Manhattan Project. See "Trinity Test Complete Takes."
70. "Crossroads B [Baker]" was preceded by "Crossroads A [Able]" as well as (of course) the Nagasaki, Hiroshima, and Trinity explosions.
71. Because of the bomb's placement ninety feet underwater, there was in fact no "mushroom cloud," and what is frequently described as such is rather the far more symmetrically composed plume of water and vapor.
72. The manifold and egregious actions and propaganda through which the environment, residents' lives, and natural and cultural history of the Bikini Atoll were destroyed by the American nuclear testing program is extensively documented.
73. For a quick example, see a current page of the website Redbubble titled "Bikini Atoll Wall Art." Redbubble is a clearinghouse website for independent artists to sell work online.
74. Compare Frances Ferguson, "The Nuclear Sublime."

Chapter Four

1. Plato, *Parmenides*, 132a, 132b. All citations of Plato and Aristotle are given with the conventional marginal notations.
2. Plato, 131d.
3. The final lines read:

> PARMENIDES. Thus, in sum, we may conclude, if there is no one, there is nothing at all. To this we may add the conclusion: It seems that, whether there is or is not a one, both that one and the others alike are and are not, and appear and do not appear to be, all manner of things in all manner of ways, with respect to themselves and to one another.
> SOCRATES. Most true. (Plato, 166b)

4. See Badiou, *Being and Event*, 31–37.

5. Plato, *Meno*, 86d.

6. Plato, 81c–d.

7. Plato, 82c–d.

8. See Euclid, Book VI, Propositions 4–5 (*Elements*, 2:200–204). If the measurements of the sides of the triangles are also the same, they will be "congruent"; the key is that, like a square, one "similar" triangle could be made "congruent" with its counterpart merely by enlarging or shrinking its sides proportionally.

9. See Euclid's *Elements*, book VI, definition I (Euclid, *Elements*, 2:188).

10. Note that in classical geometry, the only tools permissible for the construction of figures are an unmarked straightedge of indeterminate length and a compass; no measurements are done. These conventions derive from Euclid's first three postulates (see Euclid, *Elements*, 1:154). In Plato's *Republic*, book VII, geometry is recommended as "the knowledge of the eternally existent," and Plato goes as far as to propose a "direct contradiction" between the language of actual demonstrations or examples and the "essences" derived from them: the language of the adepts of geometry "is most ludicrous, though they cannot help it, for they speak as if they were doing something and as if all their words were directed toward action. For all their talk is of squaring and applying and adding and the like, whereas in fact the real object of the entire study is pure knowledge" (527b, 527a). Aristotle makes a similar point in *Posterior Analytics* (49b31; 76b40) and *Metaphysics* (1089a20).

11. Thomas Heath observes that for Plato, "geometry is concerned, not with material things, but with mathematical points, lines, triangles, squares, etc., as objects of pure thought. If we use a diagram in geometry, it is only as an illustration; the triangle which we draw is an imperfect representation of the triangle of which we think" (*History of Greek Mathematics*, 1:286–87). Note that Aristotle concurs: "The geometer bases no conclusion on the particular line being that which he has assumed it to be; he argues about what it *represents*, the figure itself being a mere illustration" (Heath, 1:337; see Aristotle, *Posterior Analytics*, 76b40).

12. Plato, *Republic*, book VII (527b).

13. Plato, *Meno*, 85c, 82e.

14. Plato, 85c.

15. Compare Alfred North Whitehead: "the space-intuition which is so essential an aid to the study of geometry is logically irrelevant; it does not enter into the premisses when they are properly stated, nor into any step of the reasoning. It has the practical importance of an example, which is essential for the stimulation of our thought" (*Introduction to Mathematics*, 180–81).

16. Barad, *Meeting the Universe Halfway*, 170–71.

17. DiCaglio, *Scale Theory*, 46–47.

18. Barad, *Meeting the Universe Halfway*, 170.

19. Horton, *Cosmic Zoom*, 11.

20. I have adapted the following illustration from Guy Ottewell (*Thousand-Yard Model*, 4–7). A number of convenient online renderings are available. Models of cosmological size and scale similar to Ottewell's have a long history. For one example, in his *Cosmotheoros* (1695), Christian Huygens asks us to imagine that if the sun is envisioned as a figure "about four inches in diameter," then "the Earth must be conceived . . . not bigger than a grain of Millet, and her Companion the Moon scarcely perceivable, moving round her in a Circle a little more than two Inches broad" (see

Huygens, *The Celestial Worlds Discovered*, 1698; cited in Van Helden, *Measuring the Universe*, 156). Albert Van Helden paraphrases Huygens's depiction of planetary distances: "A bullet shot out of a gun with the enormous speed of a hundred fathoms per pulse beat, that is, 600 ft/sec., would take 25 years to reach the Sun and 250 years to reach Saturn!" (*Measuring the Universe*, 156).

21. The scale used is approximately 6.3 billion to one (Ottewell, *Thousand-Yard Model*, 24). For present purposes I disregard a series of dwarf planets and other objects in the Kuiper Belt beyond the orbit of Neptune. Nor is it crucial that the sizes of the objects represented be strictly precise, for reasons that should become clear in the subsequent discussion.

22. Proxima Centauri is located in the Alpha Centauri system, approximately 4.2 light years (twenty-five trillion miles) from earth.

23. An interesting contrast, albeit compromised in its critical impact, is offered by Josh Worth's webpage, "If the Moon Were Only 1 Pixel: A Tediously Accurate Scale Model of the Solar System." The webpage has a button that permits a slow scroll from Sun to Pluto at the scaled speed of light, or in other words, the greatest possible physical velocity—but also lets the user shortcut this maximum using the scroll bar, and additionally interjects numerous comments and distractions along the way (Worth, "If the Moon"). Joshua DiCaglio offers a useful brief discussion of Worth's webpage in *Scale Theory*, 234.

24. See "Juno." The Juno probe is currently orbiting Jupiter, where it will remain for the indefinite future. Note that I have opted to use the Juno as my example instead of the Parker Solar Probe, launched in 2018, which as of this writing has settled into orbit around the sun, and will have achieved speeds of over 430,000 miles per hour before it eventually burns up.

25. The Parker Solar Probe, at its top speed—were it not intended to be burned up by the sun—would be capable of making the trip in about seven thousand years.

26. Approximately one and a half inches per hour, or about a quarter mile per year.

27. These estimates are given as of 2024; they regularly fluctuate.

28. Nietzsche, "On Truth and Lying," 246.

29. The estimation given is calculated as follows: 4,700 drops in one cup (20 drops per ml), 1 drop = 1/360 moles, 1 mole = 1.8×10^{24} atoms (one oxygen and two hydrogen in each water molecule).

30. Aristotle, *Categories*, 5b18.

31. Aristotle, 5b35.

32. Aristotle, 5b23.

33. Aristotle, 6a4, 6b7.

34. Aristotle, 6b27.

35. Horton, *Cosmic Zoom*, 21.

36. The era of the science-fiction pulp magazine commences with such a tale, namely, G. Peyton Wertenbaker's "The Man from the Atom," originally published in *Science and Invention* in 1923, and reprinted in 1926 by Hugo Gernsback as the first original story for his *Amazing Stories*. Wertenbaker's protagonist enlarges himself until earth "became more and more like a little ball a few feet thick"; eventually, "the stars were circling around my legs," and so on. See Wertenbaker, "Man from the Atom," 63; for further discussion, see Wittenberg, *Time Travel*, 56–60.

37. Tsing, "On Nonscalability," 505.

38. The full title of the work is *Discourses and Mathematical Demonstrations Concerning Two New Sciences Pertaining to Mechanics and Local Motions.*

39. These are the same characters who populate Galileo's earlier dialogue, *The Two Chief World Systems,* although their viewpoints are somewhat revised.

40. West, *Scale,* 38.

41. Galilei, *Two New Sciences,* 12. I have occasionally altered the translations of Galileo for the sake of clarity or literalness.

42. Galilei, 12.

43. Galilei, *Two New Sciences,* 12. Simplicio exemplifies something closer to an orthodox Scholastic, albeit one sufficiently inquisitive to demand explanations for and against his views. Stillman Drake suggests Simplicio may be a version of Galileo's younger self (Drake, "Introduction," xxxiv).

44. Galilei, *Two New Sciences,* 127.

45. Galilei, 12.

46. Galilei, 13.

47. Galilei, 86.

48. Portions of this section are adapted from my introduction, cowritten with Michael Tavel Clarke, to the edited collection *Scale in Literature and Culture*; see Clarke and Wittenberg, "Introduction."

49. Thompson, *On Growth and Form,* 2. I quote the original 1917 edition, not the 1942 revision.

50. Thompson, 28, 28–29n. Thompson observes that "problems [of dynamical similitude] have been admirably treated both by Galileo and by Borelli, but many later writers have remained ignorant of their work. Linnaeus, for instance, remarked that, if an elephant were as strong in proportion as a stag-beetle, it would be able to pull up rocks by the root, and to level mountains. And Kirby and Spence have a well-known passage directed to shew that such powers as have been conferred upon the insect have been withheld from the higher animals, for the reason that had these latter been endued therewith they would have 'caused the early desolation of the world'" (28).

51. Thompson, 30.

52. Huxley, *Problems of Relative Growth,* 1, 2. Huxley continues: "without the quantitative expression, we should be largely theorizing in the air. I would not trouble to spend my time on this point if it had not been urged on several occasions in my hearing; otherwise, one would expect that the interaction of quantitative theory with observation and experiment devoted to testing the theory, so fruitful not only in other sciences but in genetics within the field of biology, would automatically be welcomed" (2).

53. Haldane, "On Being the Right Size," 427. Similarly, Mel Siegel notes that the "generalit[y]" that "*big is weak, small is strong,* i.e., that it is large structures that collapse under their own weight, large animals that break their legs when they stumble, etc., whereas small structures and animals are practically unaware of gravity" is simultaneously "at first counterintuitive but . . . straightforwardly physics-based" ("When Physics Rules Robotics," 146).

54. Haldane, "On Being the Right Size," 424.

55. Haldane, 424.

56. Haldane, 425.

57. Bonner, *Why Size Matters,* 2, 5, 3–4. For a more general expansion of these arguments for the determinative nature of size constraints, see Barrow and Tipler's *The*

Anthropic Cosmological Principle, especially the section on "Planetary Life" (310–18) and the whole of chapter 6, "The Anthropic Principles in Classical Cosmology" (367–457), particularly the section on "The Size of the Universe" (384–85).

58. Haldane, "On Being the Right Size," 424.

59. Or speculating with special effects, as in a recent reboot of the Superman franchise in which the real physical mayhem of a fight between Kryptonian super beings is constructed digitally (see *Man of Steel*, 2013). The 2008 film *Hancock* is a parody of the same type of scenario.

60. Aristotle, *Poetics*, 1451a9.

61. Aristotle, 1450b33.

62. See Hegel, *Phenomenology of Spirit*, 55.

63. Bonner notes: "The mindset that size is not a central issue is quite understandable. To say an elephant is big says nothing about all the things that make an elephant: its anatomy, its physiology, and even its behavior" (*Why Size Matters*, 3).

64. There are also metaphysical systems that consider magnitudes and quantities as solely immanent, most notably Leibnizian monadology, which I will discuss later.

65. This way of contextualizing an antinomy of course immediately departs from Kant, for whom (a) the antinomies arise with respect solely to cosmological claims, that is, claims about empirical objects the *whole* of which can nonetheless not be given empirically, and (b) the antinomies are solved specifically through the "doctrine" of "transcendental idealism," in which "all objects of an experience possible for us, are nothing but appearances, i.e., mere representations, which, as they are represented, as extended beings or series of alterations, have outside our thoughts no existence grounded in itself" (Kant, *Critique of Pure Reason*, 511). A Kantian antinomy results from confusing a possible deduction made about the unconditioned whole of appearances—to which, according to the doctrine of transcendental idealism, we have no access—with a deduction made about the specific appearances themselves, to which we have access only through the conditions of sensory experience. Essentially, an antinomy is a "fallacy of equivocation" (515). As a practical demonstration, an antinomy works as an indirect metaphysical proof, or reductio ad absurdum, of arguments that confuse cosmological observations with deductions concerning "transcendent" (nonempirical) essences or wholes: "The conflict of the propositions drawn from it . . . uncovers a falsehood lying in this presupposition [that appearances are things in themselves] and thereby brings us to a discovery about the true constitution of things as objects of sense" (519). It is in this latter, broadly logical sense of "antinomy," as an indirect demonstration of an underlying but regularly obscured metaphysical principle, that I borrow Kant's term, sidestepping its more exclusive application to cosmological matters.

66. Kant, *Critique of Pure Reason*, 460.

Chapter Five

1. See Morton, *Hyperobjects*, 47–51.

2. See Freud, *Interpretation of Dreams*, 88n4, 341.

3. Shone, *Blockbuster*, 274.

4. For a useful discussion of this latter species of quasi sublimity, see Kristen Whissel's chapter, "The New Verticality," in *Spectacular Digital Effects*, 21–58.

5. Sontag, "Imagination of Disaster," 219.

6. Mulvey, "Visual Pleasure," 11–12.

7. I am grateful to Rosalind Galt and Adrian Goycoolea for suggesting the term "waste reveal."

8. See Kristen Whissel's essay "The Digital Multitude" for a very useful reading of "the visual, narrative, and dramatic force generated by digital multitudes in contemporary cinema" (91).

9. You are watching *Them!*, which is among the first and best of the nuclear "creature features," contemporaneous with the first *Godzilla* (*Gojira*).

10. Pierson, *Special Effects*, 65.

11. Jameson, *Postmodernism*, 385.

12. Pierson, *Special Effects*, 73.

13. It would be critically hazardous to underestimate a mainstream viewer's ability to adjudicate such multiple levels of narrative structure. I discuss this question generally in prior works: see Wittenberg, *Time Travel*, and "Time."

14. Galileo writes: "For one brief example of what I mean, I once drew the figure of a bone, lengthened only three times, and thickened in such proportion that it could function in its large animal proportionately as the smaller bone functions in the smaller animal; the figures are these, where[in] you see how disproportionate a figure the enlarged bone becomes" (*Two New Sciences*, 127–28; see figure 5.5).

15. A jaeger is approximately the height of the Statue of Liberty in New York City, including its plinth. Note that a brisk competition of record-breaking statue construction in Asia since the late 1980s has resulted in figures sometimes greatly exceeding this height, from the Dai Kannon of Kita no Miyako Park in Hokkaido, Japan (1989, 289 feet high), to the Statue of Sardar Vallabhbhai Patel in Gujarat, India (2018, six hundred feet high).

16. Tasker, *Spectacular Bodies*, 77.

17. Benjamin, "Work of Art," 40.

18. Mitry, *Aesthetics and Psychology of the Cinema*, 52.

19. I garner these approximate figures not from the film directly, but from a casual perusal of internet fan sites.

20. S. Stewart, *On Longing*, 63.

21. For a more recent example, see "Ship Sailing Under Panama Flag Runs Aground."

22. *Transformers* is from 2007. Michael Bay directed it and the following four sequels through 2017.

23. Galilei, *Two New Sciences*, 126–27.

24. Scarry, *Body in Pain*, 70.

25. Scarry, 66, 70.

26. Scarry, 70.

27. Scarry, 71.

28. Scarry, 71.

29. Horton, *Cosmic Zoom*, 16.

30. Horton, 11. Horton further remarks that "collapsing one scale into another is a profitable and productive enterprise in many fields, and is at this point demanded by global capital as one of its primary engines of extraction and circulation."

31. Sontag, "Imagination of Disaster," 218.

32. Sontag, 218.

Chapter Six

1. Swift, *Gulliver's Travels*, 78.

2. The originality of Swift's meticulously detailed approach to size change may be judged by comparison with a contemporaneous work about a very small person, Fielding's *The Tragedy of Tragedies; or The Life and Death of Tom Thumb the Great* (1731), which, despite its satirical intent, scarcely describes specific aspects of Tom's small stature beyond the mere fact of it.

3. Joshua DiCaglio usefully refers to this type of resizing as "Gulliver's scaling," which "presupposes objects, keeps them intact, and considers making them larger or smaller" (*Scale Theory*, 26).

4. Swift, *Gulliver's Travels*, 77.

5. Swift, 77–78.

6. Swift, 78.

7. Swift, 78–79. Gulliver's apology continues: "I hope the gentle Reader will excuse me for dwelling on these and like Particulars, which however insignificant they may appear to grovelling vulgar Minds, yet will certainly help a Philosopher to enlarge his Thoughts and Imagination, and apply them to the Benefit of publick as well as private Life, which was my sole Design in presenting this and other Accounts of my Travels to the World; wherein I have been chiefly studious of Truth, without affecting any Ornaments of Learning or of Style" (*Gulliver's Travels*, 78–79). Strangely, it is "vulgar Minds" who, he anticipates, will find the details of the incident "insignificant," and "Philosopher[s]" who will "certainly" discover in them a spur to "Thoughts and Imagination, and apply them to the benefit of publick as well as private Life," and so on. An editor's footnote in the Norton critical edition usefully comments that "Gulliver parrots the traditional reasons for writing and publishing travel books" (79n1).

8. Indecency or obscenity was a frequent charge against *Gulliver's Travels* by eighteenth-century critics.

9. Benjamin, "Work of Art," 37.

10. Benjamin, 37.

11. See Nicolson, "Microscope and English Imagination."

12. Benjamin, "Work of Art," 37.

13. Shklovsky, "Art as Technique," 18.

14. Swift, *Gulliver's Travels*, 99. Paul-Gabriel Boucé gives a useful survey of psychoanalytic readings of this scene, starting with Sandor Ferenczi's identification of a "Gulliver fantasy." Such readings tend, perhaps predictably, to view Gulliver's miniaturization and subsequent eroticization as a consequence or symptom of "infantile regression" (85) or of "a fear of castration associated with sexual intercourse." Such a literalistic reading of Gulliver's fantasmatic role-play is belied by Swift's own repeated and ironic intimations that the scenes themselves are a familiar and even a clichéd portrayal of the fantasy. Both Gulliver's own evident naivete and the repetition of adverbs such as "often" and "sometimes" suggest, as Boucé points out, that "Gulliver has visited the Maids of Honour on a number of occasions and is perfectly aware of what is to be expected at their fun-seeking hands," which both implies a willful indulgence in, or resignation to, fantasy role-play incompatible with mere castration anxiety, and "makes his virtuous protests of disgust, uneasiness and horror, combined with displeasure further down in the text less than entirely trustworthy" (Boucé, "Gulliver Phallophorus," 89).

15. Swift, *Gulliver's Travels*, 99.

16. Swift, 99. Gulliver's timidity here is especially ironic given that in the very next lines he describes the maids pissing into their pots "to the quantity of at least two hogsheads," which is incidentally the same quantity (of wine) the Lilliputians first gave the giant Gulliver to drink in the opening of part 1 (19–20).

17. Swift, 76.

18. S. Stewart, *On Longing*, 88.

19. Doane, *Bigger Than Life*, 59; Swift, *Gulliver's Travels*, 99.

20. Swift, *Gulliver's Travels*, 20; Adorno, *Minima Moralia*, 40.

21. Swift, "Lady's Dressing-Room," 603. See also Swift's "Strephon and Chloe" (1734).

22. See Armintor, "Sexual Politics of Microscopy," 619–40, and Baudot, "What Not to Avoid," 647–49.

23. Laura Baudot suggests that Swift's "atomistic breakdown of . . . filth" is a means of "us[ing] materialist philosophy against itself." For instance: "In describing the 'Composition' of the paste that clogs Celia's combs, Swift breaks it into its constituent parts—'Sweat, Dandriff, Powder, Lead and Hair.' The emphasis on the makeup of the material out of smaller particles, like the 'Compound of all Hues' coating the basin, suggests that Swift is taking an Epicurean/atomistic approach to describing the objects" ("What Not to Avoid," 645–46).

24. Baudot describes one of the poem's chief targets as "the pastoral tradition that nourishes the vanity of the fair and the dehumanizing naiveté of the male admirer by insisting on the divinity of women," and further suggests that "the very excesses of the poem, the lingered over and scrutinized excretions of the absent mistress, grant a kind of political imperative in determining whether the poem is as extravagantly misogynistic as it seems and to locating Swift's relationship to the material uncovered by the poem" ("What Not to Avoid," 637–38).

25. Swift, "Lady's Dressing-Room," 606.

26. Doane, *Bigger Than Life*, 59; Swift, *Gulliver's Travels*, 98.

27. Swift, *Gulliver's Travels*, 98.

28. Boucé describes Swift's reference to the English as "a casual remark fraught with razor-sharp irony when the reader bears in mind the sadly deficient state of corporal hygiene, even at Court, in eighteenth-century Britain, France, and Europe at large" ("Gulliver Phallophorus," 90). Note that a similar generalization crops up when Gulliver, within the same passages, refers to a prior incident in which his own offensive smell to a relatively diminutive Lilliputian prompts this unselfconsciously ironic admission: "I am as little faulty that way as most of my Sex."

29. Swift, "Lady's Dressing-Room," 606.

Chapter Seven

1. See "Officer Wilson's Testimony," 207. The shooting occurred on August 9, 2014; the friend walking with Brown was Dorian Johnson. The grand jury proceeding was conducted by Assistant Prosecuting Attorneys Sheila Whirley and Kathi Alizadeh of St. Louis County, Missouri. Ultimately, the grand jury chose not to indict Darren Wilson.

2. "Officer Wilson's Testimony," 212. Wilson is being questioned by Sheila Whirley.

3. "Officer Wilson's Testimony," 198.

4. "Officer Wilson's Testimony," 216.

5. "Officer Wilson's Testimony," 225.

6. "Officer Wilson's Testimony," 227.

7. "Officer Wilson's Testimony," 228–29.

8. "George Stephanopoulos."

9. The two stereotypes are distinct but related. Donald Bogle describes the brute as a "barbaric black out to raise havoc," whose "subhuman and feral" rage is a form of minimally sublimated sexual violence; bucks are more explicitly "oversexed and savage, violent and frenzied as they lust for white flesh" (*Toms, Coons, Mulattoes*, 10, 13).

10. "Officer Wilson's Testimony," 229.

11. See Bogle, *Toms, Coons, Mulattoes*, especially 1–14.

12. Griffith lifted much of the narrative from Dixon's successful 1905 theater version of *The Clansman*.

13. Dixon, *Clansman*, 323. The scene continues: "Some of the white figures had fallen prostrate on the ground, sobbing in a frenzy of uncontrollable emotion. Some were leaning against the walls, their faces buried in their arms."

14. Dixon, 204ff.

15. Conrad, *Heart of Darkness*, 40.

16. Dennis, *Critical Works*, 380–81; see also Burke, *Philosophical Enquiry*, 67.

17. Kant's phrase, again.

18. The right-wing pundit Ben Stein says of Michael Brown, "to call him unarmed is like calling Sonny Liston or Cassius Clay unarmed. . . . He was armed with his incredibly strong, scary self" (*Steve Malzberg Show*).

19. For a discussion of the "troubling bias in perceptions of the physical formidability and threat posed by Black men and boys," see Wilson, Hugenberg, and Rule, "Racial Bias," 59. Also see Goff et al., "Essence of Innocence."

20. "Campus Police Kill Student."

21. "CMPD Officer's Trial"

22. "Ex-Milwaukee Officer."

23. "Key Takeaways."

24. "No words were exchanged."

25. "L.A. Riots Anniversary." Subsequent quotations of Koon are also from this source.

26. "L.A. Officer Says."

27. Mercer, "Fear of a Black Penis," 80. Mercer further comments on both the sexual components of Koon's narrative and the extraordinary extent of his psychological projection, even in retrospect. King's movements, once he exits his car, are construed specifically as a sexual threat to the white female officer, Melanie Singer, who had initiated the car chase with King: "'He grabbed his butt with both hands and began to shake and gyrate his fanny in a sexually suggestive fashion. . . . As King sexually gyrated, a mixture of fear and offense overcame Melanie. The fear was of a Mandingo sexual encounter'" (Stacey Koon, quoted by Mercer, "Fear of a Black Penis," 80).

28. Rachel Maddow explicitly connects DiIulio's article with Darren Wilson's testimony; see *Rachel Maddow Show*.

29. DiIulio, "My Black Crime Problem."

30. DiIulio, "Coming of the Super-Predators," 23.

31. DiIulio, 24.

32. DiIulio, 23, 26.

33. Dilulio, 26. The sentiment is elaborated in the book *Body Count*, which Dilulio published with William Bennett and John P. Waters in 1996: "[Super-predators are] radically impulsive, brutally remorseless youngsters, including ever more preteenage boys, who murder, assault, rape, rob, burglarize, deal deadly drugs, join gun-toting gangs, and create serious communal disorders. They do not fear the stigma of arrest, the pains of imprisonment, or the pangs of conscience. They perceive hardly any relationship between doing right (or wrong) now and being rewarded (or punished) for it later. To these mean-street youngsters, the words 'right' and 'wrong' have no fixed moral meaning" (Bennett, Dilulio, and Waters, *Body Count*, 27).

34. Dilulio, "My Black Crime Problem."

35. A variety of such stories are documented and discussed in a series of blog posts by the television writer David Mills, who suggests that *The New York Times* employed the phrase "giant negro" more than most other papers. See "Attack of the GIANT NEGROES!!"; "Scarier Than Hitler . . . It's a GIANT NEGRO!!"; "GIANT NEGRO to the Rescue!"; "Presidential Assassin Vs. GIANT NEGRO!"; "Cute White Chick Outwits GIANT NEGRO!!"

36. See "As Ex-Theorist."

37. "Mrs. Clinton—Campaign Speech."

38. See "Hillary Clinton Still Haunted."

39. Quoted by Robinson, *Superpredator*, 16.

40. See "H.R. 3355."

41. "Congressional Record—Senate," 30088.

Chapter Eight

1. Ferriss's *The Metropolis of Tomorrow* was reissued in an influential second edition by Princeton Architectural Press in 1986. I cite the Dover republication of the original 1929 edition.

2. Ferriss, *Metropolis of Tomorrow*, 74. Ferriss adds, "the block is assumed to be two hundred by six hundred feet." Also see Koolhaas, *Delirious New York*, 114.

3. Ferriss, *Metropolis of Tomorrow*, 78, 82.

4. As Ferriss conceives them, setbacks are not an architectural design principle, per se: "they are the embodiment of legal rather than architectural concepts" (*Metropolis of Tomorrow*, 82).

5. Koolhaas, *Delirious New York*, 138–39.

6. Ferriss, *Metropolis of Tomorrow*, 16.

7. Ferriss, *Metropolis of Tomorrow*, 38. The Daily News Building was designed by John Mead Howells and Raymond Hood, completed in 1930.

8. Ferriss, 38.

9. See US Laws, Statutes, etc. The Federal "Residence Act" of July 6, 1790, finalized a compromise ceding a parcel of land from Maryland and Virginia, "not exceeding 10 miles square" and to be located on the "river Potomack, at some place between the mouths of the Eastern-Branch and Connogochegue." The precise site was to be determined by the president.

10. See L'Enfant et al., "Plan of the city."

11. For an extended discussion of "reciprocity," see Jones, "Reciprocity of Sight."

12. The relative neglect of the judicial branch is a commonly noted fault of L'Enfant's design; no anticipation of a Supreme Court appears in his original plan.

13. See *Improvement of the Park System.*

14. Eventually Tiber Creek entirely vanished into an underground tunnel.

15. Savage, *Monument Wars,* partly quoting widely reprinted comments from the *Maryland Journal,* September 26, 1791 (35, 318n23).

16. Savage, *Monument Wars,* 36, 34.

17. Savage, 46.

18. L'Enfant himself, realistic about the obstacles to his scheme, proposed a series of very large-scale engineering projects, including several to make Point A viable as the ground for a principal monument. These projects included a canal to redirect the Tiber Creek away from the center of the site and landscaping to enable the vast formal allée between Points A and L, composing the feature we would now recognize as the eastern half of the Mall.

19. Savage, *Monument Wars,* 46.

20. See Savage, 54–58.

21. Prior to the year 1311, the world's tallest structure was the Cheops pyramid in Egypt.

22. Savage, *Monument Wars,* 55.

23. Harries, *Meaning of Modern Art,* 17. I should perhaps note that I do not use the term "citizen" in its legal or juridical sense.

24. Harries discusses the simultaneous concreteness and universality of such an "ideal or transcendental subject" in Descartes's enormously influential geometry: "There is indeed something angelic about the point of view claimed by the new science, a point of view that really is no longer such, for it claims to have left behind the perspectival distortions of points of view. . . . To think a perspective as a perspective is to be in some sense already beyond its limitations" (*Infinity and Perspective,* 123).

25. Krauss, *Originality of the Avant-Garde,* 141.

26. Damisch, *Skyline,* 12.

27. Damisch, 11–12.

28. Savage, *Monument Wars,* 57.

29. Savage, 57.

30. Crary, *Techniques of the Observer,* 9.

31. Krauss, *Originality of the Avant-Garde,* 141.

32. Arendt, *Human Condition,* 250. See also Arendt's discussion of "world alienation" and "earth alienation" (261–64).

33. Crary, *Techniques of the Observer,* 4, 14.

34. Damisch, *Skyline,* 11; Benjamin, "Paris," 107. See Foucault, *Discipline and Punish,* 200–204.

35. Damisch, *Skyline,* 11.

36. Damisch, 12. Michael Tavel Clarke suggests, while speaking of Alvin Langdon Coburn's photographs of the Woolworth Building and other skyscrapers in 1912, that the skyscraper is capable of being perceived "not simply as a symbol of growth and progress but as a vehicle for new possibilities of vision" (*These Days,* 155).

37. See Toulmin, *Cosmopolis,* 68.

38. Rosalind Krauss, citing the 1920 manifesto "Purism," by Le Corbusier and Amédée Ozenfant, suggests: "Far from being cold or distancing, geometry tempts. Geometry seduces." Le Corbusier and Ozenfant directly connect the immense cartographical order of the city to its organization on minute levels of immediate human experience, for instance, in the ordered booths and displays of a modern market:

"These constant incitements of the brain, provoked by spectacles resulting from geometry, are already determined by the very presence of the city whose street plan—the houses in an almost uniform grid of windows, the neat stripes of the sidewalks, the alignment of trees with their identical circular grills, the regular punctuation of street lamps, the gleaming ribbons of tramway lines, the impeccable mosaic of paving stones—always and forever encloses us within geometry" (quoted by Krauss, *Optical Unconscious*, 161).

39. Crary, *Techniques of the Observer*, 150. Crary argues that the development of "the observer" in the nineteenth century involves "two intertwined paths," one toward "multiple affirmations of the sovereignty of and autonomy of vision derived from [the] newly empowered body," and the other "toward the increasing standardization and regulation of the observer, . . . toward forms of power that depended on the abstraction and formalization of vision" (150).

40. Crary, 150; in general, see Crary's chapter "Subjective Vision and the Separation of the Senses" (67–96).

41. Certeau, *Practice of Everyday Life*, 92.

42. See Koolhaas, *Delirious New York*, 82–85; the sketch appears on p. 83. The original sketch is from a March 1909 "Real Estate Number" of *Life* magazine (see "Buy a Cozy Cottage"); note that Koolhaas incorrectly cites the publication date of the magazine issue as October 1909.

43. Koolhaas, *Delirious New York*, 87, 83.

44. Several details in the drawing suggest that the artist is well aware of the irony of the depiction: the donkey peering over the precipice on floor eighty-two, the rustic cross-hatched wooden fence incongruously surrounding each "plot" on its steel platform, and even the fact that the house on floor seventy-nine, with its double chimney and gables suggesting (as do the others) a considerable outlay of private wealth required to situate what hardly appears to be a "cozy cottage" at such a height, has its potential vista gallingly obscured by passing clouds.

45. Koolhaas, *Delirious New York*, 85. The drawing's full caption quotes an advertising blurb from a fictional realtor: "'Buy a cozy cottage in our steel constructed choice lots, less than a mile above Broadway. Only ten minutes by elevator. All the comforts of the country with none of the disadvantages'—*Celestial Real Estate Company*." See "Buy a Cozy Cottage, etc."

46. A relatively arbitrary selection of skyscrapers described by architects or critics as "cities-within-cities," in New York and elsewhere, might include the Chicago Chamber of Commerce Building (1889; see Flinn, *Standard Guide to Chicago*, 570–71, quoted in Korom, *American Skyscraper*, 118); the New York Central Building (1929; see Korom, *American Skyscraper*, 381); Rockefeller Center (1939; see Loth, *City Within a City*); the World Trade Center (1973; see Douglas, *Skyscrapers*, 208); the Petronas Towers in Kuala Lumpur (1998; see Dupré, *Skyscrapers*, 112); the proposed Uptown München development (2003; see Wells, *Skyscrapers*, 98); and the Burj Khalifa in Dubai (2010; see Kamin, "Burj Khalifa," 78), the last of which I discuss in more detail below.

47. Article in *The New York Herald*, quoted by Koolhaas, *Delirious New York*, 89. The phrase "total architecture" is echoed by Hugh Ferriss, *Metropolis of Tomorrow*, 128.

48. Koolhaas, *Delirious New York*, 70, 82.

49. Namier, *Skyscrapers*, 8; Henry James, *American Scene*, quoted by Clarke, *These Days*, 141. Clarke notes that James was far from alone in such a view: "many

observers at the turn of the century believed that tall buildings were analogous to trusts"; opponents of skyscrapers "used the same rhetoric as those who wrote about big business . . . : 'soulless agglomerations,' 'Frankenstein monsters,' and 'monstrous parasites'" (141).

50. "The Oakland Museum."

51. Henry, "Psyche and the Psyscraper," 173; Mumford, *Sticks and Stones*, 175. See Adrienne R. Brown, who usefully discusses a number of similar criticisms ("Between Mythic and Monstrous").

52. See Clark and Kingston, *Skyscraper*, 87.

53. Koolhaas, *Delirious New York*, 88.

54. Sullivan, "Tall Office Building," 205.

55. Sullivan, 205.

56. Sullivan, 207.

57. Sullivan, 205, 206.

58. Sullivan, 203.

59. Hitchcock and Johnson, *International Style*, 67.

60. Koolhaas, *Delirious New York*, 27.

61. Sullivan, "Tall Office Building," 203.

62. Mumford, *Sticks and Stones*, 176; also quoted by Clarke, *These Days*, 149.

63. Clarke, *These Days*, 149.

64. See Le Corbusier, *Toward an Architecture*, 88; see Sullivan, "Tall Office Building," 208.

65. Schuyler, "'Sky-scraper' Up to Date," 236.

66. Schuyler, 234, 255.

67. Schuyler, 234.

68. Schuyler, 236.

69. Schuyler, 257.

70. Schuyler, "'Towers of Manhattan,'" 182.

71. Schuyler, "'Sky-scraper' Up to Date," 243.

72. Koolhaas, *Delirious New York*, 143.

73. Schuyler, "'Towers of Manhattan,'" 182.

74. Jencks rightly suggests that the bird's-eye view that sees (and even sees over) the top of the skyscraper "*is* the privileged view—likely that of the designer who works on a model and plan drawings," regardless of the fact that "one rarely sees the building from this position"; indeed, the view of and from the top is a "conceptual one which is inferred as we walk through the tall building" (*Skyscrapers—Skyprickers—Skycities*, 80n13). In general, see Fox's discussion of "the profound change" in the images of cities, both in photography and in painting, that were provoked in Paris by the Eiffel Tower and subsequently in other "vertical cities" such as New York. Indeed, as soon as construction on the Eiffel Tower had begun in 1887, photographers, many of whom had previously used balloons for such a purpose, began "clambering up its steel beams" to photograph the city below, gaining a new "typical view" that the Eiffel Tower allowed by its height and centrality (Fox, *Aereality*, 175; see Fox, 175–83).

75. Nye, "The Sublime and the Skyline," 265.

76. Jencks, *Skyscrapers—Skyprickers—Skycities*, 12.

77. A new entrance, more functional especially in terms of security but aesthetically questionable, was added in 2019. The additional small round holes above the rectangular windows are aircraft warning lights, added in 1958.

78. As David Nye comments, the "new vantage point" offered by the skyscraper, and eventually commoditized with the advent of public observation decks, "offered a reconception of urban space, miniaturizing the city into a pattern. . . . Lifted up to the sky, one was invited to see the city as a vast three-dimensional map" ("Sublime and the Skyline," 264).

79. Quoted by Kaika, "Autistic Architecture," 987. Formerly known as the Swiss Re Building, 30 St. Mary Axe is frequently called "the Gherkin." It was designed by Norman Foster and completed in 2004.

80. Berman, "When Bad Buildings Happen"; Graham, *Vertical*, 156; Huxtable, *Will They Ever Finish*; James, *American Scene*, 96; Wright, "Tyranny of the Skyscraper," 168, 180.

81. Virilio, *War and Cinema*, 4.

82. That Virilio describes the action of this eye as equivalent to "the function of a weapon" entails his own analysis of the totalizing intersection of war and vision in modern combat, and such analysis can be a caution against assuming the innocence of either vision or viewpoint, which is inevitably tied to structures of power and political manipulation. Arguably, this confluence is the source of typical pop-cultural assumptions about urban and institutional plans such as L'Enfant's, that they are designed to allow militaries easily to suppress insurrections, a conjecture no doubt borrowed from later schemes such as Hausmann's of Paris, but which has surprisingly lasting power in the mythology of urban design.

83. See Le Corbusier's *Aircraft*; *Toward an Architecture*, 159–76. See also Baudrillard, *System of Objects*, 5.

84. Virilio, *War and Cinema*, 1.

85. Virilio, 5.

86. Kaplan, "Balloon Prospect," 29.

87. Tolkien, *Return of the King*, 235.

88. Tolkien, 235.

89. Davis, "Fear and Money in Dubai," 53.

90. See, for instance, "Real Estate Collapse."

91. Mike Davis calls the development of the region "a hallucinatory pastiche of the big, the bad, and the ugly" ("Fear and Money in Dubai," 51).

92. See "Corporate News."

93. "Burj Khalifa: At the Top."

94. "Burj Khalifa: Vision." The webpage goes on to quote Mohamed Alabbar, chairman of Emaar Properties: "Burj Khalifa goes beyond its imposing physical specifications. In Burj Khalifa, we see the triumph of Dubai's vision of attaining the seemingly impossible and setting new benchmarks. It is a source of inspiration for every one of us at Emaar. The project is a declaration of the emirate's capabilities and of the resolve of its leaders and people to work hand-in-hand on truly awe-inspiring projects."

95. "Burj Khalifa: Facts and Figures."

96. I paraphrase Crary's term here, although the "technique of the observer" on which I am remarking, particular to both the publicizing of overall city plans and the construction of very tall buildings in the very late nineteenth and early twentieth century, operates in contrast to the type of viewing Crary discovers constructed "over the course of the nineteenth century," during which "an observer had to function within disjunct and defamiliarized urban spaces, the perceptual and temporal dislocations of railroad travel, telegraphy, industrial production, and flows of typographical and visual

information" (*Techniques of the Observer*, 10–11). In a sense, the skyscraper serves as a redress to such an increasingly amorphous observer, consolidating a fully urbanistic viewpoint at a specific physical location and aligning it with the monarchal "eye" of the city designer. Also see Damisch, *Skyline*, 11.

97. Nye, "Sublime and the Skyline," 264.

Chapter Nine

1. With slight leeway in its west coast time zone, the *Los Angeles Times* dispenses with qualifiers and declares, "The World's Greatest Steamship Wrecked: Titanic Strikes Giant Iceberg and Sinks on Maiden Voyage," adding the melodramatic subtitle, "The Displeasure of Neptune"—and then, with a jingoistic provincialism prevalent in disaster reportage ever since, begins to enumerate the "Many Prominent . . . Americans Aboard."

2. The *Columbus Ledger* of Georgia was so anxious to rush its account to print that it failed to correct blatant typographical errors and redundancies in its headline and sub-headlines: "On Maiden Trip, Great White Star Liner Hits Iceberg, Endangering the Lives of Over Two Thousand Persons: The Titantic [*sic*], Largest Steamship Afloat, on Maiden Voyage Across the Atlantic, Is in Trouble Today."

3. Franklin was vice president and general manager of International Mercantile Marine at White Star (see Heyer, *Titanic Century*, 70).

4. "Titanic Sinks."

5. Biel, "'Unknown and Unsung,'" 306. Biel notes that the "conventional narrative" was "centered around a myth of the heroism of the first-cabin male passengers." See also Biel, *Down with the Old Canoe*, especially chapter 2.

6. Žižek, *Welcome to the Desert*, 15; Biel, *Down with the Old Canoe*, 8.

7. Biel, "'Unknown and Unsung,'" 305.

8. These headlines are from, respectively, *The New York Times*, the *Chicago Tribune*, *The Aberdeen Daily News*, and *The New York Sun*.

9. See Boorstin, *The Image*.

10. See Žižek, *Welcome to the Desert*, 15.

11. Jane Feuer, in analyzing the "aesthetics of television," notes that "even the simplest meaning of 'live'—that the time of the event corresponds to the transmission and viewing times—reverberates with suggestions of 'being there' . . . bringing it to you as it really is'" ("Concept of Live Television," 14, Feuer's ellipsis).

12. See Grusin, "Premediation."

13. Stephen Kern makes a similar point: "The actual sinking was witnessed visually by hundreds of survivors who made it into the lifeboats; in a sense it was also witnessed electronically by telegraph operators in numerous ships at sea and by wireless operators in telegraph and newspaper offices across North America and even Europe, where messages were sent by Atlantic cable" (*Culture of Time and Space*, xiii; see also 66–67).

14. See Virilio, *Vision Machine*, 1–2. Virilio adopts the term "mechanical witness" from Paul Gsell.

15. Heyer, *Titanic Century*, 71.

16. Heyer, 71.

17. Koldau, *Titanic on Film*, 143.

18. Bullock, "Death of Thomas Andrews," 341–42.

19. B. Shaw, "*Titanic*: Some Unmentioned Morals," 214.

20. Doane, "Information, Crisis, Catastrophe," 231. Note that the *Hindenburg* crash was far from the world's worst airship disaster; just its most (re)viewable one.

21. Marks, *Skin of the Film*, xvii.

22. Merleau-Ponty, *Phenomenology of Perception*, 477.

23. "S.S. Titanic Launching."

24. In general, see Koldau, *Titanic on Film*; Bottomore, *Titanic and Silent Cinema*.

25. See Koldau, *Titanic on Film*, 6.

26. Independent of the film as a whole, this single, very expensive shot is famous, often referred to as "The Million Dollar Shot."

27. Ernest Borgnine offers a useful and entertaining description of the budget woes of the film (see Borgnine, *Ernie*, 178–79).

28. Bazin, "Evolution," 24.

29. Deleuze, *Cinema I*, 81.

30. Leibniz, *Monadology*, ¶14. Note: here and subsequently, I cite Leibniz's *Monadology* by paragraph number.

31. Leibniz, ¶60.

32. See Leibniz, ¶¶14–15, 17.

33. Žižek, *Welcome to the Desert*, 15. The original article that became Žižek's book was composed as early after 9/11 as October 17, 2001.

34. See *Secrets of the Titanic*; Ballard, *Discovery of the Titanic*.

35. Žižek, *Sublime Object of Ideology*, 70.

36. Žižek, 71.

37. Žižek, 71.

38. Burke, *Philosophical Enquiry*, quoted by Kant, *Critique of Judgment*, 138.

39. Žižek, *Sublime Object of Ideology*, 71.

Chapter Ten

1. Shinohara, "House with Triangular Windows," 67.

2. Kerez, "Thoughts on Seven Houses," 25.

3. "Jap Savagery," 73.

4. In a 2017 interview with Seiko and Tetsuo Ōtsuji, the original owners of the House in Uehara, the interviewer asks, "Weren't you bothered by the diagonal column?" and Seiko Ōtsuji responds: "Not at all. The children would lean, climb, and slide on them." Later, Tetsuo Ōsuki comments: "When people see the diagonals, they often say, 'A lot of heads get bumped there, right?' But till now there hasn't been a single bumped head." See Hosaka, "Interview," 199, 200.

5. "Jap Savagery," 73; Bognar, *Contemporary Japanese Architecture*, 313. See also Sanderson, "Kazuo Shinohara's 'Savage Machine,'" 112–13.

6. In a conversation with Kenzo Tange, discussing Tange's famously enormous *Plan for Tokyo*, Shinohara comments: "You said that the two systems, one working from the outside and one working from the inside, should join in one, that a man should have experience with both. I, however, doubt that creating a large mass from the outside and developing a concept from the inside involve compatible abilities" (see Tange, "Kenzo Tange on Residential Design," 20).

7. Taki, "Oppositions."

8. See Seike, *Art of Japanese Joinery*, 97; Engel, *Japanese House*, 114–28.

9. Shinohara employs diagonals elsewhere, albeit less audaciously: Two Houses at Hanayama (1969), Tanikawa House (1974), and House in Hanayama, No. 3 (1977). These and most other designs are available in Shinohara, *Katsuo Shinohara: Complete Works*, in addition to the original publications, chiefly in the journal *Japan Architect*.

10. Heidegger, *Nietzsche*, 1:189.

11. Shinohara, "Towards Architecture," 31.

12. Inoue, *Space in Japanese Architecture*, 3–8.

13. Shinohara, "Savage Machine," 50; Matsunaga, "Architecture as Text," 2.

14. Shinohara, "House in Uehara," 163.

15. Shinohara, 163.

16. See Massip-Bosch, Stewart, and Okuyama, *Kazuo Shinohara*, 163.

17. Shinohara, "House in Uehara," 163.

18. Shinohara, "House with Triangular Windows," 66.

19. Shinohara, "House in Uehara," 163.

20. *Kenchiku Bunka* 32.363, quoted in "Jap Savagery," 73.

21. In his role as judge for a competition of house design, Shinohara comments: "From my standpoint, creating houses is tantamount to criticizing the Japanese residential tradition and the residential designs created by others in the world around me. In other words, I regard the criticism of houses and the designing of houses as essentially the same thing" (Shinohara, "Judge's Comments," 47).

22. The house is sometimes called "House *Under* High Voltage Lines."

23. Daniell, *After the Crash*, 168; Shinohara, "Toward a Super-Big," 282.

24. Suzuki, Banham, and Kobayashi, *Contemporary Architecture of Japan*, 84; Bognar, *Contemporary Japanese Architecture*, 318; Massip-Bosch, Stewart and Okuyama, *Kazuo Shinohara*, 206.

25. Daniell, *After the Crash*, 168.

26. Shinohara, "Toward a Super-Big," 278–81, 282.

27. Matsunaga, "Architecture as Text," 1–2.

28. Shinohara, "Savage Machine," 46.

29. Shinohara, 46.

30. Shinohara, "Toward a Super-Big," 279. See also Okuyama, "The Meaning of Writing," 82–83.

31. Shinohara, "Beyond Symbol Spaces," 81. "Japanese-looking" is David Stewart's term.

32. Shinohara, 81.

33. Taki, "Oppositions," 44.

34. Taki, 47; Shinohara, "Savage Machine," 48.

35. Taki, "Oppositions," 47.

36. Taki, 46.

37. Shinohara, "Toward a Super-Big," 277.

38. "Japan-ness" is Arato Isozaki's term; see *Japan-ness in Architecture*, 11, 45; Shinohara, "Beyond Symbol Spaces," 82. David Stewart suggests that in this house "no aspect, excepting Shoji, is related to the conventional vocabulary of Japanese interior spaces"; he calls the height of the ceiling "extreme" (*Making of a Modern Japanese Architecture*, 205).

39. Shinohara, "Savage Machine," 49. Shinohara himself divides his work into four periods or "styles"; the House in White belongs to the first style, and the Uehara

House and Tanikawa House (discussed below) to his third style. See Shinohara, "Program for the 'Fourth Space.'"

40. James Curl and Susan Wilson explicitly link the House in White to the later House in Uehara: "His best-known works were the house in Uehara, Tokyo (1975–6), with its massive truss-like structure inside, a development of the free-standing columnar theme first used in the 'House in White'" (*Oxford Dictionary of Architecture*, 705).

41. Hiroshi Watanabe, discussing the later House Beneath High Voltage Lines (analyzed below), refers to "the distinctly Japanese fascination with columns as physical objects" ("Kazuo Shinohara's 'House,'" 66). Also see Inoue, *Space in Japanese Architecture*, 12, 46–48. Note that another traditional-Japanese reference point for the central post is the "Great Buddha" style, which David Stewart explicitly connects to the House in White (see D. Stewart, "Fashioning Change," 172).

42. Taki, "Oppositions," 47.

43. D. Stewart, *Making of a Modern Japanese Architecture*, 205.

44. Shinohara, "When Naked Space Is Traversed," 66.

45. Shinohara, "Third Style," 265. Compare Isozaki's discussion of "interstices" (*ma*) in *Japan-ness in Architecture*, 27, 94.

46. Shinohara, "When Naked Space Is Traversed," 64.

47. Shinohara, 64, 68.

48. Shinohara, 64, 65.

49. See Inoue, *Space in Japanese Architecture*, 146.

50. Shinohara, "When Naked Space Is Traversed," 65.

51. Shinohara, 66.

52. Shinohara, 68.

53. Shinohara, 69.

54. Shinohara, 67.

55. Shinohara, 67.

56. Shinohara, 67.

57. Enric Massip-Bosch observes: "Many of the instances in which juxtaposition plays an emotional role in Shinohara's work involve the contrast between a private interior (which I will call 'cocoon') and an external figure (which I will term 'transgressor') that apparently does not belong there. Most of the times the role of transgressor in his designs is given to structural elements that pierce or occupy the cocoon, seemingly regardless of its inhabitants" ("Emotion Devices," 69).

58. Shinohara, "When Naked Space Is Traversed," 66.

59. Shinohara, "Towards Architecture," 35.

60. Le Corbusier, *Toward an Architecture*, 87.

61. Shinohara, "Towards Architecture," 35.

62. Shinohara, "When Naked Space Is Traversed," 69.

63. Botond Bognar describes the "radically negative attitude of those architects [including Shinohara] toward the contemporary city and its conversion into Megalopolis" ("Art and Technique," 7).

64. Bognar, 7.

65. Kuan, "The Small Japanese House," 41. See also Kuan, "Traversing the House and the City," 11.

66. Shinohara, "Toward a Super-Big," 283–85.

Chapter Eleven

1. Kaufman and Rock, "Moon Illusion," 120.

2. See Plug and Ross, "Historical Review."

3. Enright, "Moon Illusion Examined," 87.

4. Molyneux, "Concerning Apparent Magnitude," 314.

5. Molyneux, 314–15.

6. Molyneux, 322.

7. See Alhacen [Ibn al-Haytham], *Alhacen on Refraction*, 327–31.

8. Molyneux, "Concerning Apparent Magnitude," 314.

9. Ptolemy, *Almagest*, 39.

10. Helen Ross notes that "the popular press today continues to report the refraction account," and cites at least one example from 1994. See Ross, "The Sun/Moon Illusion," 2.

11. Berkeley, *New Theory of Vision*, 31–32.

12. See Plug and Ross, "Historical Review," 76–77. In addition to a variety of "atmospheric refraction" (52) and "aerial perspective models" (76), Plug and Ross list "perceptual learning" (121), "brightness effects" (78), "colour effects" (83), "pupil size" and "focusing" effects (88), the "flattened dome" or "sky illusion" (99), "intervening objects" (117), "perceptual learning" (121), "size assimilation" or "size scaling" (142), "angle of regard" (153), and a number of other models, as well as subcategories of those mentioned.

13. See Hershenson, "That Most Puzzling Illusion," 1; Plug and Ross, "Historical Review," 22.

14. Molyneux, "Concerning Apparent Magnitude," 315.

15. Euclid, "Optics," 357. See also Lindberg, *Theories of Vision*, 12.

16. Euclid, "Book on Vision," 189; note that in this passage I opt for Theisen's more literal translation over the standard one of Burton, who interposes the word "object" where it doesn't appear in the Greek; Burton has "Let there be two objects of equal size, *AB* and *GD*, and let the eye be indicated by *E*, from which let the objects be unequally distant, and let *AB* be nearer. I say that *AB* will appear larger" (Euclid, "Optics," 358). The diagram, however, I take from Burton's version (357, fig. 5).

17. Kilpatrick and Ittelson, "Size-Distance Invariance Hypothesis," 223ff.

18. Kilpatrick and Ittelson, 230. The more precise formula is $S'/D' = \tan\theta'$, which distinguishes between physical quantities and perceived quantities (i.e., S' is the perceived size as opposed to S, the physical size); see Plug and Ross, "Historical Review," 31–32; Gilinsky, "Perceived Size and Distance," 462.

19. Carr, *Introduction to Space Perception*, 365.

20. Kilpatrick and Ittelson, "Size-Distance Invariance Hypothesis," 230.

21. See Kim, "Oculomotor Effects," 123ff.

22. Pecham, *Perspectiva communis*, 145; Bacon, *Perspectiva*, 225; Desaguliers, cited by Wade, *Perception and Illusion*, 104. Also compare Descartes: "the axiom of the ancient Optics, which says that the apparent size of objects is proportional to the size of the angle of vision, is not always true" (*Optics*, 111).

23. Baird, *Psychophysical Analysis of Visual Space*, 285.

24. Ibn al-Haytham, *Optics*, 174, 176; Bacon, *Perspectiva*, 207. E. H. Gombrich interestingly reiterates the point, citing Beloff: "Perception . . . may be regarded as

primarily the modification of an anticipation" (*Art and Illusion*, 172); later, Gombrich refers to the process of perception as "the rhythm of schema and correction" (270).

25. Helmholtz, *Physiological Optics*, 3:283.

26. Pecham, *Perspectiva communis*, 147; I have altered the translation slightly.

27. Gilinsky, "Perceived Size and Distance," 460; Hershenson, "The Puzzle Remains," 383; Ono, "Different Perceptual Tasks," 143; Joynson, "Problem of Size and Distance," 134; Epstein and Baratz, "Relative Size," 512; Kilpatrick and Ittelson, "Size-Distance Invariance Hypothesis," 223; Haber and Levin, "Independence of Size Perception," 1140; Gibson, *Perception of the Visual World*, vii; Carr, *Introduction to Space Perception*, 403.

28. Petermann, *Gestalt Theory*, 3–4. See also Koffka, *Principles of Gestalt Psychology*, 87–91, and Merleau-Ponty's general critique of "the 'sensation' as a unit of experience," in *Phenomenology of Perception*, 3–12.

29. Petermann, *Gestalt Theory*, 3–4. Also see Köhler, "Mind-Body Problem," 80–82.

30. See Köhler, "On Unnoticed Sensations," 15; see also Koffka, *Principles of Gestalt Psychology*.

31. See Köhler, "Mind-Body Problem," 80–81. Note that Merleau-Ponty suggests up front that the notion of sensation as the unit of objective perception "seems immediate and obvious," but that "nothing in fact could be more confused, and . . . because they accepted it readily, traditional analyses missed the phenomenon of perception" (*Phenomenology of Perception*, 3). Koffka is more blunt in his refutation of what he calls the "interpretation" model of perception, based on the constancy hypothesis: "Why, you may ask, such a long discussion of so palpably bad a theory" (*Principles of Gestalt Psychology*, 87).

32. See also, Köhler, "Old Pseudoproblem," especially 138–41; Merleau-Ponty, *Phenomenology of Perception*, 3.

33. Köhler, *Gestalt Psychology*, 71, 78.

34. Köhler, 78.

35. Köhler, 79. I sidestep the complex and powerful arguments against the "constancy hypothesis"—or against the hypothesis of an ultimately consistent relation between physical stimuli and perceptual effects—initiated by Köhler in his 1913 paper "On Unnoticed Sensations and Errors of Judgment." This refutation underlies much of Gestalt psychology as well as those aspects of phenomenology and cognitive psychology akin to it. Essentially, what Köhler refutes is not the constancy hypothesis, per se, but rather the range of empiricist assumptions or dogmas required to maintain it in light of the many ways it is violated in both everyday perception and putatively exceptional cases of illusion or error. Also see Koffka, *Principles of Gestalt Psychology*, 74–105.

36. Köhler, *Gestalt Psychology*, 79.

37. Köhler, 84, 116, 103. Compare Wertheimer: "The basic thesis of gestalt theory might be formulated thus: there are contexts in which what is happening in the whole cannot be deduced from the characteristics of the separate pieces, but conversely; what happens to a part of the whole is, in clear-cut cases, determined by the laws of the inner structure of its whole" ("Gestalt Theory," 84).

38. Köhler, *Gestalt Psychology*, 103. See also 139.

39. Merleau-Ponty, *Phenomenology of Perception*, 304.

40. Merleau-Ponty, 299.

41. Merleau-Ponty, 303.

42. Merleau-Ponty, 298.

43. Merleau-Ponty, 302; I have altered the translation here. Note also: "Apparent size is, therefore, not definable independently of distance; it is implied by distance and it also implies distance. Convergence, apparent size and distance are read off from each other, naturally symbolize or signify each other, are the abstract elements of a situation and are, within it, mutually synonymous, not because the subject of perception posits objective relations between them, but on the contrary because he does not posit them separately and therefore has no need to unify them expressly" (304). The touchstone for this type of analysis is Husserl's discussion of the "natural attitude" (Husserl, *Ideas*, 5).

44. Merleau-Ponty, *Phenomenology of Perception*, 301.

45. Merleau-Ponty, 31.

46. Merleau-Ponty, 327, 378. Compare: "The constancy of forms and sizes in perception is therefore not an intellectual function, but an existential one, which means that it has to be related to the prelogical act by which the subject takes up his place in the world. When a human subject is placed at the center of a sphere on which discs of equal diameter are fixed, it is noticed that constancy is much more perfect in the horizontal than in the vertical plane. The huge moon on the horizon contrasted with the very small one at the zenith is merely a particular case of the same law" (353n2).

47. Merleau-Ponty, 304.

48. Merleau-Ponty, 299.

49. I assume it goes without saying, if perhaps not without further analysis, that there is a range of ways in which one might commit the "error" of overestimating the size of a man approaching on a street. Someone walking alone at night in a dangerous town, approached by some man or men, may be correct to lean on the side of this putative "error"; Officer Stacey Koon confronting Rodney King, or Officer Darren Wilson confronting Michael Brown, clearly not so much.

50. See the section of Hegel's *Phenomenology* titled "Self-Sufficiency and Non-Self-Sufficiency of Self-Consciousness: Mastery and Servitude" (*Phenomenology of Spirit*, 109–16).

51. See Hegel, 110–11.

52. Hegel, 110; I have altered the translation slightly.

53. See Rousseau, "Essay," 293. I have altered the translation of Rousseau, more strictly retaining the complex grammatical tenses of the French. For the original French, see chapter 3 in Rousseau, *Essai*, 12–13.

54. See Rousseau, "Essay," 294–95.

55. See Rousseau, 295.

56. Derrida, *Of Grammatology*, 299.

Bibliography

Addison, Joseph. *The Spectator*, no. 412 (June 23, 1712). In *The Spectator*, 6:65–69. London: J. and R. Tonson, 1744.

Addison, Joseph. *The Spectator*, no. 418 (June 30, 1712). In *The Spectator*, 6:89–93. London: J. and R. Tonson, 1744.

Adorno, Theodor. *Minima Moralia: Reflections from Damaged Life*. Translated by E. F. N. Jephcott. New York: Verso, 2005.

Adorno, Theodor. "Valéry Proust Museum." In *Prisms*, translated by Samuel Weber and Shierry Weber, 173–85. Cambridge, MA: MIT Press, 1984.

Alhacen [Ibn al-Haytham]. *Alhacen on Refraction* [*De aspectibus*, book 7]. Edited and translated by A. Mark Smith. Transactions of the American Philosophical Society, n.s., vol. 100, no. 3, sec. 2 (2010), 213–550.

Ant-Man. Directed by Peyton Reed. Walt Disney Studios, 2015.

Apocalypse Now. Directed by Francis Coppola. United Artists, 1979.

Arendt, Hannah. *The Human Condition*. 2nd ed. Chicago: University of Chicago Press, 1958.

Aristotle. *Categories*. In Aristotle, *Complete Works*, 1:3–24.

Aristotle. *The Complete Works of Aristotle*. Vols. 1 and 2. Revised Oxford translation. Edited by Jonathan Barnes. Princeton, NJ: Princeton University Press, 1984.

Aristotle. *Metaphysics*. In Aristotle, *Complete Works*, 2:1552–1728.

Aristotle. *Poetics*. In Aristotle, *Complete Works*, 2:2316–40.

Aristotle. *Posterior Analytics*. In Aristotle, *Complete Works*, 1:114–66.

Armageddon. Directed by Michael Bay. Touchstone Pictures, Jerry Bruckheimer Films, and Valhalla Motion Pictures, 1998.

Armintor, Deborah Needleman. "The Sexual Politics of Microscopy in Brobdingnag." *Studies in English Literature, 1500–1900* 47, no. 3 (Summer 2007): 619–40.

"As Ex-Theorist on Young 'Superpredators,' Bush Aide Has Regrets." *New York Times*, February 9, 2001, A19.

Ashfield, Andrew, and Peter de Bolla, eds. *The Sublime: A Reader in British Eighteenth-Century Aesthetic Theory*. New York: Cambridge University Press, 1996.

"Assignment Four Documentary—The Oakland Museum." Directed by Dan Riley. Chronicle Broadcasting Co, KRON 4, 1970.

Avatar. Directed by James Cameron. Twentieth Century Fox, 2009.

Avengers: Infinity War. Directed by Anthony Russo and Joe Russo. Walt Disney Studios, 2018.

Bacon, Roger. *Perspectiva*. In *Roger Bacon and the Origins of "Perspectiva" in the Middle Ages*, edited and translated by David C. Lindberg, 1–339. New York: Oxford University Press, 1996.

Badiou, Alain. *Being and Event*. Translated by Oliver Feltham. New York: Bloomsbury, 2007.

Baird, John C. *Psychophysical Analysis of Visual Space*. New York: Pergamon, 1970.

Ball, Philip. "World's Smallest Magazine Cover Is the Size of a Red Blood Cell." *Guardian*, April 25, 2014. www.theguardian.com/science/2014/apr/25/world-smallest-magazine-cover-national-geographic-kids?CMP=share_btn_url.

Ballard, Robert D. *The Discovery of the Titanic*. New York: Warner Books, 1986.

Barad, Karen. *Meeting the Universe Halfway: Quantum Physics and the Entanglement of Matter and Meaning*. Durham, NC: Duke University Press, 2007.

Barrow, John D., and Frank J. Tipler. *The Anthropic Cosmological Principle*. New York: Oxford University Press, 1986.

Bataille, Georges. "Concerning the Accounts Given by the Residents of Hiroshima." Translated by Alan Keenan. *American Imago* 48, no. 4 (Winter 1991): 497–514. Also in Caruth, *Trauma*, 221–35.

Baudot, Laura. "What Not to Avoid in Swift's 'The Lady's Dressing Room.'" *Studies in English Literature* 49, no. 3 (Summer 2009): 637–66.

Baudrillard, Jean. *The System of Objects*. Translated by James Benedict. New York: Verso, 1996.

Baumgarten, Alexander Gottlieb. *Ästhetik*. German-Latin ed. Translated by Dagmar Mirbach. Hamburg: Felix Meiner Verlag, 2009.

Baumgarten, Alexander Gottlieb. *Metaphysics*. Edited and translated by Courtney D. Fugate and John Hymers. New York: Bloomsbury, 2013.

Baumgarten, Alexander Gottlieb. *Reflections on Poetry* [*Meditationes philosophicae de nonnullis ad poema pertinentibus*]. Translated by Karl Aschenbrenner and William B. Holther. Berkeley: University of California Press, 1954.

Bazin, André. "The Evolution of the Language of Cinema." In *What Is Cinema?*, vol. 1, translated by Hugh Gray, 23–40. Berkeley: University of California Press, 1967.

Benjamin, Walter. "Paris, the Capital of the Nineteenth Century." Translated by Howard Eiland. In *The Work of Art in the Age of Its Technological Reproducibility and Other Writings on Media*, edited by Michael W. Jennings, Brigid Doherty, and Thomas Y. Levin, 96–115. Cambridge, MA: Harvard University Press, 2008.

Benjamin, Walter. "The Work of Art in the Age of Its Technological Reproducibility: Second Version." In *The Work of Art in the Age of Its Technological Reproducibility and Other Writings on Media*, translated by Edmund Jephcott, Rodney Livingstone, Howard Eiland, et al., and edited by Michael W. Jennings, Brigid Doherty, and Thomas Y. Levin, 19–55. Cambridge, MA: Harvard University Press, 2008.

Bennett, William, John J. Dilulio Jr., and John. P. Waters. *Body Count: Moral Poverty . . . And How to Win America's War Against Crime and Drugs*. New York: Simon and Schuster, 1996.

Bergson, Henri. *Time and Free Will*. Translated by F. L. Pogson. New York: Harper and Row, 1960.

Berkeley, George. *An Essay Towards a New Theory of Vision*. In *Berkeley: Philosophical Writings*, edited by Desmond M. Clarke, 1–66. Cambridge: Cambridge University Press, 2008.

Berman, Marshall. "When Bad Buildings Happen to Good People." In *After the World Trade Center: Rethinking New York City*, edited by Michael Sorkin and Sharon Zukin, 1–12. New York: Routledge, 2002.

Biel, Steven. *Down with the Old Canoe: A Cultural History of the Titanic Disaster*. New York: Norton, 2012.

Biel, Steven. "'Unknown and Unsung': Feminist, African American, and Radical Responses to the *Titanic* Disaster." In *American Disasters*, edited by Steven Biel, 305–38. New York: New York University Press, 2001.

"Bikini Atoll Wall Art." Redbubble. www.redbubble.com/shop/bikini+atoll+prints.

Birth of a Nation. Directed by D. W. Griffith. David W. Griffith Corp. and Epoch Producing Corp., 1915.

Bogle, Donald. *Toms, Coons, Mulattoes, Mammies, and Bucks: An Interpretive History of Blacks in American Films*. 5th ed. New York: Bloomsbury, 2016.

Bognar, Botond. "An Art and Technique of Fragmentation: The New Urban Architecture of Japan." *Japan Architect* 398 (June 1990): 6–10.

Bognar, Botond. *Contemporary Japanese Architecture*. New York: Van Nostrand Reinhold, 1985.

Bonner, John Tyler. *Why Size Matters: From Bacteria to Blue Whales*. Princeton, NJ: Princeton University Press, 2006.

Boorstin, Daniel. *The Image: A Guide to Pseudo-Events in America*. 50th anniversary ed. New York: Vintage, 2012.

Borgnine, Ernest. *Ernie: The Autobiography*. New York: Citadel, 2008.

Bottomore, Stephen. *The Titanic and Silent Cinema*. London: Projection Box, 2000.

Boucé, Paul-Gabriel. "Gulliver Phallophorus and the Maids of Honour in Brobdingnag." *Bulletin de la société d'études anglo-américaines des XVIIe et XVIIIe siècles* 53 (2001): 81–98.

Breuer, Josef, and Sigmund Freud. *Studies in Hysteria*. Translated by Nicola Luckhurst. New York: Penguin, 2004.

Brown, Adrienne R. "Between the Mythic and the Monstrous: The Early Skyscraper's Weird Frontiers." *Journal of Modern Literature* 35, no. 1 (Fall 2011): 165–88.

Brown, Bill. *Other Things*. Chicago: University of Chicago Press, 2015.

Brown, Bill. "Thing Theory." *Critical Inquiry* 28, no. 1 (Autumn 2001): 1–22.

Bukatman, Scott. "Zooming Out: The End of Offscreen Space." In *The New American Cinema*, edited by Jon Lewis, 248–72. Durham, NC: Duke University Press, 1998.

Bullock, Shan F. "The Death of Thomas Andrews." In *The Titanic Reader*, edited by John Wilson Foster, 339–42. New York: Penguin, 1999.

Bunyan, John. *The Pilgrim's Progress*. New York: Dover, 2003.

"Burj Khalifa: At the Top." www.burjkhalifa.ae/en/the-tower/.

"Burj Khalifa: Facts and Figures." www.burjkhalifa.ae/en/the-tower/facts-figures/.

"Burj Khalifa: Vision." www.burjkhalifa.ae/en/the-tower/vision/.

Burke, Edmund. *A Philosophical Enquiry into the Origin of Our Ideas of the Sublime and the Beautiful*. Edited by Adam Philips. New York: Oxford University Press, 1990.

Burnet, Thomas. *The Sacred Theory of the Earth.* 4th ed. London: John Hooke, 1719.

"Buy a Cozy Cottage, etc." Illustration. *Life* 53, no. 1375 (March 4, 1909): 299.

"Campus Police Kill Student." *Los Angeles Times,* December 10, 2012.

Carr, Harvey A. *An Introduction to Space Perception.* New York: Longman's, Green, 1935.

Caruth, Cathy, ed. *Trauma: Explorations in Memory.* Baltimore: Johns Hopkins University Press, 1995.

Certeau, Michel de. *The Practice of Everyday Life.* Translated by Steven Rendall. Berkeley: University of California Press, 1984.

Citizen Kane. Directed by Orson Welles. RKO Radio Pictures, 1941.

Clark, W. C., and J. L. Kingston. *The Skyscraper: A Study in the Economic Height of Modern Office Buildings.* New York: American Institute of Steel Construction, Inc., 1930.

Clarke, Michael Tavel. *These Days of Large Things: The Culture of Size in America, 1865–1930.* Ann Arbor: University of Michigan Press, 2007.

Clarke, Michael Tavel, and David Wittenberg. "Introduction." In *Scale in Literature and Culture,* edited by Clarke and Wittenberg, 1–32. New York: Palgrave Macmillan, 2017.

Clash of the Titans. Directed by Louis Leterrier. Warner Brothers, 2010.

Cleopatra. Directed by Joseph Mankiewicz. Twentieth Century Fox, 1963.

Close Encounters of the Third Kind. Directed by Steven Spielberg. Columbia Pictures, 1977.

Cloverfield. Directed by Matt Reeves. Paramount Pictures, 2008.

"CMPD Officer's Trial—Kerrick: Ferrell Wouldn't Stop." *Charlotte Observer,* August 8, 2015.

"Congressional Record—Senate." Vol. 139, part 21 (November 18, 1993). www.congress.gov/bound-congressional-record/1993/11/18/senate-section.

Conrad, Joseph. *Heart of Darkness.* New York: Penguin, 2012.

Conselice, Christopher J., Aaron Wilkinson, Kenneth Duncan, and Alice Mortlock. "The Evolution of Galaxy Number Density at z < 8 and Its Implications." *Astrophysical Journal* 830, no. 83: 1–17.

Coole, Diana, and Samantha Frost. "Introducing the New Materialisms." In *New Materialisms: Ontology, Agency, and Politics,* edited by Coole and Frost, 1–43. Durham, NC: Duke University Press, 2010.

"Corporate News." *Arab News,* January 1, 2010. www.arabnews.com/node/332035.

Crary, Jonathan. *Techniques of the Observer: On Vision and Modernity in the Nineteenth Century.* Cambridge, MA: MIT Press, 1990.

Curl, James Stevens, and Susan Wilson. *The Oxford Dictionary of Architecture.* 3rd ed. New York: Oxford University Press, 2015.

Damisch, Hubert. *Skyline: The Narcissistic City.* Translated by John Goodman. Stanford, CA: Stanford University Press, 2001.

Daniell, Thomas. *After the Crash: Architecture in Post-Bubble Japan.* Princeton, NJ: Princeton University Press, 2008.

Davis, Mike. "Fear and Money in Dubai." *New Left Review* 51 (September/October 2006): 47–68.

Deleuze, Gilles. *Cinema I: The Movement-Image.* Translated by Hugh Tomlinson and Barbara Habberjam. Minneapolis: University of Minnesota Press, 1986.

Dennis, John. *The Advancement and Reformation of Modern Poetry. A Critical Discourse, In Two Parts*. London: Richard Parker, 1701.

Dennis, John. *The Critical Works of John Dennis*. Vol. 2. Edited by E. N. Hooker. Baltimore: Johns Hopkins University Press, 1939.

Dennis, John. *The Grounds of Criticism in Poetry*. London: George Strahan, 1704.

Derrida, Jacques. *Of Grammatology*. 40th anniversary ed. Translated by Gayatri Chakravorty Spivak. Baltimore: Johns Hopkins University Press, 2016.

Derrida, Jacques. *Truth in Painting*. Translated by Geoff Bennington and Ian McLeod. Chicago: University of Chicago Press, 1987.

Descartes, René. *Optics*. In Descartes, *Discourse on Method, Optics, Geometry, and Meteorology*, rev. ed., translated by Paul J. Olscamp, 65–173. Indianapolis: Hackett, 2001.

DiCaglio, Joshua. *Scale Theory: A Nondisciplinary Inquiry*. Minneapolis: University of Minnesota Press, 2021.

DiIulio, John J., Jr. "The Coming of the Super-Predators." *Weekly Standard* 1, no. 11 (November 27, 1995): 23–28.

DiIulio, John J., Jr. "My Black Crime Problem, and Ours." *City Journal* (Spring 1996): n.p. www.city-journal.org/article/my-black-crime-problem-and-ours.

Dixon, Thomas. *The Clansman: A Historical Romance of the Ku Klux Klan*. New York: Grossett and Dunlap, 1905.

Doane, Mary Ann. *Bigger Than Life: The Close-Up and Scale in the Cinema*. Durham, NC: Duke University Press, 2021.

Doane, Mary Ann. "Information, Crisis, Catastrophe." In *Logics of Television*, edited by Patricia Mellencamp, 222–39. Bloomington: Indiana University Press, 1990.

Doctor Strange in the Multiverse of Madness. Directed by Sam Raimi. Walt Disney Studios, 2022.

Douglas, George H. *Skyscrapers: A Social History of the Very Tall Building in America*. Jefferson, NC: McFarland, 1996.

Downsizing. Directed by Alexander Payne. Paramount Pictures, 2017.

Drake, Stillman. "Introduction." In Galileo Galilei, *Two New Sciences, Including Centers of Gravity and Force of Percussion*, 2nd ed., translated by Drake, xiii–xliii. Toronto: Wall and Emerson, 1989.

Dubois, Philippe. "Le gros plan primitive." *Revue belge du cinéma* 10 (Winter 1984–85): 11–34.

Dunkirk. Directed by Christopher Nolan. Warner Brothers, 2017.

Dupré, Judith. *Skyscrapers: A History of the World's Most Extraordinary Buildings*. Rev. ed. New York: Black Dog and Leventhal, 2013.

Eckes-Wahl, Suzanne. "Social History, Social Change and Public History." MA thesis, California State University, Sacramento, 2014. scholars.csus.edu/esploro/outputs/99257831361401671.

Engel, Heinrich. *The Japanese House: A Tradition for Contemporary Architecture*. Rutland, VT: Charles E. Tuttle, 1964.

Enright, J. T. "The Moon Illusion Examined from a New Point of View." *Proceedings of the American Philosophical Society* 119, no. 2 (April 16, 1975): 87–107.

Epstein, William, and Stephen S. Baratz. "Relative Size in Isolation as a Stimulus for Relative Perceived Distance." *Journal of Experimental Psychology* 67, no. 6 (1964): 507–13.

Euclid. "A Book on Vision." Translated by Wilfred Robert Theisen. In "The Mediaeval Tradition of Euclid's Optics," by Wilfred Robert Theisen, PhD dissertation, University of Wisconsin, 1972 (Ann Arbor, MI: University Microfilms, Inc.), 185–271.

Euclid. "The Optics of Euclid." Translated by Harry Edwin Burton. *Journal of the Optical Society of America* 35, no. 5 (May 1945): 357–72.

Euclid. *The Thirteen Books of Euclid's Elements*. Vol. 1 (books 1–2) and vol. 2 (books 3–9). Translated by T. L. Heath. Cambridge: Cambridge University Press, 1908.

"Ex-Milwaukee Officer Won't Be Charged in Dontre Hamilton Shooting." *Milwaukee Journal Sentinel*, December 23, 2014.

Eyewitness Testimonies: Appeals from the A-bomb Survivors. 3rd ed. Hiroshima: Hiroshima Peace Center, 2003.

Feis, Herbert. *Between War and Peace: The Potsdam Conference*. Princeton, NJ: Princeton University Press, 1960.

Ferguson, Frances. "The Nuclear Sublime." *Diacritics* 14, no. 2 (Summer 1984): 4–10.

Ferriss, Hugh. *The Metropolis of Tomorrow*. New York: Ives Washburn, 1929. Reprinted in facsimile with restored illustrations. London: Architectural Press, 1986.

Feuer, Jane. "The Concept of Live Television." In *Regarding Television: Critical Approaches*, edited by E. Ann Kaplan, 12–22. Frederick, MD: University Publications of America, 1983.

Fielding, Henry. *The Tragedy of Tragedies; or The Life and Death of Tom Thumb the Great*. In *Plays*, vol. 1, *1728–1731*, edited by Thomas Lockwood, 539–609. New York: Oxford University Press, 2004.

Flinn, John J. *The Standard Guide to Chicago for the Year 1892*. Chicago: Standard Guide, 1892.

Foucault, Michel. *Discipline and Punish: The Birth of the Prison*. Translated by Alan Sheridan. New York: Vintage, 1977.

The Fountain. Directed by Darren Aronofsky. Warner Bros. Pictures, 2006.

Fox, William L. *Aereality: On the World from Above*. Berkeley, CA: Counterpoint, 2009.

Freud, Sigmund. *The Interpretation of Dreams*. 1st ed. Translated by Joyce Crick. New York: Oxford University Press, 1999.

Freud, Sigmund. "The Unconscious." In Freud, *General Psychology Theory*, edited by Philip Rieff, 116–50. New York: Collier Books, 1963.

Fried, Michael. "Art and Objecthood." In *Art and Objecthood: Essays and Reviews*, 148–72. Chicago: University of Chicago Press, 1998.

Galilei, Galileo. *Dialogue Concerning the Two Chief World Systems: Ptolemaic and Copernican*. Translated by Stillman Drake. New York: Modern Library, 2001.

Galilei, Galileo. *Two New Sciences, Including Centers of Gravity and Force of Percussion*. 2nd ed. Translated by Stillman Drake. Toronto: Wall and Emerson, 1989.

Game of Thrones. HBO, 2011–19.

Gandhi. Directed by Richard Attenborough. Columbia Pictures, 1982.

"George Stephanopoulos: Full Interview with Police Officer Darren Wilson." *ABC News*, November 26, 2014. abcnews.go.com/GMA/video/exclusive-watch-george-stephanopoulos-full-interview-police-officer-27186831.

Gibson, James J. *The Perception of the Visual World*. Boston: Houghton Mifflin, 1950.

Gilinsky, Alberta S. "Perceived Size and Distance in Visual Space." *Psychological Review* 58, no. 6 (1951): 460–82.

Godzilla [*Gojira*]. Directed by Ishirō Honda. Toho Studios, 1954.

Godzilla. Directed by Roland Emmerich. Tristar Pictures, 1998.

Godzilla. Directed by Gareth Edwards. Warner Bros. Pictures, 2014.

Goff, Phillip Atiba, Matthew Christian Jackson, Carmen Marie Culotta, Brooke Allison Lewis Di Leone, and Natalie Ann DiTomasso. "The Essence of Innocence: Consequences of Dehumanizing Black Children." *Journal of Personality and Social Psychology* 106, no. 4 (2014): 526–45.

Gombrich, E. H. *Art and Illusion: A Study in the Psychology of Pictorial Representation*. Princeton, NJ: Princeton University Press, 1960.

Gone with the Wind. Directed by Victor Fleming. Loew's, 1939.

Graham, Stephen. *Vertical: The City from Satellites to Bunkers*. New York: Verso, 2016.

Greenberg, Joel. *A Feathered River Across the Sky: The Passenger Pigeon's Flight to Extinction*. New York: Bloomsbury, 2014.

Grusin, Richard. "Premediation." *Criticism* 46, no. 1 (Winter 2004): 17–39.

Haber, Ralph Norman, and Charles A. Levin. "The Independence of Size Perception and Distance Perception." *Perception and Psychophysics* 63, no. 7 (2001): 1140–52.

Haldane, J. B. S. "On Being the Right Size." *Harper's Monthly* 152 (March 1926): 424–27. Reprinted in Haldane, *Possible Worlds*, 18–26. New York: Routledge, 2017.

Hancock. Directed by Peter Berg. Sony Pictures, 2008.

Harries, Karsten. *Infinity and Perspective*. Cambridge, MA: MIT Press, 2001.

Harries, Karsten. *The Meaning of Modern Art: A Philosophical Interpretation*. Evanston, IL: Northwestern University Press, 1968.

Heath, Thomas. *A History of Greek Mathematics*. Vols. 1 and 2. Oxford: Oxford University Press, 1921.

Hegel, George Wilhelm Friedrich. *The Phenomenology of Spirit*. Edited and translated by Terry Pinkard. New York: Cambridge University Press, 2018.

Heidegger, Martin. *Nietzsche*. Vols. 1 and 2. Translated by David Farrell Krell. San Francisco: HarperCollins, 1991.

Helmholtz, Hermann von. *Helmholtz's Treatise on Physiological Optics*. Vol. 3. Edited and translated by James P. C. Southall. Menasha, WI: Optical Society of America, 1925.

Henry, O [pseud.]. "Psyche and the Psyscraper." In O. Henry, *Strictly Business: More Stories of the Four Million*, 173–82. New York: Doubleday, Page and Co, 1910.

Hersey, John. "Hiroshima." *New Yorker*, August 31, 1946, 15–68.

Hersey, John. *Hiroshima*. 2nd ed. New York: Vintage, 2020.

Hershenson, Maurice. "The Puzzle Remains." In *The Moon Illusion*, edited by Hershenson, 377–84. Hillsdale, NJ: Lawrence Erlbaum Associates, 1989.

Hershenson, Maurice. "That Most Puzzling Illusion." In *The Moon Illusion*, edited by Hershenson, 1–4. Hillsdale, NJ: Lawrence Erlbaum Associates, 1989.

Hertz, Neil. *The End of the Line: Essays on Psychoanalysis and the Sublime*. New York: Columbia University Press, 1985.

Hewlett, Richard G., and Oscar E. Anderson Jr. *A History of the United States Atomic Energy Commission*, vol. 1, *The New World, 1939–1946*. Washington, DC: US Atomic Energy Commission, 1972.

Heyer, Paul. *Titanic Century: Media, Myth, and the Making of a Cultural Icon*. Santa Barbara, CA: Praeger, 2012.

"Hillary Cliton Still Haunted by Discredited Rhetoric on 'Superpredators.'" *The Intercept*, February 25, 2016. theintercept.com/2016/02/25/activists-want-hillary-clinton-apologize-hyping-myth-superpredators-1996/.

Hiroshima and Nagasaki: The Physical, Medical, and Social Effects of the Atomic Bombings. Compiled and edited by the Committee for the Compilation of Materials on Damage Caused by the Atomic Bombs in Hiroshima and Nagasaki. Translated by Eisei Ishikawa and David L. Swain. New York: Basic Books, 1981.

Hiroshima: Three Witnesses. Translated by Richard H. Minear. Princeton, NJ: Princeton University Press, 1990.

Hiroyuki, Agawa. "August 6." In *The Atomic Bomb: Voices from Hiroshima and Nagasaki*, edited by Kyoko Selden and Mark Selden, 3–23. New York: M. E. Sharpe, 1989.

Hitchcock, Henry-Russell, and Philip Johnson. *The International Style*. New York: Norton, 1966.

Honey, I Shrunk the Kids. Directed by Joe Johnston. Buena Vista Pictures, 1989.

Horton, Zachary. *The Cosmic Zoom: Scale, Knowledge, and Mediation*. Chicago: University of Chicago Press, 2021.

Hosaka, Kenjirō. "Interview with Ōtsuji Seiko and Ōtsuji Tetsuo." In Kuan, *Kazuo Shinohara*, 199–201.

"H.R. 3355–103rd Congress (1993–1994): Violent Crime Control and Law Enforcement Act of 1994." September 13, 1994. www.congress.gov/bill/103rd-congress/house-bill/3355/text.

Husserl, Edmund. *Ideas Pertaining to a Pure Phenomenology and to a Phenomenological Philosophy: First Book*. Translated by F. Kersten. Boston: Martinus Nijhoff, 1983.

Huxley, Julian S. *Problems of Relative Growth*. New York: Dial, 1932.

Huxtable, Ada Louise. "Architecture: A Museum Is Also Art, Exhibition Shows." *New York Times*, September 25, 1968.

Huxtable, Ada Louise. *Will They Ever Finish Bruckner Boulevard? A Primer on Urbicide*. New York: Macmillan, 1970.

Huygens, Christian. *The Celestial Worlds Discovered*. 1st English ed. London, 1698.

Ibn al-Haytham, Abū 'Alī al-Ḥasan [Alhacen]. *The Optics of Al-Haytham, Books I–III: On Direct Vision*. Translated by A. I. Sabra. London: Warburg Institute, 1989.

The Improvement of the Park System of the District of Columbia: 1. Report of the Senate Committee on the District of Columbia, 2. Report of the Park Commission. Edited by Charles Moore. Washington, DC: Government Printing Office, 1902.

Inception. Directed by Christopher Nolan. Warner Brothers, 2010.

The Incredible Shrinking Man. Directed by Jack Arnold. Universal Pictures, 1957.

Independence Day. Directed by Roland Emmerich. Twentieth Century Fox, 1996.

Inoue, Mitsuo. *Space in Japanese Architecture*. Translated by Hiroshi Watanabe. New York: Weatherhill, 1985.

Intolerance. Directed by D. W. Griffith. Triangle Distributing Corporation, 1916.

"In2White." www.in2white.com/.

Isozaki, Arato. *Japan-ness in Architecture*. Translated by Sabu Kohso. Cambridge, MA: MIT Press, 2006.

James, Henry. *The American Scene*. London: Chapman and Hall, 1907.

Jameson, Fredric. *Postmodernism, or The Cultural Logic of Late Capitalism*. Durham, NC: Duke University Press, 1991.

"Jap Savagery." *Architectural Review* 162 (July–December 1977): 73–74.

Jay, Martin. *Downcast Eyes: The Denigration of Vision in Twentieth-Century French Thought*. Berkeley: University of California Press, 1993.

Jencks, Charles. *Skyscrapers—Skyprickers—Skycities*. New York: Rizzoli, 1980.

Jones, Jennifer L. "Reciprocity of Sight: The Rhetorics of Contestation and Commemoration on the National Mall." PhD dissertation, University of Illinois at Urbana-Champaign, 2006. UMI Microform 3250265.

Joynson, R. B. "The Problem of Size and Distance." *Quarterly Journal of Experimental Psychology* 1, no. 3 (1949): 119–35.

Jungk, Robert. *Brighter Than a Thousand Suns: A Personal History of the Atomic Scientists*. Translated by James Cleugh. New York: Harcourt Brace Jovanovich, 1958.

"Juno." NASA. science.nasa.gov/mission/juno.

Jurassic Park. Directed by Stephen Spielberg. Universal Pictures, 1993.

Jurassic World Dominion. Directed by Colin Trevorrow. Universal Pictures, 2022.

Kaika, Maria. "Autistic Architecture: The Fall of the Icon and the Rise of the Serial Object of Architecture." *Environment and Planning D: Society and Space* 29 (2011): 968–92.

Kamin, Blair. "Burj Khalifa, Dubai." *Architectural Record* 198, no. 8 (2010): 78.

Kant, Immanuel. *Critique of Pure Reason*. Translated and edited by Paul Guyer and Allen W. Wood. New York: Cambridge University Press, 1998.

Kant, Immanuel. *Critique of the Power of Judgment*. Translated by Paul Guyer and Eric Matthews. New York: Cambridge University Press, 2000.

Kaplan, Caren. "The Balloon Prospect: Aerostatic Observation and the Emergence of Militarized Aeromobility." In *From Above: War, Violence and Verticality*, edited by Peter Adey, Mark Whitehead, and Alison J. Williams, 19–40. New York: Oxford University Press, 2013.

Kaufman, Lloyd, and Irvin Rock. "The Moon Illusion." *Scientific American* 207, no. 1 (July 1962): 120–31.

Kerez, Christian. "Thoughts on Seven Houses I Have Visited." In Kuan, *Kazuo Shinohara*, 19–27.

Kern, Stephen. *The Culture of Time and Space: 1880–1918*. Cambridge, MA: Harvard University Press, 2003.

"Kevin Roche." In *Conversations with Architects*, edited by John W. Cook and Heinrich Klotz, 52–89. New York: Praeger, 1973.

"Key Takeaways from Former Cop's Testimony in Fed Trial over George Floyd's Death." Abcnews, February 15, 2022. abcnews.go.com/US/police-officer-charged-violating-george-floyds-civil-rights/story?id=82900618.

Kilpatrick, F. P., and W. H. Ittelson. "The Size-Distance Invariance Hypothesis." *Psychological Review* 60, no. 4 (July 1953): 223–31.

Kim, Nam-Gyoon. "Oculomotor Effects in the Size-Distance Paradox and the Moon Illusion." *Ecological Psychology* 24 (2012): 122–38.

King Kong. Directed by Merian C. Cooper and Ernest B. Schoedsack. RKO Radio Pictures, 1933.

King Kong. Directed by John Guillermin. Paramount Pictures, 1976.

King Kong. Directed by Peter Jackson. Universal Pictures, 2005.

Kittler, Friedrich. *Optical Media: Berlin Lectures 1999*. Translated by Anthony Enns. Cambridge: Polity, 2010.

Koffka, Kurt. *Principles of Gestalt Psychology*. London: Routledge and Kegan Paul, 1935.

Köhler, Wolfgang. *Gestalt Psychology: An Introduction to New Concepts in Modern Psychology*. New York: Liveright, 1947.

Köhler, Wolfgang. "The Mind-Body Problem." In Köhler, *Selected Papers*, 62–82.

Köhler, Wolfgang. "An Old Pseudoproblem." Translated by Erich Goldmeier. In Köhler, *Selected Papers*, 125–41.

Köhler, Wolfgang. "On Unnoticed Sensations and Errors of Judgment." Translated by Helmut E. Adler. In Köhler, *Selected Papers*, 13–39.

Köhler, Wolfgang. *The Selected Papers of Wolfgang Köhler*. Edited by Mary Henle. New York: Liveright, 1971.

Koldau, Linda Maria. *The Titanic on Film: Myth Versus Truth*. Jefferson, NC: McFarland and Company, 2012.

Koolhaas, Rem. *Delirious New York: A Retroactive Manifesto for Manhattan*. New York: Monacelli, 1994.

Koolhaas, Rem. *S, M, L, XL*. New York: Monacelli, 1997.

Korom, Joseph J., Jr. *The American Skyscraper, 1850–1940: A Celebration of Height*. Boston: Branden Books, 2008.

Kostov, Spiro. *A History of Architecture: Settings and Rituals*. New York: Oxford University Press, 1985.

Krauss, Rosalind E. *The Optical Unconscious*. Cambridge, MA: MIT Press, 1993.

Krauss, Rosalind E. *The Originality of the Avant-Garde and Other Modernist Myths*. Cambridge, MA: MIT Press, 1985.

Kuan, Seng, ed. *Kazuo Shinohara: Traversing the House and the City*. Zurich: Lars Müller, 2021.

Kuan, Seng. "The Small Japanese House." In Kuan, *Kazuo Shinohara*, 29–41.

Kuan, Seng. "Traversing the House and the City." In Kuan, *Kazuo Shinohara*, 11–17.

Lanzmann, Claude. "Hier ist kein Warum." In *Au sujet de Shoah: Le Film de Claude Lanzmann*, edited by Bernard Cuau and Michel Deguy, 279. Paris: Belin, 1990.

Lanzmann, Claude. "The Obscenity of Understanding: An Evening with Claude Lanzmann." *American Imago* 48, no. 4 (Winter 1991): 473–95. Also in Caruth, *Trauma*, 200–20.

"L.A. Officer Says He Tried Not to Use Force on King." *Washington Post*, March 24, 1993. www.washingtonpost.com/archive/politics/1993/03/24/la-officer-says-he-tried-not-to-use-force-on-king/053ecfa1-2187-4e93-9d26-db6c0502ab93/.

"L.A. Riots Anniversary: Stacey Koon's Disturbing Testimony." *The Daily Beast*, April 28, 2012 (updated July 13, 2017). www.thedailybeast.com/la-riots-anniversary-stacey-koons-disturbing-testimony.

Laub, Dori. "Truth and Testimony: The Process and the Struggle." In Caruth, *Trauma*, 61–75.

Laurence, William L. *Dawn over Zero: The Story of the Atomic Bomb*. New York: Alfred A. Knopf, 1946.

Le Corbusier. *Aircraft*. English and French ed. Hong Kong: Parenthèses, 2017.

Le Corbusier. *Toward an Architecture*. Translated by John Goodman. Los Angeles: Getty Research Institute Publications, 2007.

Leibniz, Gottfried Wilhelm. *Monadology*. In Leibniz, *Philosophical Texts*, translated by Richard Francks and R. S. Woolhouse, 268–81. New York: Oxford University Press, 1998.

L'Enfant, Pierre Charles, and US Commissioner of Public Buildings. "Plan of the city intended for the permanent seat of the government of the United States: projected agreeable to the direction of the President of the United States, in pursuance of an act of Congress, passed on the sixteenth day of July, MDCCXC, 'establishing the permanent seat on the bank of the Potowmac': Washington D.C." Map. 1791. www.loc.gov/item/88694205/.

Leys, Ruth. *Trauma: A Genealogy*. Chicago: University of Chicago Press, 2000.

Lindberg, David C. *Theories of Vision from Al-Kindi to Kepler*. Chicago: University of Chicago Press, 1976.

Lippit, Akira Mizuta. *Atomic Light (Shadow Optics)*. Minneapolis: University of Minnesota Press, 2006.

"London 320 Gigapixel Panorama Photo." Photograph. BT Tower in Partnership with British Telecom. 2012. 360gigapixels.com/london-320-gigapixel-panorama/.

The Lord of the Rings: The Return of the King. Directed by Peter Jackson. New Line Cinema, 2003.

Loth, David Goldsmith. *The City Within a City: The Romance of Rockefeller Center*. New York: W. Morrow, 1966.

Man of Steel. Directed by Zack Snyder. Warner Brothers, 2013.

Marks, Laura U. *The Skin of the Film: Intercultural Cinema, Embodiment, and the Senses*. Durham, NC: Duke University Press, 2000.

Marx, Karl. *Economic and Philosophic Manuscripts of 1844*. Translated by Martin Milligan. Amherst, MA: Prometheus, 1988.

Massip-Bosch, Enric. "Emotion Devices: The Role of Concrete Frame Structures in the Architecture of Kazuo Shinohara." *En Blanco (Nueva Escuela de Arquitectura de Granada)*, no. 20 (2016): 66–74.

Massip-Bosch, Enric, David B. Stewart, and Shin-Ichi Okuyama, eds. *Kazuo Shinohara: Casas/Houses [2G]*. Spain: Gustavo Gili, 2011.

Masters of the Universe. Directed by Gary Goddard. Cannon Group, 1987.

The Matrix. Directed by the Wachowski siblings. Warner Brothers, 1999.

Matsunaga, Yasumitsu. "Architecture as Text: Kazuo Shinohara in His Third Phase." In *Kazuo Shinohara (17 IAUS)*, 1–10. New York: Rizzoli, 1982.

Mercer, Kobena. "Fear of a Black Penis." *Artforum* 32, no. 8 (1994): 74–80.

Merleau-Ponty, Maurice. *Phenomenology of Perception*. Translated by Colin Smith. New York: Routledge, 2002.

Metz, Christian. *Film Language: A Semiotics of the Cinema*. Chicago: University of Chicago Press, 1990.

Mighty Joe Young. Directed by Ernest B. Schoedsack. RKO Radio Pictures, 1949.

Mills, David. "Attack of the GIANT NEGROES!!" *Undercover Black Man*, July 10, 2007. undercoverblackman.blogspot.com/2007/07/attack-of-giant-negroes.html.

Mills, David. "Cute White Chick Outwits GIANT NEGRO!!" *Undercover Black Man*, September 18, 2007. undercoverblackman.blogspot.com/2007/09/cute-white-chick-outwits-giant-negro.html.

Mills, David. "GIANT NEGRO to the Rescue!" *Undercover Black Man*, July 15, 2007. undercoverblackman.blogspot.com/2007/07/giant-negro-to-rescue.html.

Mills, David. "Presidential Assassin Vs. GIANT NEGRO!" *Undercover Black Man*, June 16, 2007. undercoverblackman.blogspot.com/2007/07/presidential-assassin-vs-giant-negro.html.

Mills, David. "Scarier Than Hitler . . . It's a GIANT NEGRO!!" *Undercover Black Man*, June 11, 2007. undercoverblackman.blogspot.com/2007/07/scarier-than-hitler-giant-negroes.html.

Mitry, Jean. *The Aesthetics and Psychology of the Cinema*. Translated by Christopher King. Bloomington: University of Indiana Press, 1997.

Molyneux, William. "Concerning the Apparent Magnitude of the Sun and Moon, or the Apparent Distance of two Stars, when nigh the Horizon, and when Higher elevated." *Philosophical Transactions of the Royal Society of London* 16, issue 187 (1687): 314–23.

"Mont Blanc: 365 Gigapixel Panorama (World's Largest Photo!)." ourplnt.com/mont-blanc-365-gigapixel-panorama-worlds-largest-photo/.

Morton, Timothy. *The Ecological Thought*. Cambridge, MA: Harvard University Press, 2010.

Morton, Timothy. *Hyperobjects: Philosophy and Ecology After the End of the World*. Minneapolis: University of Minnesota Press, 2013.

Moudry, Roberta. *The American Skyscraper: Cultural Histories*. New York: Cambridge University Press, 2005.

"Mrs. Clinton Campaign Speech—Super-Predators." *C-Span*, January 28, 1996. https://www.c-span.org/video/?c4558907/user-clip-mrs-clinton-campaign-speech-super-predators.

Mulvey, Laura. "Visual Pleasure and Narrative Cinema." *Screen* 16, no. 3 (Autumn 1975): 6–18.

Mumford, Lewis. *Sticks and Stones: A Study of American Architecture and Civilization*. New York: W. W. Norton, 1924.

Murphy, Douglas. *Last Futures: Nature, Technology and the End of Architecture*. New York: Verso, 2016.

Nagai, Takashi. *The Bells of Nagasaki*. Translated by William Johnston. New York: Kodansha International, 1984.

Namier, L. B. *Skyscrapers, and Other Essays*. London: Macmillan, 1931.

Nicolson, Marjorie Hope. "The Microscope and English Imagination." *Smith College Studies in Modern Languages* 16, no. 4 (July 1935): 1–92.

Nietzsche, Friedrich. "On Truth and Lying in the Extra-Moral Sense." In *Friedrich Nietzsche on Rhetoric and Language*, edited and translated by Sander L. Gilman, Carole Blair, and David J. Parent, 246–57. New York: Oxford University Press, 1989.

Nietzsche, Friedrich. *The Will to Power*. Translated by Walter Kaufmann. New York: Vintage, 1968.

"Northern Polar Mosaic." lroc.sese.asu.edu/posts/gigapan.

"No Words Were Exchanged Before a White Homeowner Shot a Black Teen Who Rang His Doorbell, According to Statements to Police." WHDH.com, Boston, April 18, 2023. Reposted from CNN. whdh.com/news/no-words-were-exchanged-before-a-white-homeowner-shot-a-black-teen-who-rang-his-doorbell-according-to-statements-to-police/.

"Nuclear Test Film—Trinity Shot." Film (TF 0800001). US Department of Energy, 1945. Archive.org/details/gov.doe.0800001.

Nye, David E. *American Technological Sublime*. Cambridge, MA: MIT Press, 1994.

Nye, David E. "The Sublime and the Skyline: The New York Skyscraper." In *The American Skyscraper: Cultural Histories*, edited by Roberta Moudry, 255–70. New York: Cambridge University Press, 2005.

"The Oakland Museum." Kevin Roche and John Dinkeloo and Associates (KRJDA). krjda.com/projects/oakland-museum.

Oe, Kenzaburo. *Hiroshima Notes*. Translated by David L. Swain and Toshi Yonezawa. New York: Grove, 1981.

"Officer Wilson's Testimony—Annotated." State of Missouri v. Darren Wilson, Grand Jury Testimony, vol. 5. September 16, 2014. www.documentcloud.org/documents/1371222-wilson-testimony.html.

Ogura, Toyofumi. *Letters from the End of the World: A Firsthand Account of the Bombing of Hiroshima*. Translated by Kisaburo Murakami and Shigeru Fujii. New York: Kodansha International, 2001.

Okuyama, Shin-ichi. "The Meaning of Writing: Agitation and Pronouncement." In Kuan, *Kazuo Shinohara*, 77–93.

Ono, Hiroshi. "Some Thoughts on Different Perceptual Tasks Related to Size and Distance." *Psychonomic Monographs Supplements* 3 (1970): 143–51.

Ottewell, Guy. *The Thousand-Yard Model, or The Earth as a Peppercorn*. 2nd ed. Raynham, MA: Universal Workshop, 2016.

Pacific Rim. Directed by Guillermo del Toro. Warner Bros. Pictures, 2013.

"Panaxity." www.panaxity.com/?s=1-kl-tower.

Pearl Harbor. Directed by Michael Bay. Buena Vista Pictures, 2001.

Pecham, John. "*Perspectiva communis*: Text and Translation." In *John Pecham and the Science of Optics: Perspectiva communis*, edited and translated by David C. Lindberg, 59–239. Madison: University of Wisconsin Press, 1970.

Petermann, Bruno. *The Gestalt Theory and the Problem of Configuration*. Translated by Meyer Fortes. New York: Harcourt, Brace, 1932.

Petroski, H. "Vitruvius's Auger and Galileo's Bones: Paradigms of Limits to Size in Design." *Journal of Mechanical Design* 114 (1992): 23–28.

Pevsner, Nikolaus. *A History of Building Types*. Princeton, NJ: Princeton University Press, 1976.

Piaget, Jean. *The Child's Conception of Number*. Translated by C. Gattegno and F. M. Hodgson. New York: Norton, 1965.

Piaget, Jean. *Judgment and Reasoning in the Child*. Translated by Margorie Warden. Totowa, NJ: Littlefield, Adams, 1972.

Piaget, Jean. *Structuralism*. Edited and translated by Chaninah Maschler. New York: Harper and Row, 1970.

Pierson, Michele. *Special Effects: Still in Search of Wonder*. New York: Columbia University Press, 2002.

Plato. *The Collected Dialogues*. Edited by Edith Hamilton and Huntington Cairns. Princeton, NJ: Princeton University Press, 1961.

Plato. *Meno*. In Plato, *Collected Dialogues*, 353–84.

Plato. *Parmenides*. In Plato, *Collected Dialogues*, 920–56.

Plato. *Republic*. In Plato, *Collected Dialogues*, 575–844.

Plug, Cornelis, and Helen E. Ross. "Historical Review." In *The Moon Illusion*, edited by Maurice Hershenson, 5–27. Hillsdale, NJ: Lawrence Erlbaum Associates, 1989.

Ptolemy. *Ptolemy's Almagest*. Translated by G. J. Toomer. New York: Springer-Verlag, 1984.

"'Quiet Revolution' on in Museum." *Oakland Tribune*, February 21, 1967.

The Rachel Maddow Show. November 25, 2014, MSNBC.

"Real Estate Collapse Spells Havoc in Dubai." *New York Times*, October 6, 2010. www.nytimes.com/2010/10/07/business/global/07dubaibuild.html.

Reynolds, Frances. *An Enquiry Concerning the Principles of Taste, and of the Origin of Our Ideas of Beauty, &c*. London: J. Smeeton, 1789.

Rhodes, Richard. *Dark Sun: The Making of the Hydrogen Bomb*. New York: Simon and Schuster, 1995.

Rhodes, Richard. *The Making of the Atomic Bomb*. New York: Simon and Schuster, 1986.

Robinson, Nathan J. *Superpredator: Bill Clinton's Use and Abuse of Black America*. Somerville, MA: Current Affairs Press, 2016.

Rosen, Jonathan. "The Birds: Why the Passenger Pigeon Became Extinct." Review of Joel Greenberg's *A Feathered River Across the Sky*. *New Yorker* (January 6, 2014): 62–67.

Ross, Helen E. "The Sun/Moon Illusion in a Medieval Irish Astronomical Tract." *Vision* 3, no. 39 (2019): 1–5.

Rousseau, Jean-Jacques. *Essai sur l'origine des langues*. Paris: L'Harmattan, 2009.

Rousseau, Jean-Jacques. "Essay on the Origin of Languages." In Rousseau, *Essay on the Origin of Languages and Writings Related to Music*, edited and translated by John T. Scott, 289–332. Hanover, NH: University Press of New England, 1998.

Sanderson, Warren. "Kazuo Shinohara's 'Savage Machine' and the Place of Tradition in the Modern Japanese Residence." *Journal of the Society of Architectural Historians* 43, no. 2 (May 1984): 109–18.

Sankichi, Tōge. *Poems of the Atomic Bomb*. Translated by Richard H. Minear. In *Hiroshima: Three Witnesses*, edited by Minear, 275–366. Princeton, NJ: Princeton University Press, 1990.

Savage, Kirk. *Monument Wars: Washington, D.C., the National Mall, and the Transformation of the Memorial Landscape*. Berkeley: University of California Press, 2005.

Scarry, Elaine. *The Body in Pain: The Making and Unmaking of the World*. New York: Oxford University Press, 1985.

Schuyler, Montgomery. "The 'Sky-Scraper' Up to Date." *Architectural Record* 8, no. 3 (Winter 1899): 231–60.

Schuyler, Montgomery. "'The Towers of Manhattan' and Notes on the Woolworth Building." In *Skyscraper: The Search for an American Style*, edited by Roger Shephard, 181–89. New York: McGraw-Hill, 2003.

Secrets of the Titanic. Directed by Robert D. Ballard and Nicolas Noxon. National Geographic Video, 1999.

Seike, Kiyosi. *The Art of Japanese Joinery*. Translated by Yuriko Yobuko and Rebecca M. Davis. New York: Weatherhill/Tankosha, 1977.

Selden, Mark. "Introduction: The United States, Japan, and the Atomic Bomb." In *The Atomic Bomb: Voices from Hiroshima and Nagasaki*, edited by Kyoko Iriye Selden and Mark Selden, xi–xxxvi. New York: M. E. Sharpe, 1989.

Shaftesbury, Anthony Ashley Cooper, Earl of. *The Moralists: A Philosophical Rhapsody.*

Shapley, Harlow, and Heber D. Curtis. "The Scale of the Universe." *Bulletin of the National Research Council* 2, part 3, no. 11 (1921): 171–217.

Shaw, Bernard. "The *Titanic*: Some Unmentioned Morals." In *The Titanic Reader*, edited by John Wilson Foster, 214–16. New York: Penguin, 1999.

Shaw, Philip. *The Sublime.* New York: Routledge, 2017.

Shinohara, Kazuo. "Beyond Symbol Spaces." *Japan Architect* 46, no. 4 (April 1971): 81–88.

Shinohara, Kazuo. "House Beneath High-Voltage Lines." *Japan Architect* 293 (September 1981): 18–29.

Shinohara, Kazuo. "House in Uehara." In Massip-Bosch, et al., eds, *Kazuo Shinohara*, 162–63.

Shinohara, Kazuo. "House with Triangular Windows." *Japan Architect* 52, no. 2 (1977): 66–67.

Shinohara, Kazuo. "Judge's Comments." *Japan Architect* 47, no 8 (September 1972): 44–48.

Shinohara, Kazuo. *Kazuo Shinohara: Complete Works in Original Publications (The Japan Architect* 93). Edited by Atsuko Nishimaki. Tokyo: Shinkenchiku-Sha, 2014.

Shinohara, Kazuo. "A Program for the 'Fourth Space.'" *Japan Architect* 353 (September 1986): 28–35.

Shinohara, Kazuo. "The Savage Machine as Exercise." *Japan Architect* 54, no. 3 (March 1979): 46–51.

Shinohara, Kazuo. "The Third Style." In Massip-Bosch, et al., eds, *Kazuo Shinohara*, 260–76.

Shinohara, Kazuo. "Toward a Super-Big Numbers Set City and a Small House Beyond." In Massip-Bosch, et al., eds., *Kazuo Shinohara*, 277–87.

Shinohara, Kazuo. "Towards Architecture." *Japan Architect* 56, no. 9 (September 1981): 30–35.

Shinohara, Kazuo. "When Naked Space Is Traversed." *Japan Architect* 51, no. 2 (February 1976): 64–69.

"Ship Sailing Under Panama Flag Runs Aground in Northern Japan, Splits in Two." Reuters, August 12, 2021. www.reuters.com/world/ship-sailing-under-panama-flag-runs-aground-northern-japan-oil-leaking-kyodo-2021-08-12/.

Shklovsky, Viktor. "Art as Technique." In *Russian Formalist Criticism: Four Essays*, 2nd ed., translated by Lee T. Lemon and Marion J. Reis, 3–24. Lincoln: University of Nebraska Press, 2012.

Shone, Tom. *Blockbuster: How Hollywood Learned to Stop Worrying and Love the Summer.* New York: Free Press, 2004.

Siegel, Mel. "When Physics Rules Robotics." *2nd International Conference on Autonomous Robots and Agents*, Palmerston North, New Zealand (December 13–15, 2004): 146–51.

Sontag, Susan. "The Imagination of Disaster." In *Against Interpretation and Other Essays*, 212–28. New York: Dell, 1969.

Spaceballs. Directed by Mel Brooks. Metro-Goldwyn-Mayer, 1987.

Speer, Albert. *Inside the Third Reich: Memoirs by Albert Speer.* Translated by Richard and Clara Winston. New York: Macmillan, 1970.

"S.S. Titanic Launching and Officers." Advertisement. *New York Times*, April 18, 1912.

Starship Troopers. Directed by Paul Verhoeven. Tristar Pictures, Touchstone Pictures, and Jon Davison Productions, 1997.

Star Wars. Directed by George Lucas. Twentieth Century Fox, 1977.

Star Wars Episode II: Attack of the Clones. Directed by George Lucas. Twentieth Century Fox, 2002.

The Steve Malzberg Show. Newsmax, August 16, 2014.

Stewart, David B. "Fashioning Change." In *Kazuo Shinohara: 3 Houses*, edited by Christian Dehli and Andrea Grolimund, 169–79. Lucerne: Quart Verlag, 2019.

Stewart, David B. *The Making of a Modern Japanese Architecture: 1868 to the Present*. New York: Kodansha, 1988.

Stewart, Susan. *On Longing: Narratives of the Miniature, the Gigantic, the Souvenir, the Collection*. Durham, NC: Duke University Press, 1993.

Sullivan, Louis H. "The Tall Office Building Artistically Considered." In Sullivan, *Kindergarten Chats and Other Writings*, 202–13. New York: Dover, 1979. Originally published in *Lippincott's* 57 (March 1896): 403–9.

Super 8. Directed by J. J. Abrams. Paramount Pictures, 2011.

Suzuki, Hiroyuki, Reyner Banham, and Katsuhiro Kobayashi. *Contemporary Architecture of Japan, 1958–1984*. New York: Rizzoli, 1985.

Swift, Jonathan. *Gulliver's Travels*. Edited by Albert J. Rivero. New York: Norton, 2002.

Swift, Jonathan. "The Lady's Dressing-Room." In *The Essential Writings of Jonathan Swift*, edited by Ian Higgins and Claude Rawson, 603–6. New York: Norton, 2009.

Swift, Jonathan. "Strephon and Chloe." In *The Essential Writings of Jonathan Swift*, edited by Ian Higgins and Claude Rawson, 610–17. New York: Norton, 2009.

"Swiss Lab 'Nano Chisels' World's Tiniest Magazine Cover." NBC News, April 15, 2014. www.nbcnews.com/science/science-news/swiss-lab-nano-chisels-worlds-tiniest-magazine-cover-n90096.

Szasz, Ferenc Morton. *The Day the Sun Rose Twice: The Story of the Trinity Site Nuclear Explosion, July 16, 1945*. Albuquerque: University of New Mexico Press, 1984.

Taki, Koji. "Oppositions: The Intrinsic Structure of Kazuo Shinohara's Work." Translated by Neil Warren and Jorge M. E. Ferreras. *Perspecta: The Yale Architecture Journal* 20 (1983): 43–60.

Tange, Kenzo. "Kenzo Tange on Residential Design: Interviewed by Kazuo Shinohara." *Japan Architect* 41, no. 3 (March 1966): 17–22.

Tange, Kenzo, and Arata Isozaki. "Directions in Today's Architecture: A Discussion Between Kenzo Tange and Arata Isozaki." *Japan Architect* 45, no. 7 (July 1970): 23–28.

Tasker, Yvonne. *Spectacular Bodies: Gender, Genre and the Action Cinema*. New York: Routledge, 1993.

The Ten Commandments. Directed by Cecil B. DeMille. Paramount Pictures, 1956.

"Thank You, London: A Portrait of Our Capital During the Games." btlondon2012.co.uk/pano.html.

Them! Directed by Gordon Douglas. Warner Bros. Pictures, 1954.

"This Is the Tiniest Color Picture Ever Printed." *Futurity*, December 15, 2015. www.futurity.org/smallest-inkjet-printed-color-image-1070172/.

Thompson, D'Arcy Wentworth. *On Growth and Form*. 1st ed. Cambridge: Cambridge University Press, 1917. Revised and republished in 1942.

Thomson, William (Lord Kelvin). "Lord Kelvin on Ether and Gravitational Matter Through Infinite Space." *Philosophical Magazine* 2, 6th ser., no. 8 (August 1901): 161–77.

"The Thousand Yard Model, or The Earth as a Peppercorn." Electronic presentation of Guy Ottewell's *Thousand Yard Model*. United States N.S.F. Optical-Infrared Astronomy Research Laboratory. noirlab.edu/public/products/educational-programs/eduprog032/.

"365-Gigapixel Panorama of Mont Blanc Becomes the World's Largest Photo." Petapixel, May 24, 2015. petapixel.com/2015/05/24/365-gigapixel-panorama-of-mont-blanc-becomes-the-worlds-largest-photo/.

Titanic. Directed by James Cameron. Paramount, Twentieth Century Fox, and Lightstorm Entertainment, 1997.

"Titanic Sinks Four Hours After Hitting Iceberg." *New York Times*, April 16, 1912.

Tolkien, J. R. R. *The Return of the King*. New York: Del Rey, 1986.

Toulmin, Stephen. *Cosmopolis: The Hidden Agenda of Modernity*. Chicago: University of Chicago Press, 1990.

Transformers. Directed by Michael Bay. Paramount Pictures, Dreamworks Pictures, Hasbro, and De Bonaventura Pictures, 2007.

"Trinity Test Complete Takes." AtomCentral.com. www.youtube.com/watch?v=7dfK9G7UDok.

Troy. Directed by Wolfgang Peterson. Warner Brothers, 2004.

Trubowitz, Lara. *Civil Antisemitism, Modernism, and British Culture, 1902–1939*. New York: Palgrave Macmillan, 2002.

Tsing, Anna Lowenhaupt. "On Nonscalability: The Living World Is Not Amenable to Precision-Nested Scales." *Common Knowledge* 18, no. 3 (2012): 505–24.

US Laws, Statutes, etc., 1790. *An act for establishing the temporary and permanent seat of the government of the United States. New York: F. Childs and J. Swaine,* 1790. www.loc.gov/item/rbpe.21500600/.

Van Helden, Albert. *Measuring the Universe: Cosmic Dimensions from Aristarchus to Halley*. Chicago: University of Chicago Press, 1985.

Venturi, Robert, Steven Izenour, and Denise Scott Brown. *Learning from Las Vegas: The Forgotten Symbolism of Architectural Form*. 2nd ed. Cambridge, MA: MIT Press, 1977.

Virilio, Paul. *The Vision Machine*. Translated by Julie Rose. Bloomington: Indiana University Press, 1994.

Virilio, Paul. *War and Cinema: The Logistics of Perception*. Translated by Patrick Camiller. New York: Verso, 1989.

Wade, Nicholas J. *Perception and Illusion: Historical Perspectives*. Dordrecht, Netherlands: Springer, 2005.

Watanabe, Hiroshi. "Kazuo Shinohara's 'House Beneath High-Voltage Lines.'" *AIA Journal* 71 (August 1982): 66–67.

Waterworld. Directed by Kevin Reynolds. Universal Pictures, 1995.

Weller, George. *First into Nagasaki: The Censored Eyewitness Dispatches on Post-Atomic Japan and Its Prisoners of War*. Edited by Anthony Weller. New York: Three Rivers, 2006.

Wells, Matthew. *Skyscrapers: Structure and Design*. New Haven, CT: Yale University Press, 2005.

Wertenbaker, G. Peyton. "The Man from the Atom." *Amazing Stories* 1, no. 1 (1926): 62–66. Originally published in *Science and Invention* 11, no. 4 (1923): 329–30.

Wertheimer, Max. "Gestalt Theory." Translated by N. Nairn-Allison. *Social Research* 11, no. 1 (February 1944): 78–99.

West, Geoffrey. *Scale: The Universal Laws of Life, Growth, and Death in Organisms, Cities, and Companies*. New York: Penguin, 2017.

Whissel, Kristen. "The Digital Multitude." *Cinema Journal* 49, no. 4 (Summer 2010): 99–110.

Whissel, Kristen. *Spectacular Digital Effects: CGI and Contemporary Cinema*. Durham, NC: Duke University Press, 2004.

Whitehead, Alfred North. *An Introduction to Mathematics*. New York: Oxford University Press, 1948.

The Wild Bunch. Directed by Sam Peckinpah. Warner Brothers–Seven Arts, 1969.

Wilson, John Paul, Kurt Hugenberg, and Nicholas O. Rule. "Racial Bias in Judgments of Physical Size and Formidability: From Size to Threat." *Journal of Personality and Social Psychology* 113, no. 1 (2017): 59–80.

Wittenberg, David. "Bigness as the Unconscious of Theory." *ELH* 86, no. 2 (Summer 2019): 333–54.

Wittenberg, David. "Time." In *The Cambridge Companion to Narrative Theory*, edited by Matthew Garrett, 120–31. New York: Cambridge University Press, 2018.

Wittenberg, David. *Time Travel: The Popular Philosophy of Narrative*. New York: Fordham University Press, 2013.

"World's Smallest Magazine Cover Measures 11 x 14 Micrometers (w/ Video)." PhysOrg, April 25, 2014. phys.org/news/2014-04-world-smallest-magazine-micrometers-video.html.

Worth, Josh. "If the Moon Were Only 1 Pixel: A Tediously Accurate Scale Model of the Solar System." joshworth.com/dev/pixelspace/pixelspace_solarsystem.html.

Wright, Frank Lloyd. "The Tyranny of the Skyscraper." In Wright, *The Future of Architecture*, 163–80. New York: Plume, 1953.

Žižek, Slavoj. *The Sublime Object of Ideology*. New York: Verso, 1989.

Žižek, Slavoj. *Welcome to the Desert of the Real!* New York: Verso, 2002.

Index

Page numbers in italics refer to figures.